Parent Anger Management

The PAMP Programme

Gerry Heery

Russell House Publishing

First published in 2007 by:
Russell House Publishing Ltd.
4 St. George's House
Uplyme Road
Lyme Regis
Dorset DT7 3LS

Tel: 01297-443948
Fax: 01297-442722
e-mail: help@russellhouse.co.uk
www.russellhouse.co.uk

British Library Cataloguing-in-publication Data:
A catalogue record for this book is available from the British Library.

ISBN: 978-1-905541-04-1

Layout by Jeremy Spencer
Printed by Antony Rowe, Chippenham

Russell House Publishing

We aim to publish innovative and valuable materials to help
managers, practitioners, trainers, educators and students.

Our full catalogue covers: social policy, working with young people, helping children
and families, care of older people, social care, combating social exclusion,
revitalising communities and working with offenders.

Full details can be found at www.russellhouse.co.uk
and we are pleased to send out information to you by post.
Our contact details are on this page.

We are always keen to receive feedback on publications and new ideas for future projects.

Contents

About the Author

Gerry Heery is a training consultant with over twenty years front line experience as a social worker and extensive involvement in developing and delivering domestic violence related interventions within Northern Ireland's criminal justice, social services and voluntary sectors. He is the author of *Preventing Violence in Relationships* (JKP, 2000). He lives with his wife Maire in Belfast and they have five children.

Acknowledgements

To Michael, Colm, Clare, Nuala and Declan
Precious gifts that have challenged my wisdom.

This publication reflects my experiences of working with many people, clients and colleagues over the past 25 years within the Childcare, Youth Justice and Probation sectors in N Ireland. Although often challenging, I have been privileged to receive much encouragement and support that has contributed richly to my learning and development.

More specifically I am indebted to Pip Jaffa from the Parents Advice Centre in N Ireland who first approached me with the idea of trying to tailor my experience in anger management work specifically for the needs of parents. I would also express my appreciation to Shirley Hayes who not only co-facilitated the PAMP pilot during dark winter evenings in central Belfast in 2005 but also provided me with helpful feedback on the manual design and content. From the parents who attended these sessions, I also received useful advice. I am thankful to Brian Taylor from The University of Ulster for accessing the evidence base on parents anger management work and also to Dorota Iwaniec from Queens University Belfast, who so readily provided me with some of her material. Martin Calder was a source of guidance and encouragement in putting this manual together.

Finally, I wish to acknowledge the continuous support and advice I have received from my wife Maire during this project. As well as designing the "Taking care of Yourself" elements in the sessions, she also proof read all the material helping me to control my tendency towards lengthy torturous sentences and hopefully making the material more accessible to those who wish to use it.

Of course, none of the above is responsible for any errors or shortcomings in *Parents Anger Management: The PAMP Programme.*

Introduction

> *Being a parent tests your patience, your flexibility, wisdom and endurance like no other career or relationship.*
>
> McKay, Rogers and McKay, 1989: 241

A personal story

I am fortunate to be the parent of five children, who at the time of writing range in ages from 4 to 22 years and all live at home. In one sense, this has provided me with ample opportunities to learn about how my own anger has been aroused, and managed or mismanaged by various situations involving my children. I have learnt that difficulties do not diminish as children get older; they just are different.

My own limitations in this area, and they are numerous, were fully realised in the early stages of putting this programme together. I had just spent a very profitable two hours working on the computer, going between websites, gathering various bits of information; copying, cutting, pasting and downloading etc. My youngest son was in the house. He was just over two years old at the time, and had been looking for some attention from me. I had generally been ignoring him or trying to get him to do something else. The next think I knew the computer screen went blank. He had come up behind me and switched off the plug! Within an instant I was flooded with feelings of anger and rage and despair. Oh God my work has been lost! Why did he do that? I have wasted my time this morning! I will have to do it all again! At the back of my head was the thought that I hadn't been saving everything as I went along. There was no excuse for this and was my fault. However, it was easier to blame my young son. I shouted at him 'Don't do that!' which was obviously a stupid thing to say as the harm was already done. I was tense, stressed, feeling hard done by, and angry. I felt like lashing out at anybody.

It took me some time to realise that my son had actually provided me with a real learning opportunity and also a stark reminder that I am on a journey myself in working at these things. Even though I knew that much, if not all, of the information was retrievable or no-one was hurt or had died, I had to question the effects this had on myself. How would I cope if life really dealt me a difficult hand and I had to face some of the situations and experiences that those I work with often have to endure and deal with? What about the distress and upset I caused my son who was following his natural inclination in wanting to engage with me? It was a salutary lesson.

The old saying goes that we teach that which we most need to learn. As the above example shows, I am not in a position to present myself as someone who has mastered and managed the anger within myself in a perfect way. It is an area that I need to attend to and work at. The point is that I have been fortunate enough in my professional life to read and study this area and to have experience in helping people address it and try to overcome problems they were having in relation to their anger. My experience has been as a practitioner within the NI Probation Service in helping develop and deliver both their Anger Management and Domestic Violence Programmes. These were cognitive behavioural programmes offered to people whose mismanagement of anger or whose domestic violence had brought them into the criminal justice system. I also subsequently developed and published the Preventing Violence in Relationships Programme (Heery, 2000) which again was an educational, cognitive-behavioural programme aimed at men who wished to address their use of controlling and abusive behaviour as a result of the problems it was causing in their lives. I have been privileged to be able to continue my interest and commitment to this work with this publication.

Why anger management for parents?

The importance of parenting to the life chances of children is now well established in a wide body of research literature. Most parents recognise it as the most important and ultimately the most rewarding thing that they will do. It is also tough! It is a role that involves long hours; incredibly messy noisy children; constantly carrying out many time consuming and repetitive tasks; being pushed to the limit; having to continuously give attention and approval; and always trying to stay alert! There are many aspects of parenting: no two parents are the same and there is no prescribed formula for 'perfect parenting'. Most of us find a way through it and give our children as secure and loving a start in life as we can. This book will not cover or do justice to the many facets of parenting. It focuses on one particular area that for some may be causing difficulties in their parenting role and that is the appropriate management of anger.

It is clear that parents, all parents, regularly experience high levels of anger (Dix, 1991). Parents, and I include myself in this, will often come to the brink of despair and rage in terms of dealing with the children they love. The hopes, the expectations and the fears we have around our children's behaviour, futures and outcomes will often lead us to feel the anger rising within us. It comes with the territory! Studies carried out on 'average parents' report high levels of anger with their children and the fear that they will sometimes loose control and harm their children. For example, research carried out by the UK based NSPCC indicated that parents of babies and toddlers said they lose their temper with their child on average once a week. Six out of ten parents of babies and toddlers (61 per cent) said they have hit their child (NSPCC, 2005).

The problem is not the anger per se. Anger is a normal, natural, necessary human emotion. Indeed, because anger is almost universally present in parent/child relationships, the illusion may be created that it is harmless. In many cases, this is so. However, when anger is not expressed or managed in a healthy way then problems may arise. Anger leading to aggression can have a devastating impact on children, potentially distorting their sense of self and causing long lasting emotional problems. In addition, anger mismanagement is something that can cause problems not only for those who are the objects of uncontrollable anger but also the angry person themselves. There are some parents who will have to find methods to manage the anger that arises as part of the parenting process in ways which do less harm to their children or themselves.

In discussing these issues with various parents, voluntary and community agencies operating in Northern Ireland, the need for a tool to help parents to address issues around anger was identified. This needed to be something accessible, experiential and creative in helping people think about and learn to manage their anger better. The result is the PAMP programme, an intervention of eight two hour sessions, which can be delivered individually or in groups, and is designed to facilitate an ongoing process of exploration and learning for parents who acknowledge that they need and want to better manage their anger.

The programme

The starting point with any endeavour in life is to be clear about the principles and values that give it drive and direction. Part One provides this foundation to the programme, the ethical base of values, the knowledge upon which it rests, and the elements required to deliver the work in an effective and positive way. It will identify the theoretical underpinnings but not go into these in detail. Rather, these various perspectives will be integrated into Part Two in order to give clear guidance on the approach required from the facilitator of the programme. Part Two begins with guidance on the structure and make up of each of the eight sessions, which are then fully outlined in separate chapters. Session 1 is focused on the challenge of change, which is about encouraging the person to think about why they are doing the programme and their readiness for participation. The programme then moves through a detailed exploration and analysis of anger, allowing each participant to assess their own anger and begin to identify how it relates to their thinking, emotions, and actions and beginning to identify what they need to do to manage it (Sessions 2, 3 and 4). The emphasis in Session 5 then moves to looking at the impact of mismanaged parental anger and parenting styles on children and their development, and how children learn to manage their own anger. Session 6 explores the links between gender and anger, and also the need for recognition of how past traumatic life experiences may impact on managing anger. The penultimate Session 7 concentrates on exploring anger, power, control and conflict issues; helping people find safer ways of handling conflict as parents. The final session is about encouraging participants to bed in the material that has been covered and to sustain the learning and progress they have made. It is also about endings and action planning for what they need for the future.

Part Three will address issues around quality assurance, monitoring and evaluation issues. It will clearly lay out the requirements on workers and agencies who choose to use this programme to ensure practice which is both ethical and effective.

Who this book is for

This programme is a significant intervention that can be used by workers from various professional backgrounds including social work, counselling, mental health, justice or community work. However, those intending to use it need to ensure that they are sufficiently clear about the material and have built in various support and monitoring systems to ensure programme integrity and a positive service to users.

There is the old story about the newly qualified psychologist wishing to devote his life to helping parents with their children. He developed his course called Ten Rules for Parents. His first child came along and he changed the course to Ten Hints for Parents. Another child arrived and he modified his course to Ten Suggestions for Parents. His third child arrived and he stopped lecturing! It is within such a spirit that PAMP is offered to those interested in this type of work. That said, the elements it contains and those outlined above, are those that have been identified in the research as necessary in helpful interventions with people experiencing anger management problems (Deffenbacher, 1996). PAMP seeks to be innovative in targeting this material specifically at parents. It is presented as an important accessible resource that may be of assistance to those working with parents in helping them enhance their capacity in carrying out their essential role.

TESTIMONIAL

Translating the theory and research into user friendly materials is the biggest challenge in practice currently. It is for this reason that Heery's book is a timely and priceless addition to the busy practitioner. The material covered will have a broad appeal ranging from criminal justice providers, child care and protection workers and advocates for children in private and public law. This book deserves recognition as a key academic text as well as a regularly used operational tool, with huge potential as a training resource. All readers will emerge at the end of the book with an enhanced view in their professional and personal lives.

Martin C. Calder November 2006

PART ONE

THE FOUNDATION

> *Making the simple complex is commonplace, making the complicated simple, awesomely simple…that's creativity.*
>
> Charles Mingus

PAMP is a structured programme of intervention, with pre-set aims, measurable objectives and relevant content. The challenge has been to pull together a wide range of theoretical material and present it in ways that meet the needs and learning styles of individual participants. Its about allowing and challenging people to think about, reflect on, and then to make changes in their behaviour. It offers the opportunity to take responsibility to do tough personal work. The ultimate goal is to provide a creative, constructive, challenging learning experience to those who are motivated to address their anger as parents. To do this in an effective and ethical way, the programme needs firstly and primarily to be clear and explicit as to what it is and what it is based on.

The ethical practice base: values

As a social worker my commitment is to work with people in ways which promotes social change and problem solving in human relationships. The key values that I have endeavoured to build into this programme and which will require the commitment of those who choose to facilitate it are respect for the individual person; promotion of user self-determination; promotion of social justice; and working for the interests of users. These are congruent with the values underpinning social work in many countries of the world (Banks, 2006).

What this means is that participants are viewed as human beings, not as problems to be solved. Each participant will be seen as an individual with a dignity beyond measure, and a personal core which is unique to that individual. Furthermore, they will be viewed as the experts in their own role as parents who have been offered, and have agreed, to take part in a process of adult learning. Each participant is recognised and valued as an individual with her or his own viewpoints and learning styles. The programme is not about the notion that people's problems can be solved by professionals who know better. It recognises the fact that people are aware of their needs and an understanding of the roots of those needs will come to the surface through a positive process of learning and discovery. The value base is therefore one of giving people what they want, recognising their experiences and expertise, striving to meet their needs and providing them with a challenging, stimulating learning and developmental experience. The involvement of users in the piloting and design of this programme has been a commitment to this process. This ethical value base comes before the science.

The ethical practice base: knowledge

However, ethical practice demands that it is founded on reliable knowledge. It is important that those of us who have a little more time to access the literature and research which is continually emerging, are able to put this together in ways that allow practitioners to take it forward and continuously improve and develop practice. It is about gathering a wide variety of diverse but relevant material and trying to re-assemble it in a useful and creative way. It is about trying to help practitioners deliver this material in a down to earth language that can connect to people and avoids the use of jargon that can have the effect of creating unnecessary barriers by reinforcing power differences and also of alienating people we are trying to help (Thompson, 2003). This is not straightforward for various reasons. Primarily, in dealing with human behaviour the science can be inconsistent, contested and difficult to apply. Nevertheless, the challenge is to base the programme on a reasonable body of evidence based material. It needs to be grounded in the research that indicates what is likely to be most helpful to people seeking to make changes in their behaviour and in particular with anger related problems. Anger management programmes derived from cognitive – behavioural theories have been implemented globally and have been demonstrated to be effective in altering thinking processes associated with aggression (Goldstein, et al. 2004).

Other relevant theoretical perspectives including adult learning, person centred, motivational, change, solution focused and group work theories are also relied on to varying degrees in the design and delivery of the programme. Detailed descriptions and analyses of these various perspectives will not be presented in detail at this point, but will be integrated into the programme as required. Thorough explanation and guidance will then be given to the potential facilitator to give them a sense of why the exercise is being used, the approach taken and how this relates to the theory/research. There will also be extensive referencing for further reading for those who wish to follow up particular areas.

The contested nature of the knowledge base is already evident in the fact that this programme is primarily cognitive behavioural as opposed to being a psychodynamic intervention. This is not to rule out the relevance and importance of the understanding that may come from understanding the person's early childhood experiences and subconscious. It may be the case that various deep rooted difficulties are present in the situations of some participants and referral to more in depth counselling services may be required. However, in choosing to go down the learning and cognitive behavioural routes, the programme reflects the research that these approaches have the most empirical support. This direction, therefore, needs to be made clear to any potential participant.

Facilitating the programme

One positive consequence of taking this more educational and cognitive behavioural line is that facilitation of the programme is feasible to a wide range of workers from various disciplines operating within the social and community care fields. It is aimed at busy but reasonably experienced workers (social workers, counsellors, mental health workers, family workers, community and group workers etc.), who want to have an accessible, easy to use, and effective and ethical tool which may help those they are working with make progress on an area of difficulty in their lives. However, although the manual is designed to be easy to use, this does not mean that the facilitators task is easy. Firstly, there is considerable onus on potential facilitators to ground themselves in the knowledge base, to have a good sense of it and to know where they are coming from. This manual is intended to provide sufficient material for this task. Indeed, there will often be more in the guidance parts than will be necessary to present to the individual or the group. Potential facilitators should not feel that they need to regurgitate the extensive notes which are provided in relation to each element of each session (there are 48 of these in total). The facilitator needs to acquire a good sense of the piece and then find their own way to present it.

There is a need to find the balance between being clear about the knowledge base but not allowing it to totally dominate the work. In one sense, although the knowledge base is important there needs to be more reliance on the process of learning rather than the more static knowledge. This is fundamental and what makes sense as a goal for education and development in the modern world (Rogers, 1988). Furthermore, each socio-emotional problem experienced by an individual is unique, open to many different explanations and cannot be resolved by the simple application of a body of knowledge.

In following the programme, the facilitator should be more concerned with creating an atmosphere and a relationship that allows the participant to identify their problems, name and frame them and begin to test strategies which may help address them. The skills of facilitation, with individuals and groups, are about following through on the value base in giving equal value and status to all, being clear about purpose and helping to create an enjoyable, pleasant, cooperative, harmonious, supportive atmosphere where differing perspectives, ideas and conflicts are accepted. At the same time, the leadership responsibility cannot be abdicated. Participants will want clear guidance and structure going through the programme and will need to be confident that a safe, encouraging and empowering learning experience is maintained.

There may be issues for facilitators in terms of whether they themselves are parents or not and the degree to which they may wish to share personal material. It should be possible for someone who is not a parent to facilitate the group. This will fit with the approach of not claiming to be an expert on the parenting of other people's children. It is better to be 'up front' about one's lack of actual hands on experience in the subject of the programme. As for parents, the sharing of personal material may well be appropriate (as I did in the introduction) but care should be taken in the choice of the examples.

Working with groups

The emphasis in this manual will be on the group work medium. As with the other theoretical perspectives, material on group work will be integrated as appropriate into the respective sessions. It is the ethos and value base of the group model that is critical in terms of how this programme is delivered. The core process of group work is the interaction between a group of people, based on mutuality, as the means to achieving the purpose of the group. It refers to 'the conscious, disciplined, and systematic use of knowledge about the process of collective human interaction in order to intervene in an informed way, or promote some desired objective in a group setting' (Benson, 1996: 11). At the heart of group work theory is the capacity for groups to bring about change both by feedback and access to coping skills.

Facilitating a group is a highly skilled and sometimes very demanding activity, particularly to someone who is new to this type of intervention. The challenges involved in leading the group and in communicating clearly with participants in taking them through a structured programme will be addressed in future chapters. At this point, the onus is on potential facilitators to be open and honest with themselves as to their ability to take on this task. Some previous experience of group work is required as well as ensuring that support and supervision will be provided whilst facilitating a group. Co-facilitation, as well as being a justifiable approach to the programme in its own right, may also be a way of building in more support. Benson (1996) provides useful guidance on this. Each facilitator needs to be aware of their own role and contribution, to be clear and in agreement with each other on the purpose of the group, and to be prepared to fully discuss conflicts, tensions, and feelings aroused by the joint work. Each should be willing to permit and invite differences in perception, style, and approach as long as there is agreement about purpose. Its about trying to develop a working relationship that is around collaboration, sharing, trusting, talking to each other both within and outside the group setting.

As with most things, the biggest single factor in the breakdown of group work is a lack of preparation. This begins when thinking about group size and composition. Groups of about eight people are probably ideal for this type of programme, although some authorities in this area suggest aiming for an original number of ten or so to allow for drop outs and absences (Brown, 1992). The group make up is important. Homogenous characteristics may be more important since they may help the group to gel. Having one person with learning difficulties in a group of people with significantly higher intellectual abilities is going to be problematic. Similarly, there may well be issues in having a group of seven men and one woman. (gender issues are considered below). Again, there may be difficulties for a member of a particular ethnic group attending a group totally comprised of members of another race. There may also be the issue of whether to bring a married couple or partners into a group programme. The literature varies on this. One commentator has suggested that this may help reduce inconsistencies and contradictions in child-management and increase mutual support within the couple (Iwaniec, 1997). However, another source takes a different view, suggesting that couples should be advised to do separate programmes arguing that this approach 'avoided conflict between couples, and also effectively helped battered women to use the group as a support' (Acton, 1997: 14). All these issues need to be carefully considered prior to commencement of the programme just as much as being clear about the purpose and content. Commitment to do this, in order to deliver a positive learning experience to participants will pay off.

Working with individuals

Although the sessions are written for a group setting, they can be used individually as well. Additional guidance will be provided if an exercise needs some modification to be delivered individually. There are pros and cons for each approach. We do not yet have the quality research to make definitive statements as to the 'best' approach – group or individual (Iwaniec, 1997). From a personal point of view, I am coming to the end of a long and not very illustrious career in amateur football. I know that when I go out to train I tend to do better with a group. I push a little harder, I find the fact that we are all out on a cold night encouraging and I often feel and think that I am getting more out of this than if I was out on my own. Having said that, there are always some in the group who don't appear to be trying that hard with the danger that this can rub off on the others! Also, if I was out with a coach just one-to-one, I think I would probably give a lot of effort!

The fact remains, that whether in a group or individually, ultimately change in any area requires strong personal work. It may well come down to what will best meet the needs of potential participants and what they are most comfortable with. The points made earlier about the value base, the quality of the relationship, the style of working alongside and with participants, creating an encouraging positive and challenging experience equally apply to the individual one-to-one approach. Whether delivering this programme individually, or in a group, either facilitating it alone or co-facilitating, remember always that participants see and feel the worker as a person, they just don't hear the worker. The essence of how the facilitator is with people, how they relate to them and treat them is fundamental to the chances of a successful intervention in their lives.

Promoting inclusion and diversity: programme content

The value base outlined earlier needs to be taken deeper and further. Choices have to be made as to the knowledge base of the programme and the approaches that are taken to the subject of anger. As we shall see, there are far reaching consequences from some of these choices in terms of the messages they give to different groups of people. The programme content, and how this has been decided upon needs to be made explicit and to what degree the values, prejudices, history and learning experiences of the author has influenced these. The fact that the author is someone who is a white, middle class, middle aged (nearly, although of course it depends when you read this!) Catholic, Irish, a husband and father and with a host of other important characteristics will no doubt have impacted on the content of the programme.

The fundamental view of anger as an emotion that is potentially positive and indeed necessary for our survival as a species is one that is presented in the programme. This reflects some of the influences on the author coming from a Christian, Western and humanist background. Although research evidence will be given for this approach, it does not tally with that, for example, of someone from the Buddhist culture who may view anger as an 'afflictive emotion' and not a positive thing. They may also have differing perspectives on emotions themselves (Goleman, 2004). Another author tells the story of an anthropologist carrying out research on the Eskimo people. Initially, she was accepted by the group, but when she displayed her anger in a way that would be perfectly acceptable in her own culture, she was shunned for three months! (Dryden, 1996). So there are cultural differences in how anger is viewed and these need to be recognised.

It doesn't stop there. If we then venture into the area of gender, things can get even murkier. There is the ongoing contentious and divisive issue of the similarities and differences between men and women. Do we assign human traits to males and females on the basis of their sex? These are important considerations in helping mothers and fathers have an understanding of their own experience and expression of anger. The view taken in the programme is a commitment to a common human nature and to the uniqueness of each individual. However, the programme leans towards, but does not impose the perspective, that there are differences between men and women that are not all to do with historical, cultural and political factors. Session 7 addresses these issues in terms of how women and men experience anger and allow participants to explore their own experiences of this. Of course the issue of specifying the distinctiveness of the masculine and feminine species is difficult and highly controversial. It is not imposed on participants and different views and perspectives are acknowledged and accepted. Each participant will have the opportunity to look at their experience and expression of anger in their lives as a mother or a father and come to their own conclusions.

A related concern is the fact that a lot of research into parenting has been focused on just one gender and that is mothers. As a result, there is the need to take care and be cautious about over – generalising research in the programme content. Similarly, with regard to the effectiveness of anger management interventions, most of those that have been subject to evaluation have been within the criminal justice system and have involved males. So, there is limited research on the effectiveness of cognitive – behavioural and educational approaches with women, although research in the criminal justice field reported findings that supported interventions applying equally well to women offenders (Dowden and Serin, 2001). There is also the issue of mixed gender groups and concerns that women may find these intimidating and do not open up as much with important issues as in single gender groups. Despite this, the programme seeks to offer parents of both sexes the opportunity to work together on these issues and strives to ensure an atmosphere that is positive and safe for all participants. The onus then is clearly on the facilitator to ensure that no participant, whatever their age, gender, culture, religion or sexual orientation, is subject to negative and abusive behaviours.

Another potentially divisive area of the programme content is that on change and lifestyle issues. Again, there is varied and conflicting evidence on the degree that people can change deeply ingrained and long established patterns of behaviour. Because of the author's Christian background and beliefs, the possibility of a spiritual dimension in our lives that can play a key part in trying to change is acknowledged. Again this is not imposed, and the possibility of change coming entirely from within people themselves and more humanist perspectives are recognised and encouraged.

We live in a complex world. There are many and conflicting explanations put forward to explain various aspects of human behaviour. The science is complicated, contradictory and open to challenge. The preceding paragraphs have not just been about getting into tortuous debate, navel gazing and running the risk of paralysing ourselves from offering anything in case it offends someone. There is always a danger of ideologies of one form or another creeping in and distorting the approach that needs to be taken. All one can do is be up front as to where the programme is coming from, what it is based on and recognising its tendency to view people and behaviour in a way that reflects a western cultural view of anger as well as what some of the current evidence and research base says about it. At the same time, the challenge remains to strive to accommodate cultural, gender, psychological or intellectual differences.

Promoting inclusion and diversity: accessing the programme

There is also the need to proactively seek to engage with a wide range of individuals and groups from society who may experience needs in this area and wish to participate in the programme. The challenge is to use the insights from the above wide and complex range of knowledge and translate it into a language and an approach which can help adults from a wide variety of backgrounds work together in addressing what is a difficult area of behaviour for them. To help with this the programme has been piloted with a group of parents from the greater Belfast area and their views have been incorporated into its final design. The commitment is to present the material in ways that may foster concrete experiential learning of abstract concepts and transferable skills. Participants need to really get into the material in their own ways and not through basic information giving approaches. This will also help the participation of people who may struggle with literacy based material, for whom English may not be their first language or who come from different backgrounds. Of course the option for people to put ideas or thoughts on paper, for example, by keeping an anger diary or working up an action plan should also be encouraged as the power of committing personal material to paper should not be underestimated. Writing can be 'even more powerful than visualisation as it bridges the subconscious and conscious mind...and literally imprints the brain' (Covey, 2004: 157).

Agencies who choose to offer this programme, need to look at the cultures from within which they are offering this service and how they can truly try to make it accessible to a wide range of people. This involves looking at the structures and processes around the promotion, availability, delivery and support of the programme as well as being clear about its content and what it is based on. All this needs to be put on the table and offered to potential participants or service users who can make a fully informed choice as to whether they wish to take the service.

Pre programme contact

In terms of ensuring that people know what they are undertaking so that they can make real choices, the option of individual meetings or information sessions should be considered to help this process. This may be more helpful in cases where the medium of groupwork is being considered to deliver the programme. Potential participants may tend to feel ashamed, embarrassed, and reluctant to expose themselves to complete strangers and will need reassurance as to the process. It is helpful to engage with potential participants to identify and explore any personal concerns they have and try to relate these to the group. The meeting could explore how the person's needs may, or may not, be met in the social context of a group of people with similar concerns and anxieties (Brown, 1992). For example, a person with learning difficulties may find the programme much more positive if delivered on an individual basis allowing him or her to work at their own speed. An initial contact can also try to assess the degree of ownership that the person is taking of their problem and how motivated they are to address it. Research indicates that potential participants need to own their personal problem with anger and want help for the problem (Deffenbacher, 1996).

Professional responsibility and accountability

As indicated in facilitating the programme parts, it is important that professionals continue to inform themselves of the latest research and literature in their areas of work. Agencies or workers who decide to use this programme will have a readily accessible, clear and useful tool to help them in this work. As indicated in the facilitator guidance, there is an onus on the facilitator to familiarise themselves with the material and decide how they want to present it in ways that suit themselves and their groups or client. If we are going to teach or present anything to others it requires us to really get a good understanding and grasp of the subject matter (Covey, 1997).

Of course, as stated earlier, the knowledge base on its own is not enough. Agencies need to be careful of the myth of the 'new knowledge worker' (Jones, 2002). It is dangerous to make the assumption that reading the detailed guidance from the manual will be enough to know how to do the job of delivering this intervention. Ideally, there needs to be a learning culture within the agency delivering the programme. This can allow professionally curious staff to reflect on what they are doing and to be less self-conscious about learning and more explicit about the challenges of developing this programme. There needs to be interaction, problem solving, and critical thinking in terms of a team approach in taking forward this programme. It is critical that these team skills are actively in place to help staff continue to learn and grow in this area of work. This will also help ensure that the programme is delivered safely and that it does no harm to anyone. Monitoring and evaluation issues will be dealt with in Part 3.

Risk issues

Finally, there is risk. Risk assessment and management run through modern life like blood through veins. Our world is now dominated by risk related issues and fears. We have seen how even with the most sophisticated security and monitoring systems available, that, on occasion, disasters have occurred without warning. PAMP is a voluntary, educational, preventative intervention for motivated parents. There will be an ethos of respect and acceptance and an onus on the facilitators to ensure that no participant is placed in a position where they are embarrassed, humiliated or degraded.

Prospective participants need to be happy to commit to these principles both in terms of how they will be treated but also in relation to how they will treat others. Each participant will contract that they will be respectful and allow others to have their views even if they don't agree with them. The responsibility of the facilitators to monitor and maintain this contract will also be made clear. If these principles are adhered to, the likelihood of an outburst of unhealthy anger or aggression will be greatly reduced. In addition, a clearly defined programme structure will also help minimise frustration that can result from vague expectations of what is going to happen.

Of course, the fact that the people who are wishing to come on the programme do have problems in how they manage anger does indicate that the potential for aggressive behaviour may be there. It is important that the facilitators are not unduly alarmed by an exposure to anger. Remaining calm provides counterbalancing reassurance, and it also prevents giving off cues which may be misread as threat signals by an angry person (Novaco and Chemtob, 1998). It is important not to take it personally. An outburst may even provide an unexpected opportunity to teach anger coping skills. Always remember that for that person, anger may have got them what they wanted in certain situations and it may be difficult to relinquish this sense of control and effectiveness. Of course, if the participant's anger is not possible to manage within the group and it is causing distress and being disruptive to others in the group then a supported withdrawal from the programme will be required.

Basic common sense measures should be incorporated into the structure and delivery of the programme. These should include a public and protected location for the programme, personal details about the facilitators being kept confidential, consideration given to the arrangement of the physical surroundings and that there is a security response to a crisis.

Information about a potential member's past aggressive behaviour needs to be taken seriously and considered. The programme is not suitable as a response to people who have known histories of serious violence. It is not a response to domestic violence. In particular, it is not suitable for those who are known to be perpetrators of serious domestic violence. This behaviour should be addressed formally within the criminal justice system and decisions taken in terms of legal or other responses to it. Domestic violence is not an anger management issue. There are underlying beliefs involved which need to be addressed. There are dangers in the perpetrator seeing anger management as a solution to their problems, and it can also create a false sense of security for the victim. Much more in-depth work may need to be carried out with perpetrators in terms of them being held accountable and taking responsibility for their behaviour (Heery, 2000).

If it becomes clear that some of the participants have been on the receiving end of domestic violence, they should immediately be offered access to advice and support in helping them address this difficulty. Along with children safety issues, prospective participants need to be made aware of the clear policy and procedures in relation to addressing domestic violence. With regard to children there is little room for discretion. If there is information coming from any of the participants which indicate that children have been abused, or are at risk of serious abuse, the details should be passed onto the relevant statutory child protection agency.

Conclusion

A lot of issues have been raised which are important for the potential facilitators to think about and address before embarking on delivery of this intervention. Part 2 contains more detailed guidance and the detailed outlines for each of the sessions of the programme. It also returns to and addresses in more depth some of the themes raised above. The sessions will build upon this foundation and provide all that is required to deliver the programme.

PART TWO

THE PAMP PROGRAMME: THE SESSIONS

Session structure

PAMP is comprised of eight sessions, each lasting approximately two hours. As indicated in Figure 1.1, each session has a similar structure with six distinct elements. The sessions are designed to allow some flexibility to facilitators although about 20 minutes or so should be allocated to each element. In terms of adult learning theory the sessions are designed to maximise participants' engagement with, and concentration on the task. They will work in bursts of 20 minutes or so with a short break between segments. This will also allow the facilitators some discretion in the time allocated to each element and to build some flexibility into the programme (sessions may be slightly shorter for individual delivery).

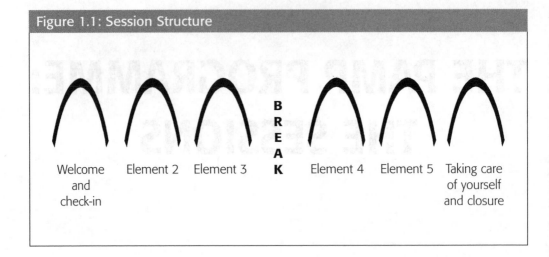

Figure 1.1: Session Structure

| Welcome and check-in | Element 2 | Element 3 | B R E A K | Element 4 | Element 5 | Taking care of yourself and closure |

The first and final element of each session is the same. Each session will begin with a welcome. The content and objectives will then be outlined to participants. The objectives for each session are outcome based and each element within the session will relate to one or more of these. The aim is to break down the overall challenge of better anger management as a parent into smaller, more achievable tasks; in other words, to facilitate participants to 'work on focused, goal limited objectives, rather than on a global 'anger problem' that can otherwise seem impenetrable and insolvable' (Novaco and Chemtob, 1998: 181). From Session 2 on, the first element will also include the opportunity for participants to check in. The check in encourages participants to monitor how they are doing and guidance is provided on this in Sessions 1 and 2.

The final element in all the sessions is called 'taking care of yourself'. This acts both as a relaxing way to finish off the session and also has a wider focus on helping participants begin to think about stress and lifestyle issues. Each session will end with a short closure aimed at encouraging participants to briefly identify one piece of learning.

In terms of how each of the remaining elements are constructed, a variety of approaches are used as indicated below. The aim is to relate to participants' differing learning styles and preferences, whether this be visual, aural, through reading and writing or of a more participatory active mode. It is important to clarify the needs of the participants in relation to literacy before commencing, and the material then delivered in the way which best suits their learning needs. Participants should be advised that written work will not be a demand of the programme but it is a helpful aid for those who prefer to do so. They can use a notebook for this purpose. Session outlines and the figures can also be provided for participants as a resource. The overall approach is designed to provide opportunities for participants to connect to an adult learning cycle of experiencing learning needs around their management of anger, having the chance to reflect on these, consider various ideas and perspectives on them and finally have the opportunity on an ongoing basis to try out and test new learning (Kolb, 1984). The various approaches used will be clearly indicated as follows in each of the sessions:

1. **Presentations:** The facilitators will present information to the individual or group. This material will be clearly outlined in the guidance and will usually not take more than five or ten minutes. The onus is on the facilitator to get a good sense of this critical material and in their own way to share it with participants.

2. **Discussions:** These will usually follow on from the above, and will involve the opportunity for participants to discuss issues raised by the input either in groups or with the facilitator.

3. **Exercises:** More experiential activities including drawing, collage work and role play will also be used in some of the elements. Not all of these inputs will be suitable for individual delivery and alternative options will be offered.

4. **Individual work:** This will comprise of time for participants to relate material to their own situations, to complete self-assessments, hand outs, plans etc., which they may wish to keep or use to reflect on some of the implications and learning for themselves.

5. **Theory – evidence base:** Finally, for many of the elements, additional material will be provided for the facilitators' information reflecting a wide range of the literature.

This will include some rationale for the approach being taken and also more specific guidance. This is intended to deepen facilitators' knowledge and may help with issues that arise in discussions or from the exercises. This material does not need to be formally presented to the individual or group.

Session 1
Choice, Change and Minding the Gap!

Lord, give me the serenity to accept the things I can't change, the courage to change the things I can, and the wisdom to know the difference.

Serenity Prayer

1.1 Welcome, introduction and objectives

The objectives of the session are that you will:
- Feel welcome, understand and contract to the programme.
- Decide how motivated you are to better manage your anger as a parent.
- Identify helps and hindrances in achieving your goal of managing your anger better as a parent.
- Learn about managing your stress.

1.2 The programme's aims, objectives, approach and contract
The anger diary, working between sessions and checking in
Contracting

1.3 Ready, willing and able: thinking about change

Break

1.4 Exploring an abusive anger outburst

1.5 Facing the challenge

1.6 Taking care of yourself and closure

Facilitators' Guidance for Session 1

1.1: Welcome, introduction and objectives

Warmly welcome participants, or the individual, to Session 1 and acknowledge their commitment to partake. Indicate that introductions will take place shortly. Display the session title, objectives and outline. In this, the first of eight sessions, the focus will be on change and in particular on the choice they have made to try and make changes in relation to their behaviour. Explain the idea of the word 'gap' in the session title and how this refers to the gap between where they are now and where they want to be – to manage their anger better as parents! In this first session, they will begin to think about how committed they are to getting across this gap.

Following this, briefly outline the objectives of the session. Emphasise that the first objective is about making sure that everyone feels welcome in the group and knows exactly what they are getting into. Objectives two and three are aimed at giving people the opportunity to think about their motivation for doing this personal work and what may help or hinder them in doing so. Objective four is to help people with stress and lifestyle issues. This will be how each session will end and will be developed as the programme progresses. Briefly run through the content of the session.

The facilitators need to introduce themselves and share a little about their background and experiences. It is important to stress one's interest and commitment to working alongside people in helping them to undertake the work. It can also be helpful to point out that *all* parents have to work hard at managing their anger. This can be demonstrated by a short personal story about the facilitators own difficulties with anger (see author's example in the Introduction). Following this, and to conclude this first element of the session, each participant should be invited to introduce themselves, using their preferred first name, and to briefly give an indication of why they have come. Thank people for their input and check that everyone is clear about what is going to happen before moving onto the next element. Encourage them to ask questions if they need any clarification.

Theory/evidence base

As indicated in the introduction, some pre-group work should have been done and prospective participants will have had an opportunity to get some information on the programme. Nevertheless, the first session is critical. From the outset, the venue needs to be comfortable and the approach warm, gentle, friendly and accepting. Remember Maslow's hierarchy of needs. He argued that certain basic physiological needs have to be met first before the individual can then think about other higher level needs.

22

Basically, participants need to feel physically safe and comfortable. Similarly with emotional needs, they need to feel secure. The way the programme begins can help take this process forward and encourage participants' motivation towards meeting higher needs around learning and self-actualisation (Maslow, 1970).

The theme of this first session is around positive beginnings and emphasising choice and responsibility in terms of why people are in the group (Deffenbacher, 1996). It is about trying to build on participants' courage and commitment in undertaking a difficult journey of change. At the same time, it is critical to highlight at this early stage that the programme will encourage and challenge participants to make changes to their thinking and behaviours.

One writer on group work refers to the three Cs: compassion, commitment and competence (Benson, 1996). These need to be conveyed at the outset. It is critical that the approach is clear, particularly in this first element of the programme. This will set up the next element which is about continuing to foster members' attraction to the group, establishing structure and control, developing trust and cohesion and negotiating an agreement on the work of the group.

1.2: The programme's aims, objectives, approach and contract

Presentation

Using Figure 1.2, present the aims and objectives of the programme. Emphasise that the aim is clear – to help parents learn to better manage their anger with their children. To this end participants will need to make progress across the range of objectives that either can be read out, or displayed in the room if appropriate:

Figure 1.2: PAMP Aims and Objectives

To learn to manage my anger as a parent by:

1. Increasing awareness of my anger, stress and aggression.

2. Identifying a personal list of my main anger arousing situations and circumstances as a parent (my triggers).

3. Challenging and making changes in my thinking in relation to anger arousing situations.

4. Learning ways to calm myself, such as breathing focused relaxation, progressive muscular relaxation, and guided imagery training.

5. Improving my coping skills in dealing with provocative, problem and conflict situations.

6. Reducing the frequency, intensity and duration of my anger as a parent and my use of aggression.

Point out that the approach throughout will be about helping people to make progress in relation to these objectives. Before getting into the work, it is important to make the following points:

- Acknowledge each participant's courage in being prepared to state that they have a problem with their anger and the resultant behaviours. Point out that, as with any difficulty in life, the starting point in beginning to deal with it is to take ownership.

- Research, and our own experience, tell us that most, if not all of us, become mildly to moderately angry anything from several times a day to several times a week. Studies carried out on even 'average parents' report high levels of anger with their children and the fear that they will sometimes lose control and harm their children. So it is something all parents experience to varying degrees.

- Stress that this course is not about an 'expert' telling parents how they should improve what they do, or telling them how to deal with their anger and parenting. They are responsible for their own parenting and they will make their own decisions on what to take from this course.

- Emphasise that it is an educational course based on adult learning principles. It will not be lectures. Information will be provided, and they will be challenged to think about a wide range of areas. However, it will be much more than just listening to a facilitator. There will be opportunities to watch, move and take part in physical activities, talk, share opinions, practise skills, plan, problem solve etc. In short, they will be offered a wide range of learning opportunities. What will be required from them is an open mind along with commitment, determination, concentration and dedication. It will be their choice and responsibility to do the work.

- Everyone is different. Each participant has his or her own unique history and experiences. The course is designed to cover as full a range of relevant issues as possible but some parts may be more relevant than others. Try to stay with it. There are common themes that run through the course and learning may come from somewhere unexpected if the person or group can stay alert and involved. However, at the end of the day it will be their right to take what fits and leave the rest.

- Suggest that participants may at times experience feelings of confusion, embarrassment and distress. This is not the purpose of the course although they are here to have themselves challenged. Such feelings may in fact be a good sign, that *'you're shaking yourself up'*.

- Finally, learning can be fun! Encourage participants to open their minds and hearts to the material, process it, and, at least, give it a fair chance. This course is about giving an opportunity to participants to take some time out to think about anger in their family life in general and particularly as a parent, to explore and reflect on it. This should lead to some participants learning specific ways of coping and managing anger in ways which are not harmful to themselves or others whom they care for.

Before moving on, check if anyone has any issues with the approach.

The anger diary, working between sessions and checking in

To illustrate that the course is about people deciding and committing to the work themselves, the idea of the anger diary should be introduced at this point. In relation to this, each future session will begin with a brief check in, where participants will be given the opportunity to share briefly how their anger has been in the period since the last session. They need to keep some sort of record for themselves of how they are dealing with their anger with their children. A very simple recording system can be suggested and provided to them as outlined in Figure 1.3. They should make a point at the end of each day to reflect back on how their anger has gone and if they haven't been angry as a parent during the day they should note it down. However, if they have been angry during the day they should score themselves against the questions in Figure 1.3. They can use a diary notebook for this purpose. At the start of each session they will have the chance to make a brief statement of how often they became angry, how long their anger episodes lasted and what were the scores they gave themselves in terms of their level of arousal and aggression. This allows one way of monitoring how they are doing on the programme and if they can identify any movement for themselves at home with their children.

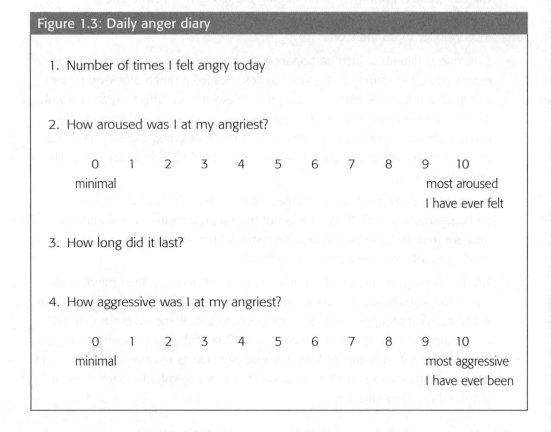

Figure 1.3: Daily anger diary

1. Number of times I felt angry today

2. How aroused was I at my angriest?

   0   1   2   3   4   5   6   7   8   9   10
   minimal   most aroused
                                                  I have ever felt

3. How long did it last?

4. How aggressive was I at my angriest?

   0   1   2   3   4   5   6   7   8   9   10
   minimal   most aggressive
                                                  I have ever been

Contracting

Although it is preferable that all potential participants have already signed the main programme contract (see Appendix 2) they need to have the chance to think about how they want to work together as a group. They will probably already be getting a sense of a structured course and it is important that everyone doing the course understands and agrees to this, as well as to the original contract and to the non-negotiable ground rules. Briefly take the group through the following core ground rules and guidelines, which should be displayed (see Figure 1.4).

Figure 1.4: PAMP contract

Respect

Confidentiality

Participation

Safety

Time

Respect

Facilitators and participants will be required to show respect to each other. Each participant needs to feel comfortable with the group and know that they have the right to express their views and to be heard. It is important that participants feel able to share emotionally charged or difficult material without disruption or judgement. This does not mean that everyone has to agree with them! Disagreement and debate are welcome but no-one should feel pressurised or forced to accept ideas that they are not happy with, even if it means that participants and facilitators agree to disagree.

The facilitators and participants have a responsibility to challenge abusive and discriminatory attitudes and behaviour.

Confidentiality

Nothing that is said by any course participant should be disclosed to, or discussed with, anyone who is not on the course (see below). When participants talk about issues, experiences or events involving significant others (e.g. family members or friends etc.) care should be taken not to divulge details that might reveal their identity.

Confidentiality may only be breached if:
- A participant's safety may be of serious concern.
- The safety of another individual is at risk including child protection issues.
- A criminal offence has been committed, or may be about to be committed.

Participation

Participants are expected to fully commit themselves to the programme. The course is not compulsory and is designed for people who are motivated to be there and to do the work. Unless there are significant safety issues as indicated below, participants will be asked to take part in all elements of the programme. The more they put in the more they will get out of it. The use of the diary and reflecting on the work between sessions will greatly enhance the learning from the programme.

Participants should be reminded that this is a learning programme, and is not counselling or personal therapy. Disclosures of sensitive material cannot be worked on, and interpretations should not be offered on other participants' behaviours.

Safety

If participants are to feel respected within the programme, then they must be safe from any form of aggressive behaviour. Verbal, physical and any other unacceptable behaviour will not be tolerated. It may also be the case that anger related difficulties are areas that are emotionally charged, and potentially distressing for some people. It is not, however, the intention of the programme to cause distress, even though the risk is there. Every effort should be made to alert participants to the content of each session in order for them to judge the extent to which they wish to participate. If they choose, participants may opt out of exercises without having to explain their reasons.

At least one of the facilitators should be available after each session should any participant wish to talk about how the course has been affecting them.

Time

The facilitators should ensure that the sessions finish on time, and will not be extended beyond the times set out. Participants should take responsibility for attending sessions in good time. If participants are going to be late or have to leave early the facilitators should be informed.

Exercise

After the above points have been outlined, participants should be asked to form pairs, reintroduce themselves and discuss briefly how they feel about the guidelines. They need to be happy with them and feel they can suggest any additions or amendments that they wish to make. Briefly take feedback from each of the pairs and agree and confirm the contract. (If working with an individual, give them a few minutes to reflect on the guidelines and give her or him the opportunity to suggest additions or amendments).

Theory/evidence base

In this element of the session, a significant amount of direct information has to be given by facilitators to the participants in relation to programme objectives, including content, style and contract. With regard to contracting it is important to be clear about what is negotiable and what is not. Participants will need to have a clear sense of what they are agreeing to. The facilitators should take their leadership responsibility and spell out the minimum expectations of those participating (Benson, 1996). It is difficult for facilitators to achieve the right balance in terms of not being over directive and negatively impacting on the process or dynamic within the group or the individual. In line with the adult learning theory referred to below, there needs to be an ethos where participants feel they can ask questions, make points to each other, be spontaneous and learn. To this end, the importance of seeking the involvement of participants to create some sense of ownership of the process is important and should be strived for in the approach taken. It is also clear from the literature that an effective aid in obtaining commitment within the group is that of involving the group in agreeing guidelines. This may have been done to a certain degree in the selection process or the preliminary interview but the group as a unit will have to establish norms of behaviour which are acceptable to all members. It is therefore important to give the group or individual a real opportunity to reflect on or contribute to the group contract.

The idea of the check in and the anger diary is to help participants to have a sense of the problem they have with their anger and to help them contribute to self-monitor their progress. Coping with anger is an active process. Participants should be encouraged to think about the material that is covered between sessions, and whilst there will be no formal homework per se, suggestions will be given about practising some of the topics covered in the sessions.

Research in adult learning indicates that people learn in different and varying ways. For example, there are those who prefer a social style and generally communicate well with people, both verbally and non-verbally. They prefer learning in groups or classes and like to heighten learning by bouncing ideas and thoughts off other people. Those with a visual style prefer images, pictures, colour and other visual means to help their learning. The programme will aim to provide a wide range of learning approaches. It needs a flexible approach to both recognise that there is more to intelligence than just verbal reasoning ability and to meet the need to respond to people's different strengths. Ultimately this will depend on the participants' motivation as outlined later in this chapter. Adult learning theory comes to similar conclusions for example, in that the andragogical model of adult learning proposes the view that adults tend to be more motivated towards learning that helps them solve problems in their own lives (Knowles, 1984).

1.3: Ready, willing and able: thinking about change

Presentation and exercise

In this part of the session, participants are encouraged to think about and reflect on where they are in relation to their motivation to work at change in this area of their lives. This can be answered by asking them to think about how 'ready, willing and able' they really are (see Figure 1.5).

*Are they really **ready**?*
Is anger management a big enough priority for each of them at this point in their lives? Everybody has things that they know they should do something about but still don't! Do participants realise that it's going to be a process and not something that can be done quickly?

*How **willing** are they?*
Do they really feel that things need to change? Is there a gap between how things are in their lives and how things ought to be? This is the gap they need to think about. Are they really feeling the discomfort and tension in themselves because of the gap? Is the desire to get across the gap something that's coming from inside themselves or are they being pushed into this by someone else? If it's not really coming from themselves how likely is it that they can stay committed to the work?

*Finally, how **able** do they feel that they can manage their anger better?*
How confident are they that progress can be made? Have they a sense of hope? The fact that they have taken this first step may well be a demonstration of their hope. Also do they have the discipline and self-control to stick with it? Can they work to a long-term goal?

Leave the question of how ready, willing and able they are with them and point out that they will be returning to it later in the session.

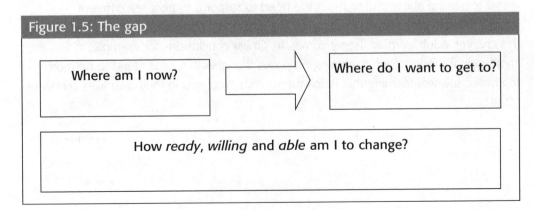

Figure 1.5: The gap

Where am I now? → Where do I want to get to?

How *ready, willing* and *able* am I to change?

Exercise

For now, the task is to show the process of change. Ask a participant to volunteer an example of a successful change they have made in another area of their life. Examples such as giving up smoking, alcohol, loosing weight, changes in lifestyle are useful, but things like changing hair colour are not! Reassure any potential volunteer that it will not be a threatening exercise. The task for the facilitator is then to try to take that person through their change process. An experiential way of doing this is to use the room layout or seats to show and illustrate the person physically moving through the process of change. Alternatively, it can be drawn out on a flip chart (see Figure 1.6).

It is vital that down-to-earth language is used to help the person bring their example to life. This process does not need to be explained in detail by the facilitator as it is self-explanatory. In my experience, usually when I have done this exercise, an appropriate example has been found within the group and the point has been made.

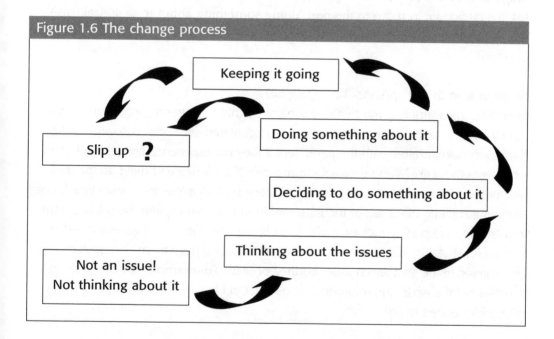

Figure 1.6 The change process

Keeping it going

Doing something about it

Slip up **?**

Deciding to do something about it

Thinking about the issues

Not an issue!
Not thinking about it

Stage or seat 1: Not an issue (pre-contemplation)
For the purpose of this exercise, the facilitator should begin by asking the person to think of a time **before** they considered the example behaviour to be a problem, when it just wasn't an issue for them at all! Refer to it as a time that the person was not thinking about the need to change. Get them to sit in the first seat, the **'not thinking about it seat'**. Ask one or two open questions as to why it wasn't an issue for them, but don't get into challenges. If doing this exercise on a flip chart, draw up the 'not thinking about it box'.

Stage or seat 2: Thinking about the issue (contemplation)
Ask the volunteer to move to the **'thinking about it seat'**. Then begin to explore, briefly and in general terms, how the person first began to think about making a change in the behaviour that they are considering. How long did it take for them to begin to see that it was an issue? What was that issue about? What exactly was it that got them to think about making the change? How long did this go on for? Was it outside pressure? Was it the growing knowledge of an issue? How did they think about the need to change?

Stage or seat 3: Deciding to do something about it (determination)
What then led the person to decide to do something about it? Move the person to the **'deciding to do something about it'** seat. What did they decide? How firm or loose was their plan?

Stage or seat 4: Doing something about it (action)
Ask the participant to move to the next **'doing something about it'** seat. Again, use the participant's example to ask some open general questions. What did they do? How did it go?

Stage or seat 5: Slip up/knock back (relapse)
Hopefully, the example given by the volunteer will not have been successful in making the change the first time and they will have encountered set backs. Following on from the action stage, explore with the participant if they did experience any set backs and what were these like? Were they able to maintain the change and move to the final seat or did they have a slip up and have to move back to a 'previous seat'? Which one? Without going into the detail of the issues referred to below explore the set back issue in relation to the participant's example. In particular use one or two general questions to explore what they did in response to the set back and have them demonstrate this by returning to the seat which reflected their position. For example, did they give up completely for a while and return to seat one? Or did they go back to thinking about what they needed to do?

Stage or seat 6: Keeping it going (maintenance)
Ask the volunteer to move to this seat and talk about the successful change they made. Is there any possibility of relapse or is it something now truly established and built into their life?

Thank the person for their example and let them know that they have summarised many years of research into change! The main point to stress is that change is rarely a one-off success. It is an ongoing process and sometimes a set back may be one step closer to eventual success. Success is on the far side of failure. Change will not be a single event or transition rather a process or series of transitions in a movement that may gradually lead to desistance from the problem behaviours.

Refocus the group on why they are here. They have each identified their behaviour in relation to their anger as a parent as being problematic and needing to change. In terms of this, where do they see themselves? Ask them to go to the seat or part of the room that represents where they are on the stages of change. Allow each person to take a place and then ask each why they have sat where they have. (If several people go to the same seat ask them to take turns or bring over extra seats!) Affirm each person's reply.

If using a flip chart allow each person come up and initial where they are in the process. The main point is to use everyday language to make the concepts clear and accessible to all participants.

Theory/evidence base

Research identifies two key elements involved in change. At the end of the day it comes down to a person's **motivation** and their **ability** to achieve it. In other words, change requires someone to accept the need to change as well as having a means or a strategy to actually make it happen. In this session the focus is mainly on participants' motivation to change. This is done through the Stages of Change Model or formerly the Trans Theoretical Model (Prochaska and DiClemente, 1994). In short, the *stages of change model* represents the temporal dimension of change and is currently among the most popular social-cognitive models of health promotion being researched. Those who have succeeded in addressing addictive behaviours appear to go through an observable process of change. This model has had enormous impact in the addictions field with stage appropriate interventions. It has just recently began to make its way into the world of social work and criminal justice in assisting with a wider range of behavioural changes. Whilst research is more limited in these areas, it nevertheless provides a useful model to help us understand change across a range of behavioural areas.

Stage 1: Pre-contemplation This is the stage where there is no acknowledgement or acceptance of a problem or difficulty or any sign of a desire for the need to change (as GK Chesterson said, 'It isn't that they can't see the solution – they can't see the problem'). The person may well be unaware of the issues, deny responsibility, blame others or may be scared. They may feel helpless and passive. This may range across a continuum from complete to partial denial, to minimising use of negative behaviours, to minimising one's responsibility for such behaviours or to denying or minimising the harm caused by such behaviours. It is marked by resistance to change which can be characterised by reluctance, rebellion, resignation, or rationalisation.

Stage 2: Contemplation At this point, the person may be open to the possibility of an issue or issues being important and the need for change. The person might be open to considering personally relevant information and feed-back and to weighing up the pros and cons of change, but continue to be ambivalent and anxious about moving forward. This early motivation may come from being subject to external intervention and therefore, as yet, there is no personal commitment. Some people may wait for a magic moment, some may act prematurely without thinking things through, some may say in a month or two, some may substitute thinking for action and talk about change for years!

Stage 3: Determination This is the stage where the person is beginning to accept that there are real problems and is adamant about doing something about them. There will be variations as to how far the determination will take the person into real change. Some may be able to identify changes and specify goals but may remain ambivalent about the process and consequences. Some people may try to convince themselves of the need to do something while others will be able to formulate a solid, realistic assessment coupled with a calm dedication to move forward usually measured as within the next month.

Stage 4: Action In the literature this action stage is the phase of implementing a plan and a period when the actual change may be observed. A sense of efficacy, of being able to do it, is important. There may be a danger of the client seeing the change as a panacea for all ills or there is only superficial compliance, old habits die hard!

Stage 5: Relapse This is an integral part of the change process. Change is viewed as cyclical and something that rarely succeeds first time. Indeed, one of the strengths of this cyclical model is that it allows for 'the reality that few people succeed the first time round' (Howarth and Morrison, 2000: 83). Change comes from repeated efforts, re-evaluation, renewal of commitment and incremental successes. It is often an uneven process of setbacks, gains and relapses. There may be naivety about the possibility of change or insecurity and vulnerability as one moves into new territory and the temptation to revert to old ways in times of crisis and complexity. So relapse, the slip up or the step back is a natural and frequent occurrence. This can actually be a sign of being closer to achieving change. It is important that facilitators maintain a positive view of the resistance of participants on programmes such as this one. Resistance should be viewed as a normal natural process, indeed it should be welcomed as a possible sign that participants are trying to engage with significant aspects of their behaviour.

Stage 6: Maintenance If someone has made and maintained successful change they have moved into this phase. Maintenance can be thought of when people have sustained the change for a significant period of time. It is also useful to see it as a continuation of change, not the absence of change. The literature varies on the amount of time required to justify the claim that the change has been made. This ranges from a minimum of six months to others who argue that the change needs to be demonstrated for much longer periods of five years and more.

The other aspect of the stages of change model, which is a theme that runs through the programme, is the responsibility on the facilitators to set the scene and work in ways that create the possibility that motivation may be increased and to encourage participants to keep working at it. The programme is aimed at people who are at least at the determination stage, and seeks to use insights from the Motivational Interviewing approach which argues for a collaborative and empowering foundation to assisting people with behaviour change. To this end, and reflecting the value base and adult learning principles already referred to, the approach of facilitators needs to be based on demonstrating empathy to participants, avoiding argumentation, encouraging them to challenge their own thinking and finally, supporting and believing in their ability to change (Miller and Rollnick, 2002). Nevertheless, the ultimate responsibility for change remains with the individual and it has to be faced that for some this may not be possible.

Break

1.4: Exploring an abusive anger outburst

Presentation and exercise

Present or show an example of a parent's mismanagement of anger leading to an abusive, aggressive incident. A scenario can be read out to the group but it will be more powerful if a short example can be presented on video or DVD. It is usually possible to get examples from TV soaps, dramas, films or various agencies such as the NSPCC. Child Care organisations may have vignettes which can be obtained. Something which shows the context, build up and how the anger is manifested is required. It does not need to show extreme violence, indeed it may be better if it doesn't, but gives a sense of an abusive angry outburst. This should last approximately five minutes.

Explain to the participants that the purpose of this exercise is just to get them thinking about different issues involved in the anger episode. After listening to or watching the unhealthy anger outburst, the group should be introduced to the triangle of behaviour which is going to be a theme for this programme. This can be handed out or drawn up on a flip chart and used as a resource for the exercise (see Figure 1.7). Ask the group to consider separately the three points of the triangle:

1. What was the angry parent thinking?

2. What emotions was the angry person experiencing?

3. What abusive actions did the angry person do?

This can be done in various ways, as a group discussion, individually, or participants could work in pairs with each pair taking a different question and then briefly giving feedback. This will also help in the process of group members getting to know each other. Another more experiential way is to create an imaginary triangle in the room using tape or furniture and identify the three corners as for thinking, feeling and action.

If required, additional questions may also be used to further the analysis:

4. What were the effects on the children and the parent?

5. Would there be any difference in the scenario if the parent was of the opposite sex?

6. What ideas do you have that may have let the parent deal with the situation in a better way?

7. What does the parent need to do to try to move away from using such behaviour?

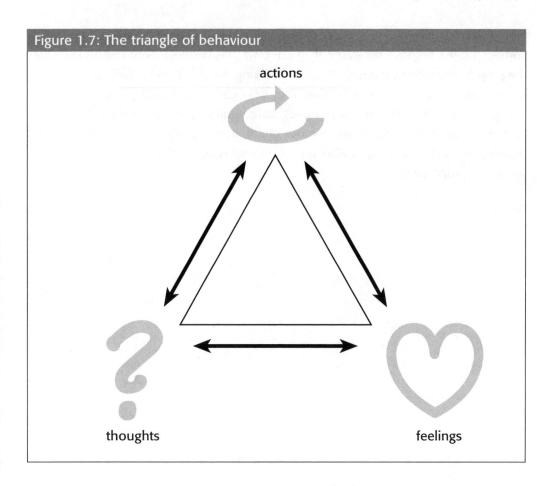

Figure 1.7: The triangle of behaviour

actions

thoughts

feelings

Emphasise that this is not a test, with right or wrong answers, nor are participants expected to provide detailed, definitive answers at this stage. Stress that the behaviour being looked at in the example is much more than just the actions of the person, but needs to be understood within the context of the persons thoughts and feelings as well. It is this triangle of thoughts, emotions and actions that need to be worked on if change to behaviour is to occur. This is what they will ultimately be doing on this programme. Point out that the triangle of behaviour, which they have applied to try to understand the behaviour of the parent in the example will be the main tool they will use in this programme in trying to understand, and more importantly begin to change, their own behaviour. To make progress in this they will have to work at all three corners of the triangle, i.e. their thinking, their feelings and their actions. That is the challenge ahead. Affirm participants' efforts as they will probably have identified many of the issues and problems that the programme will be looking at.

Theory/evidence base
The basis of this element is to allow participants to begin to open up the areas of behaviour that they will be asked to examine in the programme, but initially in a safe

way, as it is not their own behaviour. It is usually easier to look at, analyse and process someone else's negative behaviour than our own. This will help them begin to see that the programme will cover areas to do with thinking, emotions and actions and how these relate and connect to each other. They will need to continually revisit these areas and go through them in their own way, regularly, vigorously and powerfully. The cognitive behavioural analysis, and the use of the triangle to try to give a visual way of grasping this and continuing to work on behavioural issues, will become a core strand within the programme.

1.5: Facing the challenge

Presentation and exercise

For this penultimate sequence, begin by pointing out that participants have just looked at an example of someone else's anger. The challenge for each of the group now is to look at and challenge their own anger. Using Figure 1.8 overleaf, ask the participants to think about how they will meet the overall aim of the programme which states: 'To manage my anger better as a parent.' This is what is hoped for each person in the room. This is what they are taking ownership of. This is their goal.

If working with an individual, discuss and explore the issues which have been raised. If working with a group, the options of working in pairs should be considered, again aimed at helping participants get to know each other. Each pair can then feedback some of their points into a general group discussion and this can be recorded on a flipchart under the heading of helps, hindrances and ideas.

Conclude this part of the session by pointing out, that with regard to change , with all its complexity and difficulty, there are two key aspects that seem to be present in those who make this change. Firstly, with regard to motivation, they see it as a really **important** issue in their lives. Secondly, with regard to their ability to succeed, they feel **confident** about doing so. Ask participants to think about these two concepts in relation to the challenge they are facing and all the obstacles to progress they will experience.

Ask each participant to do their own score on the importance/confidence scale shown in Figure 1.8 on page 40 and share within the group.

Figure 1.8: Facing the challenge: to manage my anger better as a parent

1. What are the things that may help me achieve this goal?

2. What are the things that may block me achieving my goal?

3. What ideas do I have that will give me a better chance of success?

How important is this to me?

    0   1   2   3   4   5   6   7   8   9   10

Not important   Most important

  at all   thing in my life

How confident am I of succeeding?

    0   1   2   3   4   5   6   7   8   9   10

Not confident   Totally

  at all   confident

1.6: Taking care of yourself and closure

Point out to participants that, in this and subsequent sessions, the final element will be about relaxation, both as a way to end the session following the hard work that they have completed and to help them begin to think about stress and lifestyle issues. Inform the participants that they will be exploring stress and lifestyle issues in more detail later in the final session of the programme. Just for now, they are asked to be open to the material and give it a chance to help them judge how useful it will be to them in managing their anger.

Point out that there is much research showing how lifestyle and associated tension and stress issues have a two-way relationship with anger. Physical tension creates stress, which may predispose us to anger. Anger then causes additional body tension so it becomes easy to get locked into a vicious cycle of stress and anger. Stress can become the fuel of anger. Research has also indicated three useful approaches in managing stress and these are breathing, muscular relaxation and using guided imagery. Tell participants that they will have the opportunity to experience each of these in the remainder of the programme. Make it clear that these examples will only provide a sample of what is available in each of these areas in order to give people a sense of them.

Before starting the exercise the following points should be made:
1. Relaxation is not a state that one has to remain in at all times. Stress can be the spice of life. It is about balance and knowing when we are too stressed and tense and being able to do something about it.
2. Relaxation is something that is obtainable, although it can be difficult to achieve, depending on ones lifestyle and attitudes towards it.
3. These sessions will not be about trying to take control of their minds. They will not be hypnotised or brain washed. It is an opportunity to begin to think about and sample possible ways of dealing with the stress they experience in their lives.
4. Finally, although they are designed to be 'relaxing' and not arduous, nevertheless, particularly with the breathing exercises, if anyone feels that they do not want to partake for any reason, particularly medical, they should feel free to abstain from the practice. (It is important to reiterate this point at the start of each session.)

Explain to the group that in this first session, they will be taken through a basic relaxation method. This may be useful particularly at times when they are feeling very stressed and close to 'loosing their cool'. It is based on the evidence that deep breathing is an effective way to lower physical stress levels (Bergin and Fitzgerald, 1994).

41

Use the following script to take the individual or group through the exercise:

1. Make sure that your body is in an upright position, either sitting or standing.

2. Mentally say 'stop' to yourself.

3. Close your eyes, close your mouth and breathe in deeply through the nostrils. Exhale slowly through the nostrils.

4. Allow your shoulders to drop and the hands to relax. If standing, allow the arms and hands to hang loose. If sitting, allow the arms to slightly bend and the backs of the hand to rest on top of the thighs.

5. Allow the teeth to slightly part, the tongue to rest on the base of the mouth and the jaw to relax.

6. Breathe in deeply through the nostrils. Breathe out slowly through the nostrils. Do at least five inhalations and five exhalations.

7. Allow your breathing to return to normal allowing it to find its own speed, length, depth and rhythm.

(If necessary, the above exercise could be practised more than once.)

Closure

Ask participants to indicate in one word how they are feeling and, more importantly, one thing they are taking away from the session in terms of new learning that they will apply in their lives. 'To learn and not to do, is not to learn' (Covey, 2004: 33). The main point is to keep it quick and snappy. Indicate that the work of the session is finished. Do not go back into the work. Affirm people for doing the work and participating and leave any questions and issues with them to ponder themselves or to bring back next session. If someone is clearly upset or distressed, they can be offered the chance to stay back and discuss things with the facilitator. A quick final reminder on the anger diary or check in may be helpful.

Session 2

The Challenge of Anger

Anyone can become angry – that is easy. But to be angry with the right person, to the right degree, at the right time, for the right purpose, and in the right way – this is not easy.

Aristotle

2.1   Welcome, objectives, overview and check in

The objectives of the session are that you will:
- Increase your understanding of anger.
- Explore how you experience and express your anger.
- Reflect on one of your abusive anger outbursts.
- Learn about managing your stress.

2.2   What is anger?

2.3   The big body map: the effects of poor anger management on health and well being

Break

2.4   The stages of anger

2.5   Mismanaged anger as a parent

2.6   Taking care of yourself and closure

Facilitators' Guidance for Session 2

2.1: Welcome, objectives, overview and check in

Welcome the group or individual to the second session. Display the session title, objectives and overview. Remind the participants that they have had the chance to consider their motivation and commitment to undertake this personal work. In this session, the focus will be on taking a detailed look at their difficulties with anger. By the end of the session, they will each think and feel that they have made some progress in trying to face up to Aristotle's challenge. The first objective is to try to get a sense of what exactly anger is. The second objective is about beginning to think about how this anger is experienced and expressed. The third objective aims to take this further so that each participant will be able to explore, in some depth, one of their own angry outbursts as a parent and link this to the 'Triangle of Behaviour' presented in the first session. The final objective continues further learning on stress and lifestyle balance issues. Check that the group or individual understands the objectives and briefly run through the content of the session.

At this point, participants will be offered the opportunity to briefly check in to the session. Each person will have a minute or two to address their anger diary and make a general comment as to how they feel about their anger (see page 25). They should **briefly** address the key issues in relation to their anger as a parent, including its frequency, intensity, duration and finally the degree to which it has led to aggressive behaviours. There will not be the time to go into any detailed processing of situations, it is just an opportunity for people to touch base and monitor their own efforts to manage their anger and share this with the group. Is it getting better, getting worse or not really changing? People will be encouraged just to indicate this without any judgment or analysis. The facilitator should affirm those who appear to be making progress and encourage those who are finding it difficult but are still working at the task.

2.2: What is anger?

Presentation, discussion and individual exercise

Begin by pointing out that in this element, a lot of material will be presented for consideration and will be divided into three parts:

- understanding what anger is;
- how anger is experienced;
- how anger is expressed.

Understanding what anger is

Everyone in the room will probably have their own view and understanding of anger. Encourage people to share their views of anger, either as a short discussion or through calling out thoughts, ideas and words that they associate with trying to understand it. These can be recorded onto a flip chart. Naturally, within most groups there will be ideas and thoughts which reflect a wide range of understanding of what anger is. As with most areas of human behaviour, there are no neat answers and each of us has to come to our own conclusions about such issues. Emphasise that this diversity of views reflects the first key point that needs to be made, namely that there are differing ideas of what anger is. The PAMP view can then be put forward, as summarised in Figure 2.1. It is not imposed but offered to participants.

Figure 2.1: What is anger?

As natural as being thirsty

Feeling it inside myself – an emotional state

Occupying both mind and body

An aid to help 'fight the good fight'

Something that can help sort things out

A response to pain and hurt

An essential part of myself, of protecting myself, of making myself known to myself and others!

A lot of anger can be negative, unreasonable and destructive!

Anger is viewed as a normal, natural, useful, indeed necessary emotion that we all experience. They say that new born infants appear to express emotions comparable to anger and rage in the first few hours of life (Beck, 1999). So we are talking about something as **natural as being thirsty**. It is a healthy, non-evil part of our make-up and it is something that everyone experiences.

It is also an **emotional state** marked by feelings inside ourselves. Point out that the emotions will be looked at in Session 4 in much more detail.

Anger is something which is **of the mind and the body**. We are talking about a negative internal feeling state associated with thinking and feelings. It is a unique, subjective experience, accompanied by physical reactions. Our muscles will get tense and the nervous system becomes aroused. This will be explored further later in the session.

Without anger how much progress would have been made in tackling injustices within the world? How many of us can watch what happens to starving children in Africa or elsewhere without experiencing anger? So in one sense anger is given to us to help us **fight the good fight**.

Furthermore, anger is a signal that in many cases, can have positive consequences both for the sender and the receiver. At home, anger may sometimes allow difficult issues or problems to be brought to the surface and dealt with, and may actually strengthen relationships. **It may help us to sort things out.**

The universal trigger for anger is a sense of being endangered, a physical or symbolic threat to our self-esteem or dignity, being treated unjustly or rudely, being insulted or demeaned, or being frustrated in pursuing an important goal (Goleman, 1998). **It is a response to pain or hurt.**

Anger is, then, **an essential part of defining or protecting ourselves,** or making known to ourselves and others who we are.

However, the unpleasant reality is that there is a lot of anger in the world and **a lot of it is negative, unreasonable and destructive**. It causes serious problems if we are unable to manage it.

Before moving on, check with participants if they are comfortable with these approaches to anger.

How anger is experienced

Having made clear the programmes view of anger as a natural entity, that we all experience anger and have all been in an angry state at some point in our lives, there are wide variations among people in terms of how strong, how often and how long lasting their anger experiences are. Stress to participants that it is these three elements that they need to think about in beginning to understand the difficulties that they may have in how they experience anger. Take the participants through the questions in Figure 2.2, asking them to reflect on them from their own perspective.

Figure 2.2: Experiencing my anger

- **Is my anger too strong at times?**

- **Does my anger happen too often?**

- **Does my anger last for too long?**

- **Is my anger too much a part of myself, is it almost my personality?**

In relation to the first question, point out that anger can range from mild annoyance to all out fury and rage. Problems arise when we experience extremely intense anger, even allowing for the fact that 'the acceptable norms for such behaviour may vary by family and culture' (Golden, 2003: 281). High intensity anger can be something that can be distressing, almost a mysterious force that can take charge of us. Anger like this is sometimes viewed by people as being a passion by which one is gripped, seized or torn (Averill, 1982). Briefly ask the individual or group if they are worried by the intensity of their anger, even if only occasionally?

The second question to think about is frequency. Severe intensity alone is grounds for doing something about it, but even if less intense, frequent experiences of anger should also be addressed. Again ask if this is an issue for the person or group.

Thirdly, participants should be encouraged to think about the duration of anger episodes. Do they pass quickly or do they tend to stay with them. Anger experiences can range from transient to long term, and participants need to reflect on this issue and its importance if angry episodes go on too long.

Remind participants that each of us need to look closely at how we experience anger. That is the purpose of the diary they are keeping and the check-in at the beginning of each of the sessions will give them some indication of their own levels and intensity of the anger they are experiencing.

Finally, explore briefly whether the issue of anger almost being part of their personality is relevant for anyone? Does the individual or anyone in the group feel that they are angry almost all of the time? Suggest that the participants can reflect quietly on this issue but do not put any pressure on anyone to publicly indicate that they have such a problem at this point. They just need to be open to the possibility. In working through the programme and in trying to increase their own awareness of their behaviour between sessions, they may become clearer on these issues. It is also possible that for some, previous negative experiences may have had a bad effect on their lives and may be causing them anger difficulties. They may need more specialised help and assistance in trying to overcome their past traumas. The main point to be made is that while the programme will not do anything to exacerbate these difficulties, it will nevertheless be unable to provide psychotherapeutic or counselling intervention. The main focus will be on encouraging participants to work through their mismanagement of anger in the here and now, and develop ways of coping with it. One way of explaining this is to use the analogy of the tennis player needing to change how they hold the racket to improve their game. In one sense, it may be useful for the tennis player to have a full understanding of how they developed the faulty handling technique and the bad training experiences they had. However, it is not by understanding how they developed the poor technique that will improve their game, but the desire to learn the new grip and apply it. It is the same with anger. PAMP may not help them fully understand the roots of their anger, rather it will encourage and support them in working at how they handle it. PAMP will provide opportunities for everyone to reflect a little more on whether deeper issues may be relevant to their problems in a later session and to consider in confidence whether there are issues that may need a more specialised intervention.

How anger is expressed (letting it out or keeping it in!)

The expression of anger is the final subject in this element. To begin, take participants through the questionnaire in Figure 2.3. This can be done verbally; the questions are read out and each person notes down their choice of answer, either a, b, c, or d for each question. After reading out all the questions, participants can then be given the scores for each question to add up privately. Alternatively, if all the group is comfortable with doing written exercises the questionnaire can be handed out and completed and scored individually by participants.

Before outlining the significance of the scores stress that caution is needed in terms of interpreting the results, it will only give a sense of potential difficulties in the expression of their anger.

Figure 2.3: PAMP expressing my anger assessment

When I am angry I do the following:	often (a)	sometimes (b)	rarely (c)	never (d)

1. Become cold and overly controlled

2. Shout loudly

3. Cry

4. Completely lose control

5. Use verbal abuse

6. Become physically aggressive

7. Ignore it but find myself angry about something safe

8. Walk away

9. Damage property

10. Hope it will go away

(Used with permission of authors Faupel, Herrick and Sharp (1998) who have pointed out that because scale has not been normed on a large sample the scores should be treated cautiously)

Scoring for expressing my anger assessment questionnaire

Question No:	(a)	(b)	(c)	(d)
1.	1	2	3	4
2.	4	3	2	1
3.	1	2	3	4
4.	4	3	2	1
5.	4	3	2	1
6.	4	3	2	1
7.	1	2	3	4
8.	1	2	3	4
9.	4	3	2	1
10.	1	2	3	4

SCORE =

Scores 31-40: letting it out

This score suggests that the person has an ineffective and uncontrolled response to anger and their angry feelings are expressed in verbally or physically aggressive behaviour towards other people or objects. This can go right up to the pathological kind of anger that can lead to rage and fury easily erupting into violence (Goleman, 1996). Ask participants if they felt that they were scoring on the questions which were about getting their anger out? Point out that, apart from the issue of abusing others on the receiving end, many people nevertheless feel that it is necessary to vent or get rid of our anger. However, although this idea is popular in many quarters much of the research advises against it. Giving vent to anger does little or nothing to dispel it though it may feel satisfying at the time. In fact, it is often one of the worst ways to try to cool down as outbursts of rage typically pump up the emotional brain's arousal leaving people feeling more angry and not less, and ultimately leading to more inappropriate expressions of anger. Its a bit like giving an alcoholic a drink, the more one vents the more one enjoys the high of anger.

Scores 10-19: keeping it in

So if we can't let anger out, what about keeping or holding it in or suppressing it. Many people hesitate to admit their own anger. When anger-producing circumstances occur, they put on a good front and pretend to feel no tension at all. But how does this help meet our needs? How long can we do this without finally breaking down or blowing up? There may be some people who never really blow up but still take their anger into dark places, where it may live in the shadows to nurture destructive, hidden agendas and manipulative, exploitative or even vicious ways of dealing with other people. Its like a sort of passive aggression. There is a need to have control with the least amount of risk. But as with complete suppression there will also be a perpetuation of unwanted tension. Difficulties with anger can be just as much to do with this aspect than with the more stereotypical aspect of blowing our tops that we tend to associate with anger. (Personally, suppression and passive aggression have been areas that the author has had to work at and still does in terms of how he manages his own anger).

Scores 20-30: balance and the difficult middle road

Responses falling in middle range scores suggest a more well balanced style of anger. This is the difficult road between keeping it all in and letting it all out. This takes us back to Aristotle's challenge and can be also thought about with the idea of the pressure cooker (See Figure 2.4). Modern psychology tends to confirm the wisdom of the ancients and much of religion, that we have to find this difficult middle road. This will be the challenge for participants as they continue their work on the programme. Indicate that it is how they express and manage their anger that will be the key focus of PAMP. Like learning any new behaviour, there are no quick fixes. Coming back to the triangle of behaviour, they will each have to start working at their thinking , their emotions and their actions in making necessary changes to help them better manage their anger.

Figure 2.4: The pressure cooker

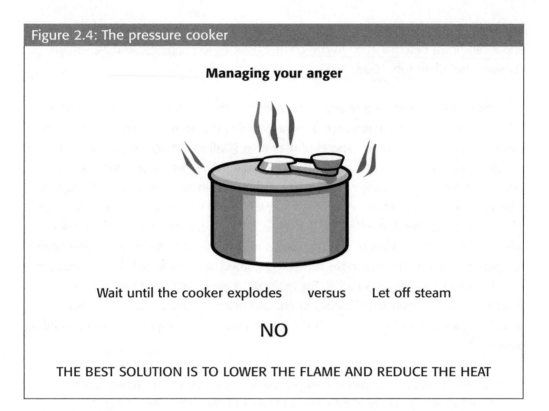

Managing your anger

Wait until the cooker explodes   versus   Let off steam

NO

THE BEST SOLUTION IS TO LOWER THE FLAME AND REDUCE THE HEAT

Theory/evidence base

The facilitator guidance already contains a significant evidence base, and there is always a danger of overwhelming ourselves and those with whom we work with too much data. There is also the issue that the field is a contested one, so caution is required. For example, with regard to the underlying premise that anger should be viewed in positive terms as a natural human emotion, this can be challenged by those who see it as unhealthy and self-defeating, taking the view that 'there is nothing inherently right or legitimate about anger' (McKay, Rogers and McKay, 1989: 56). These differing views not only represent differing psychological theories but also cultural and religious differences, as with the example of Buddhists who tend towards seeing anger as an afflictive emotion.

Despite this, and accepting individuals' rights to such views, there is a strong evidence base for seeing anger more positively. 'Indeed it is an essential part of who we are, vital to our survival in that we need anger to define boundaries' (Pert, 1997: 285). When anger is expressed appropriately and the target hears and responds appropriately it can be empowering and give those who express their anger a sense of control and well being. It is not anger that leads to violence and aggression. As long as one can talk about things, anger can lead to solutions, not to violence. It is only when one can no longer communicate that anger leads to violence. 'Anger provides for personal resilience. It is a guardian of self-esteem, it potentiates the ability to address grievances, and it can boost determination to overcome obstacles to happiness and aspirations' (Novaco and Chemtob, 1998: 172).

In relation to the experience of anger, the notion of the angry temperament or **trait** is referred to in much of the research. People with this characteristic may find that anger negatively affects most or all aspects of their lives (Deffenbacher, 1996). This relates to the group of people who naturally and easily make themselves angry, and one authority refers to an underlying biosocial tendency to do so (Ellis, 2003). Participants who find themselves experiencing anger frequently and intensely across a wide range of situations may need to reflect on this issue. Of course, it may be that the person who is suffering from a deep, unrecognised and unresolved anger may not only have a temperament issue, but may have suffered disturbed or abusive early life experiences or subsequent traumas as an adult. For example, there is significant research which indicates links between anger management difficulties and post traumatic stress disorders (Novaco and Chemtob, 1998). These areas will be explored in more depth in Session 7.

There is also a range of views on how people express their anger. 'When angered, people respond in a variety of adaptive and maladaptive ways' (Eckhart and Deffenbacher, 1996: 34). They may get self-righteous, they may sulk, they may have passive anger, and think about revenge, they may become overtly aggressive (Goleman, 2004). One authority on this subject talks about modern day men and women, especially of Anglo-Saxon descent, and how they tend to be constrained in their everyday lives. Many do not act or speak with very much passion or force. Its not that they are low key and relaxed, but that they are more controlled and bottled up. They tend to keep good and bad feelings in and when things go badly try to carry the burden without giving any outward signs (Biddulph, 1997).

There remains some disagreement in how best to express anger. It has to be conceded that the research on letting out anger and ventilating is mixed. PAMP advises against anger inciting therapies, which, as one author commented, 'may work at least to some extent, however they often end up by creating more harm than good' (Ellis, 2003: 134). Other research studies found that individuals who become aggressive against wrong doers usually end up feeling more angry (Williams and Williams, 1993). Once again, not all participants will, or be required to, accept this position.

2.3: The big body map: the effects of poor anger management on health and well being

Presentation and experiential exercise

Explain that in this section the aim is to learn about the effects of poor anger management on health. Ask the group to think about how they feel in their bodies when they begin to experience intense anger. This can be done by using a large sheet of paper which is placed on the floor. Have a volunteer lie down on it and draw an outline of their body shape. Have the group (or individual) then show on the body map the parts of their bodies that are affected by anger. Ask the participants where they first note themselves becoming tense. For some this may be tension in their neck; others might experience knots in their stomachs etc. Point out that what is being demonstrated is the 'fight or flight' response to stress which has been extensively researched for the last century or so. Basically, the body moves into automatic pilot to prepare itself to deal with the problem. (There is more detail on this in the following evidence/theory section which may be used if required). The areas identified on the body shape are those affected by the aroused state of anger. Point out that if we are talking about occasional experiences, then there is no significant harm. However, ask the group, or individual, what do they think will happen if such experiences are intense, regular and ongoing. They will probably arrive at the answer themselves but it should be stressed that there is a growing body of medical research and evidence which points to the strong possibility of significant health problems as shown in Figure 2.5. Participants can be encouraged to reflect on their own health concerns in relation to their anger.

Finish this element by asking participants if they can identify their particular bodily reactions which they are aware of as they are moving into an angry outburst. As well as reminding them that they may be doing themselves harm, their awareness of these can also be a source of help in trying to manage a specific anger inducing situation. 'These then become signals for coping rather than signals for anger' (Acton, 1997: 33). Hopefully, each person will be able to identify at least one early warning sign that they experience in their bodies as they progress up the moving stair towards an outburst of uncontrolled anger and can then take preventive action before it is too late. Indicate that we will be coming back to this issue later in the session.

Theory/evidence base

This exercise will illustrate the stress response which is now well documented in psychological research. The fight or flight research, first documented approximately a hundred years ago, demonstrated the automatic responses which were and are important as a survival mechanism when confronted with danger.

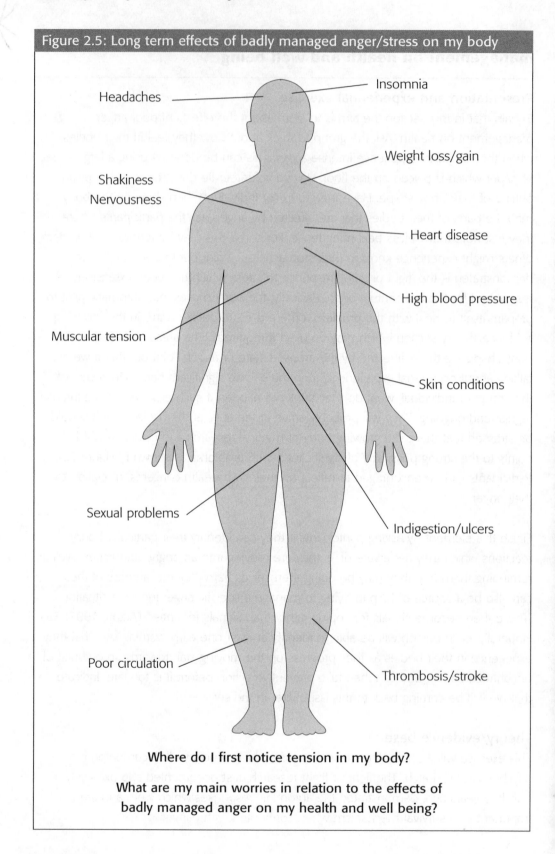

Figure 2.5: Long term effects of badly managed anger/stress on my body

Insomnia

Headaches

Weight loss/gain

Shakiness
Nervousness

Heart disease

High blood pressure

Muscular tension

Skin conditions

Sexual problems

Indigestion/ulcers

Poor circulation

Thrombosis/stroke

Where do I first notice tension in my body?

**What are my main worries in relation to the effects of
badly managed anger on my health and well being?**

A series of automatic physical events take place to prepare the body to fight to protect itself, to freeze in terror or to take flight and get away. A range of chemicals and hormones are released into the body and various things happen; the breathing speed increases; the pulse rate and blood pressure raised; the digestive system shuts down; the mouth goes dry; the muscles tense; the mind becomes more alert; the senses sharpen; the skin perspires; the hair can stand on end; the bladder and bowels are emptied; the emotions are heightened; the blood clotting mechanism is activated etc.

Of course such stress responses are not in themselves bad. They can enable a threatened person to run faster, shout louder, see more clearly, hit harder, endure more pain, etc. However, it is when the stress response is turned on persistently that serious organic damage will inevitably occur. In particular, a range of negative effects have been identified in relation to the poor management of anger. Occasional anger creates no lasting harm. However, there is now significant research to indicate that prolonged high levels of anger related stress can have detrimental effects on health. 'It seems that it doesn't matter whether anger is expressed or suppressed. Its just plain bad for you' (McKay, Rogers and McKay, 1989: 31). When we repeatedly bring on the physical changes that go with rage we can damage our cardiovascular systems. The association between anger and high blood pressure has been demonstrated by many studies on many different patient populations. 'Chronic, sustained anger keeps the body in a constant state of emergency, and the regular body functions, digestion, clearing the blood of cholesterol, and resisting infection, may be delayed, depressed or bypassed' (McKay, Rogers and McKay, 1989: 26).

Break

2.4: The stages of anger

Presentation and individual work

The purpose of this element, and the following one as well, is to allow the individual or participants to begin to explore one of their own anger outbursts. To begin, they should select an example of their own badly managed anger with one of their children. Allow a little time for them to silently identify a situation that is significant and highlights their difficulties in managing their anger. It does not have to be the 'worst' example of their badly managed parental anger – but it can be. It may be a more typical example of situations that regularly occur with their child(ren). The most important aspect is that they have a clear memory of what happened. Point out that they will be revisiting this example several times during the programme and will be using it to help progress their learning. Stress that they do not need to share their abusive episode at this point. They are going to do the work in their own heads and choose how much or little they wish to bring into the group discussion or share with the facilitator.

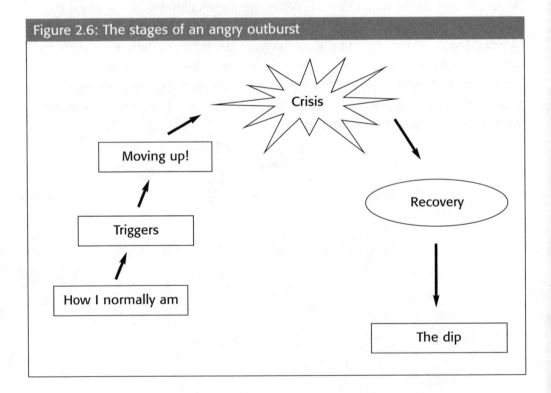

Figure 2.6: The stages of an angry outburst

They will now have an opportunity to relate their example to a well researched model which should help them to see that things just don't happen, and that however quickly things appear to happen, there is a process, and understanding this may help in doing something about it (Figure 2.6).

The first stage is how we normally are and is each person's starting point. This will obviously be different for everybody since every person has their own personality, temperament, moods, etc. There are also differences in the amounts and types of stress and pressure that people experience at various points in their lives, be they personal, social, economic or whatever, and these may impact on their 'normal' way of being. Ask participants to take a few moments to think about how they were in the period in which the example of their badly managed anger took place. They will have the opportunity in doing their personal work on this programme to continue to think about their own baseline position and whether they are able to move on this in terms of stress or lifestyle issues.

The second stage is the event that happened, with the effect of triggering the anger in the individual. Ask the individual or group to think about a thermometer and did they have a sense of their own temperature rising as a result of their child's behaviour. What was it that started to irritate or annoy them – to push their buttons? What were the prompts, the cues, or the things that got them going! What was it about the situation, events or circumstances that wound them up? They will be different for each individual. 'People take different messages from the same experiences' (Ellis, 2002: 134). Encourage each person to have in their minds at least one trigger.

Much of the research indicates that there is then a build up period. The analogy of going up the moving stairs in a shopping centre can be used. This can be an exhilarating and energising process – getting worked up with a self-righteous inner talk that gives the person convincing arguments for venting anger. This is where anger can become 'the most seductive of negative emotions; the self-righteous inner monologue that propels it along fills the mind with the most convincing arguments for venting rage' (Goleman, 1996: 59). In thinking about their examples, participants should have had a sense that the adrenalin was then starting to pump through their body and there was a definite physiological process underway. They were probably experiencing some or all of the bodily reactions referred to earlier and were having to deal with the issue of keeping it in or letting it out it! Ask participants to think about what this period was like for them. Did they shoot up quickly? Why were they not able to step back? What about the bodily reactions they were experiencing? Can they see that it may have been possible to apply these as their early warning signs because it was at this stage that these were appearing?

Do they remember their anger building? The body was flooded and pumped up with high levels of stress chemicals and blood pressure. The emotional brain heated up and reached a point at which the person was beyond reason and they behaved in a physically, verbally or emotionally abusive way to their children. They were out of control and blew their top. They lost it! Again, it will be important for participants to reflect on their own crisis points. To what extent did they completely lose it? How abusive or dangerous did they become? Did they, on the occasion they are thinking about, or on any other occasion, ever go seriously beyond a point in their behaviour that was a real worry to them? This may well be their main motivation for being in the group, in that they don't want to ever repeat these types of behaviours. Again, at this point, the main objective is just to give people the information and for them to begin to make judgements as to the degree the model fits with their own experience of anger.

The next stage identified in the research is the aftermath and when the individual starts to come back down. This takes a while and care is needed as adrenalin remains in the system for approximately 90 minutes so there is always the danger of shooting back up again. Ask participants to reflect on how they experienced this period. Did they come back down or did something else happen that led them going straight back into another explosive outburst even before the dust had hardly settled from the previous crisis?

Finally, there is the dip. The reality of what has just happened, the extent and the implications of the abusive behaviour that one has used begins to sink it. Sensations of regret, depression, feeling sorry for oneself may have been present. There may have been some initial attempts to try to sort things or make up. Of course, it's not easy to talk ourselves out of something that we've behaved ourselves into! People usually find that they end up on a new baseline, flatter, more down and depressed as a result of what they've done, with feelings of hopelessness, bitterness, frustration and hurt all too prevalent. Again, allow participants to make connections to their own example.

Participants can take a few moments to reflect on the six stages and the process involved, either individually, in pairs or as a group discussion. They are not required to share any details of the example they are considering. At this point, they need to make a judgement as to whether the framework or model fits with their own angry outbursts. The challenge, and this is what the work of the programme is about, is how they may be able to prevent themselves moving up to the outburst stage without repressing their anger.

2.5: Mismanaged anger as a parent

Presentation and individual exercise

Inform participants that after having considered a wide range of ideas and research linked to anger, and having just looked at the stages in one of their anger outbursts, they will now take their example a little further in beginning to identify ways of changing their behaviour. Display or draw Figure 2.7 and ask participants to return their minds to the situation they have chosen. Encourage them to try to place themselves back in that situation and to make it as real as possible. Ask them to once again visualise the scene just before their anger exploded. Picture the objects that made up the scene, including the colours and textures. Imagine the air, was it still or moving, dry or humid? What sounds or smells may have accompanied the setting? Each person should picture what led to the event. What actually happened? Who was there and what were their reactions as they became angry? How was this situation resolved? Think about things for a few moments. Allow each participant to then take a couple of moments to mentally note or briefly write down the incident that led to them experiencing anger and what they did in responding to it.

Participants will probably have gathered a lot of detail on the situation and the challenging or provocative behaviour they were having to respond to. Without minimising the difficulties they experience as parents, ask them now to return to the situation. Point out that the little arrow between the situation and their response is really a triangle. This triangle represents the 'gap', that is, the space between the events and their response. It is this space that they need to explore and make as big as possible so that they are 'able' to 'respond' in ways which are less destructive – this is their responsibility. Consequently, they now need to focus entirely on the **gap** between the incident and their abusive behaviour, and in particular on their own inner world in terms of what **they** were thinking ,feeling and doing. Stress again that they should pay attention to the moment immediately after the provoking event and right before they became abusive. Can they recall any thoughts they might have had, other emotions they might have experienced, or bodily reactions during the event. Use Figure 2.8 to process this, either verbally, on a flip chart, using the three corners of a 'triangle' within the room, or alternatively as an individual resource for each participant to complete. The task is to apply the triangle of behaviour which they covered in the previous session to their own behaviour. Ask participants not to complete the box at the bottom of the page at this point.

Some participants may find it difficult to identify what other emotions they experienced just before they became angry. However, encourage them to take time to reflect on their experience. If anyone finds themselves going immediately from the event to their anger, encourage them to think of the situation as if it was on video or DVD and try to reverse their imaginary film from the moment when they first experienced anger.

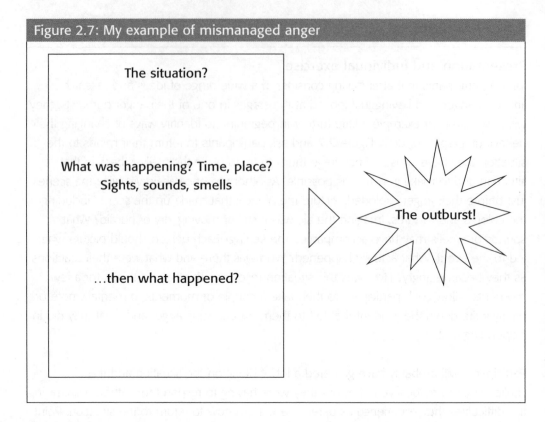

Figure 2.7: My example of mismanaged anger

The situation?

What was happening? Time, place?
Sights, sounds, smells

...then what happened?

The outburst!

Some may have identified conclusions or meanings that they gave to the event. Some may have identified feeling hurt, discounted, shamed, frightened, devalued, or embarrassed before becoming angry. It can be challenging to identify these internal reactions that preceded and accompanied anger; it is a skill that requires practice, but it can be learned. The more that participants can practise this type of self-reflection, the more they will learn about themselves. This is critical. It will be this ability to identify, to reflect on or to challenge their internal reactions that will be the basis for making sense of and managing anger. Those who don't communicate with themselves (or others) about what's going on will continue to get into trouble with their anger. They need to work out what is going on internally and why. The challenge of this work will be to analyse and work to make changes in how they think, handle their emotions and in what they do. To this end, encourage participants to complete the final section on Figure 2.8 and use a group round to take and record at least one different way that participants could have handled the situation that would have not led to them being abusive to their children.

Figure 2.8: My mismanaged anger and my inner world

Between the situation and my bad response what was I thinking, feeling and doing?

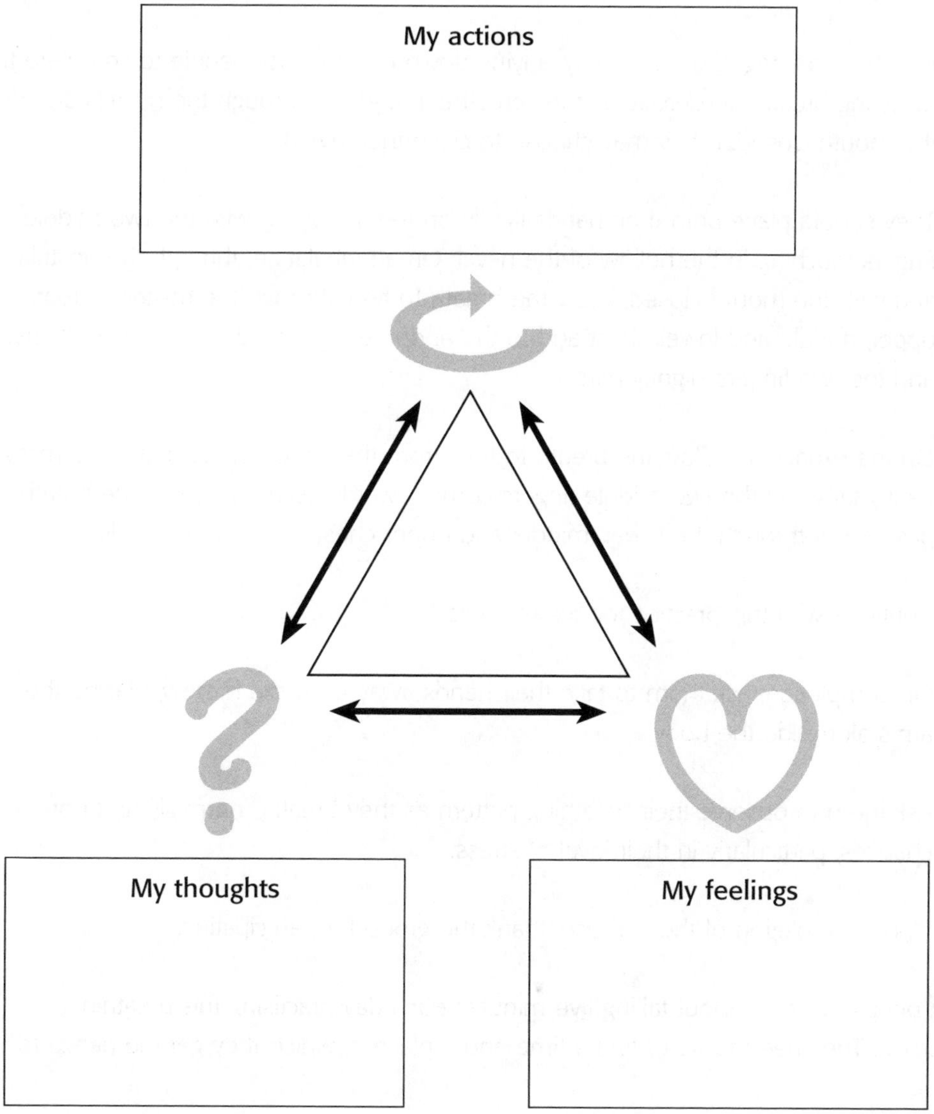

My actions

My thoughts

My feelings

Identify at least 3 changes to any of the above that may have helped me to deal with the situation better?

1.

2.

3.

2.6: Taking care of yourself and closure

This session will finish with guidance being given in relation to practising deep breathing. (Give participants the previous brief health warning.)

1. In either an upright, or preferably, a lying down position, ask people to complete the following breathing exercise as they breathe in and out through the nostrils and with the mouth closed. (They may choose to close their eyes).

2. They should place both their hands lightly on the abdomen with the two middle fingers touching in the hollow of the naval. On an inhalation, through the nostrils and with the mouth closed, allow the breath to flow through the nostrils, throat, upper, middle and lower chest and to the abdomen so that the tummy gently rises and the two fingers slightly part.

3. On the exhalation, allow the breath to flow from the abdomen so that the tummy gently falls and the two middle fingers come towards each other, and the breath passes out through the lower, middle and upper chest, throat and nostrils.

4. Continue with this practice for five minutes.

5. On completion, ask them to take their hands away from the tummy, placing the arms alongside the body.

6. Ask them to observe their breathing pattern as they breathe normally and note any changes, particularly in their level of stress.

7. Upon completion of the exercise, thank the group for participating.

Ask people to think about taking five minutes each day practising this breathing exercise. They need to try to find a time and a place in which they get the peace to do it.

Closure
(See end of Session 1, page 42.)

Session 3
The Trouble With Thinking

> *Anger is never without a reason but seldom a good one.*
>
> Benjamin Franklin

3.1   Welcome, outline, objectives and check in

The objectives of the session are that you will:
- Increase awareness of your thinking and how it relates to your anger.
- Identify one or more example of faulty thinking.
- Develop some better thinking.
- Increase awareness of relevant lifestyle and stress issues.

3.2   Thinking about thinking

3.3   Top triggers

Break

3.4   Exploring negative thinking

3.5   Challenging and changing bad thinking

3.6   Taking care of yourself and closure

Facilitators' Guidance for Session 3

3.1: Welcome, outline, objectives and check in

Welcome participants or the individual to the session and display the session title, objectives and outline. Inform the group that in this session, as the quote suggests, the focus will be on the area of thinking and how people think. This is one of the key points on the triangle of behaviour. It is about exploring the reasons behind a person's anger, the triggers or prompts, and the stages of the journey through an angry episode that they do not handle well. The first objective is aimed at providing the opportunity for participants to begin to explore their mindsets, attitudes and beliefs which may all contribute to how they manage their feelings of anger, particularly that anger which relates to their role as a parent. Participants will be asked to look at their thinking and to be prepared to have it challenged. The second objective follows on from this and by the end of this session, through exploring aspects of their own way of thinking and relating this to some of their angry outbursts, each person will have been able to identify some examples of their faulty thinking. From this, the third objective is that they will not only begin to challenge this thinking but begin to move towards identifying alternative ways of thinking about the difficult anger producing situations they encounter with their children. Emphasise that it is only a beginning, and each person can only go as far as they can, but at least they should be open to the possibility that at times the ways they think about the challenges and difficulties of parenting may not be particularly helpful. As in all sessions, the final objective relates to assisting people in learning stress management strategies and working at their overall life balance. Check that the group or individual understands the objectives, and briefly run through the content of the session.

Before preceding into these areas, participants will be offered the opportunity to briefly check in to the session. Each will have a minute or two to address their anger diary and make a general comment as to how they feel about their anger (see guidance pages 25-26 and 44).

3.2: Thinking about thinking

There are number of ways to help the group or individual to begin to think about their thinking processes and two options are outlined below.

Option 1 for group or individual (presentation and discussion)

An example of the relevance of thinking can be presented to the group in the scenario of three people waiting for a bus, and how each of them reacts differently to the same situation. The three people in question are waiting at the bus stop to take the bus to work. The bus approaches and then drives straight past them. Following this, each of the three people behaves differently:

1. Person 1 storms round to a local taxi office and rushes into work. He arrives late, and when his manager asks what kept him he aggressively tells him it was 'the bloody bus drivers fault!' He continues to behave aggressively with people in work and has a stand up row with another worker who makes a mistake later that morning.

2. Person 2 panics and starts to worry about the trouble they are going to get into at work. They end up deciding that they can't face the boss and to go home and phone into work as sick so as not to have to deal with the problem of being late. This person also convinces themselves that it is no big deal and tries to just put it out of their mind.

3. Person 3 takes a little while to deal with the situation. They decide to contact the bus company later in the day to report what happened. In the meantime, as it is such a lovely day, and the next bus isn't due for an hour, they decide to take a walk in the park and just go into work late and explain the situation to the boss. They subsequently do this, and find that they are relaxed and refreshed by the time they get to work to have a pleasant and productive day.

Ask the group to explain why the individuals reacted differently, why one reacted angrily and aggressively, one reacted passively and the third dealt positively with the situation. Bring out the importance of how each person **thought** about the situation to explain how they then felt and reacted. The critical issue is that, confronted with the same event, each person thought differently about it and as a result had different emotions and feelings and behaved in different ways. Ask the group what were the differences in thinking?

1. Person 1's thoughts might have been 'That 'bastard' drove past me on purpose, that bus driver is terrible for doing that to me, you can't trust anyone now.'

2. Person 2's thoughts might have been 'Oh God, I'm going to be in trouble. Everything always happens to me. It's awful the way I'm treated, he shouldn't

have done that to me, I can't stand the fact that I'm going to be late for work, my boss is going to blame me when I get to work.'

3. Person 3's thoughts might have been 'I wonder what happened to the bus man today, maybe he's distracted about something else, how will I deal with this, what can I do to make the best of this even though it is a bit of a nuisance.'

Finish this part of section 3.2 by referring back to the triangle of behaviour, either visually on a flip chart or drawn out on the floor, and briefly illustrate the connected thinking, feelings and action process (see Figure 1.7).

Option 2 for some groups (exercise)

This needs to be agreed, prior to the session, with one of the participants in private, without the knowledge of other group members. (Try to choose someone who will be comfortable with the exercise, since if several people are approached before someone agrees to do it, then the effect will be lost). The person should be carefully briefed as follows. As the element is being introduced by one of the facilitators the volunteer will suddenly stand up and say in a strong voice, or shout, that this course is the biggest load of rubbish, a complete waste of time, they are sick of it and then to storm out of the room! Let the participants experience the moment for a little while and then reassure them that what has taken place has just been an exercise to help them look at some issues around thinking and behaviour. Return the 'volunteer' to the group and thank him or her for their participation and performance and then get into discussing and processing the incident. Ask the participants to identify how they thought the facilitators were impacted on by the verbal onslaught of the individual. How did they think they would be feeling about it and how could it affect their behaviour in leading the work? Hopefully a range of effects will be identified including being embarrassed, hurt, angry, upset, undermined, having their confidence shattered, determined to continue, being misunderstood, relieved, etc. Agree that all these effects could be experienced by different facilitators but the key point is that no two facilitators will react in the same way. For example, one may be totally devastated and find it difficult to continue, but another may not be in the slightest way put off and will continue with the course as if nothing has happened. Ask the group what explains these possible different outcomes to the same situation? This should take the group to the point that a critical element in the behaviour of the facilitators is what they **thought** about the situation. Explore with the group how far and how deep such thinking might go. It is not only their thinking about the particular incident, but also their deeper thinking, mindset and beliefs and motivations about doing this work, how it should be done, what can go wrong, how to deal with it and their expectations of the work. The key point is that it is the facilitators thinking that can have a very significant influence on how they are impacted upon and how they react to the type of behaviour that the volunteer demonstrated. It is the importance of their inner world that was touched upon in the last session.

Finish this part of the section by referring back to the triangle of behaviour, either visually on a flip chart or drawn out on the floor, and briefly illustrate the connected thinking, feelings and action process (see Figure 1.7).

Self awareness

Continue this element by pointing out that one of the things which makes us different from the animals is we can actually think about how we think! Another way to illustrate this is to ask the participants if they can, in their own minds, step outside themselves for a moment. Ask them to put their minds up into a corner of the room and imagine that they are looking down and observing themselves as they participate in this session. They should be able to mentally think about how they are thinking in relation to what they are hearing. Can they actually experience themselves thinking? For example, this is interesting and I am agreeing with what is being said, this is rubbish, this is boring, this is challenging me, this is a load of whatever! Maybe they can see that they are not really listening that well because of some other problem or distraction that is going on in their lives at the moment. Can they bring that to awareness and say that they are going to put that on hold until they leave the session and just try to concentrate better on what is going on. It is this ability that ultimately says that human beings have the chance to make changes to their way of looking at things and to how they will ultimately behave. Every person has this gift of **self-awareness** which allows them to work at change!

To finish this part of the session, encourage each participant to try to begin addressing issues in their own thinking. How do they think? Are they aware of any flaws in their own thinking? For example, do they tend to jump to conclusions, to see things in black and white, to have certain unrealistic expectations of things? Are they impulsive, short sighted, too immediate, self – dominated in the way they think? Have they ever thought about how they think? Has their thinking always been the same way? Is it just a habit? Use Figure 3.1 as an individual exercise or prompt for a group discussion to help encourage participants begin to identify some of their own general thinking errors or weaknesses.

Theory/evidence base

This session introduces more explicitly the cognitive behavioural approach. At its simplest, it proposes that feelings and negative behaviours may come from thoughts, they do not arrive by themselves. 'What is important then is the quality of our thinking and our beliefs' (Faupel, Herrick and Sharp, 1998: 11). Once this has been accepted, the thoughts can be identified – the distorted thoughts can be righted, and the feelings will cease to arrive. The tenets of cognitive behavioural therapy (CBT) can be given the shorthand of Thoughts – Feelings – Impact – Action. Participants need to make this journey into their inner world to begin to get a sense of how and to what extent the way they are thinking connects to why their identified triggers are causing such aroused feelings and problems with anger. The approach argues that one of the most potent ways to put anger at rest is to be able to undermine the thoughts, beliefs or convictions that may be fuelling and igniting the anger in the first place.

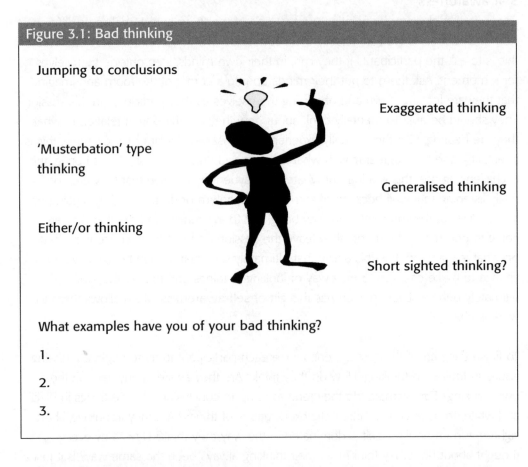

Figure 3.1: Bad thinking

Jumping to conclusions

Exaggerated thinking

'Musterbation' type thinking

Generalised thinking

Either/or thinking

Short sighted thinking?

What examples have you of your bad thinking?

1.

2.

3.

However, this is easier said than done. 'It is central to much of social psychology that people try to maintain cognitive consistency between their attitudes and their actions and that they experience a subjective sense of discomfort where there is inconsistency' (Feldman, 1993: 280). The problem is that it is often easier to change our thinking than our behaviour. So we can build up and use faulty thinking to back up behaviour that we are finding difficult to change. This can take various forms such as displacing responsibility, blaming others for the situation, moral justification or minimising the consequences. To have kept negative or distorted thinking patterns alive, individuals will have continuously repeated, reinforced and acted on them and it will take a great deal of hard personal work to challenge their own thinking. They will need to do more than just get into thinking exercises. Not only will they have to dispute their internal thinking forcefully, but they will also have to do it emotionally and behaviourally, as we shall see in future sessions.

The research is strong on the key point that participants need to be able to make inroads into how their thinking links to their anger if they are to make progress (Deffenbacher, 1996). 'Common characteristics of neglectful parents are their self-defeating thoughts and beliefs about their abilities to cope effectively with different life tasks' (Iwaniec, 2003: 57). They need, by the end of the session, to be able to identify at least some of their distorted thinking (Beck, 1999) or irrational beliefs (Ellis, 2003) that may lie underneath or at least contribute significantly to their difficulties with anger. To do this participants need to be able to identify the thoughts or cognitions that they experience which induce or at least seem to be associated with their anger episodes. They need to 'seize on and challenge the thoughts that trigger the surge of anger' (Goleman, 1996: 61). The ability to reframe a situation more positively is one of the most potent ways to put anger at rest.

It is also important to point out that the cognitive behavioural approach is not without its critics. Its emphasis on the person's internal world and their responsibility to sort themselves out may overlook and downplay the inequalities and negative situations experienced by many people. Is there a danger that the approach is too focused on helping people cope within an unfair society without causing trouble? In other words, to take all the responsibility for their inability to manage their anger and ignore wider issues around the inequalities within society with its structural discrimination and oppression. Is there a danger of urging people to make the best of things and get on with it and in so doing, teaching them not to strive for fairness or justice,? The wider picture needs to be kept in mind, and there is a real relationship between poverty, unemployment, lack of opportunities, isolation and managing anger. It is imperative that peoples difficult social circumstances are not trivialised or ignored. The importance of this type of programme being part of an overall service to parents will be returned to in Part 3.

The programme ultimately rests on the belief that people always have the power of choice – that whatever their genetic or biological inheritance, their upbringing and circumstances – they can be self-determining through their own awareness and choices (Covey, 2004). The aim is to help people think more critically and creatively to solve problems and improve their emotional life and relationship with their children. This is, in my view, a form of empowerment as long as issues of social justice are not ignored.

3.3: Top triggers

Presentation, discussion and individual work

To begin this work on a general level, encourage participants to think about the things that would irritate or cause parents to be angry. That is, the triggers and activating events that are perceived to be negative. At this point, it is not about the participants' own triggers, but what they imagine would trigger anger in most parents. Depending on the size of the group, they can discuss these in pairs first and then bring them to the group, or it can be done within the entire group and one of the facilitators can record the suggestions. As in other parts of the course, if there are literacy issues, try to find ways to represent the various triggers on the wall or flipchart. Get a list as wide-ranging as possible, from the crying or demands of a young baby, to the perceived defiance of an adolescent, to lifestyle issues of the young adult child. Accept anything that is offered as a trigger by any group member. Of course, there are various triggers that go across all areas of our lives, for example, someone cutting in front of us when we are driving on the motorway, someone criticising us at work or someone being rude and so on. Try to keep the focus on parenting triggers. This exercise may generate humour and laughter, which is fine. However, facilitators need to take care over their own reactions, and whilst humour is important in maintaining the positive working relationship, in some instances 'laughter would serve only to endorse the aggressive parental response' (Acton, 1997: 27).

When a long and full list has been produced, the task for each participant is to personalise the items for themselves (Figure 3.2 can be used as a resource). They should work up their own list of the top five or more 'parenting related' events or situations that appear to culminate in them loosing their tempers and behaving in ways that are not appropriate. Remind them of the stages of anger model from the last session and see how their own triggers fit into the model.

Explain to participants that the more challenging bit is now to reflect on their lists and see what it is telling them about themselves. At one level, it will probably highlight the real challenge involved in parenting. As one author says 'Life, whether I like it or not, usually gets spelled h-a-s-s-l-e!' (Ellis, 2003: 112). Stress to participants that parenting is tough work and this is made worse if people are also facing serious social problems in terms of income, health, child care, employment etc. The triggers they have outlined would probably be challenging to a lot of parents. However, on the other hand, particularly when working with a group, the point should be made that some of the behaviours listed as triggers are normal child behaviours and not problems in themselves. Stress that they need to begin to look hard at the triggers they have identified and to turn their perspective from their child to themselves.

Figure 3.2: My top triggers?

What are the situations with my children that are my biggest irritants and trigger my anger:

1.

2.

3.

4

5.

Can I look at any of the triggers above in a different way which would lead me not to get so annoyed and worked up? For example, am I getting angry about something that is common for all parents, or it is really normal behaviour for most children and is not as provocative as I am making it seem?

Finish this part of the session with a group round by asking each participant to focus on just one of their triggers. It does not have to be the worst. The main thing is, that if they can pick one where, if they changed the way they thought about the incident or situation, it would mean that they didn't feel quite as angry. (This is what the final section of Figure 3.2 refers to if it is being used as a resource). The new 'thinking' may still leave them feeling somewhat angry, but they would definitely feel themselves 'cooling' and going down the scale in terms of the intensity of their anger by looking at the situation in this different way. Again, it is important to be encouraging and reassuring to those who find this difficult. Point out that there will be further opportunities to look at this issue and to just go as far as they can. It is also worth distinguishing between those participants who are able to reframe their thinking in relation to the specific trigger to such a degree that the event almost ceases to be a trigger. For example, 'My child is just behaving the way most three-year-olds do when they are bored and frustrated'. This is difficult. For some participants, it may be more about being able to bring more helpful thinking to a situation that is clearly angering them. Some examples may be; 'This is going to upset me and I have recognised it but now I have recognised it I can deal with it a bit better'; 'This is not the end of the world'; or, 'I know I can deal with this, take a few deep breaths – I can be angry and relaxed at the same time!'

Break

3.4: Exploring negative thinking

Presentation and discussion

In this sequence, participants will be encouraged to reflect on two issues:

1. Their underlying and core mindset as to their role as a parent.

2. The degree to which some of their thinking around parenting and its frustrations may be causing them difficulty.

Once again, emphasise that this is just a beginning and there are further layers to add on as the programme continues and these should continue to help participants increase their awareness of their inner thinking world. Point out that there will be no magic wand type cure, nor formula for personal happiness. Rather, the first step is about becoming more aware of what it is in each person that upsets or angers him or her inappropriately. It is about recognising some of the relevant issues that have arisen from exploring their triggers.

Core beliefs about parenting

Read out the quotes on Figures 3.3 and 3.4. This is more effective if carried out 'in role' and the emotional messages of the statements are conveyed to the group. (A male and female facilitator could read the respective parts). Ask the group whether they feel there would be a relationship between what each of the persons quoted is saying and how they may manage their anger as a parent. Process the feedback and try to reach the point that their views on their role as a parent is bound to have some link to how they will manage the frequent anger producing events that are part and parcel of parenting.

Each participant should then be given the opportunity to address this fundamental question as to their commitment and motivation to being a parent, and how this may relate to the difficulties in relation to parenting and their anger becoming magnified. They should review their top triggers and ask themselves:

- What do they say about how I think about my role as a parent?

- What do they say about why I want to be a parent?

- What do they say about how important my role as a parent is to me?

Let each person reflect on this personal material around their core beliefs about being a parent for a moment or two.

Figure 3.3: Views on parenting from two fathers

Sometimes I pinch myself and I say, how did I get such an extraordinary stroke of luck? Here I am, 59, with these two wonderful children. I get to see a lot of them so it means we have terrible quarrels and also the time and space to get over them. I support them at school and run around organising their social life and I think – this is incredible!

Kids are just a nuisance. If I was to marry again, I wouldn't have any. My old lady wanted to have them. Only trouble was, that made me a father. To start with they killed our sex life. They made so much noise. And they're stupid. Its not their fault, but you've got to admit their conversation is boring. And they cost money. Add that lot together and what does a father get out of it? Damn all!

Two fathers quoted in Burgess, 1997: 108

Figure 3.4: Views on parenting from two mothers

My son was the best thing that ever happened to me. He has brought so much happiness to our whole family. He has helped me really appreciate the important things in life…

My whole life evolves around feeding John and coping with his crying and screaming. I tried to defeat him but he has defeated me instead. He does not want me and I do not want him. One of us has to go. He does not fit into this family: I feel that someone has dumped him on me and forgotten to take him away.

Two mothers quoted in Iwaniec, 2003: 50

Thinking in relation to the frustration of parenting

Moving on from participants' core fundamental beliefs about their role as parents, explain that the second part of this element of the session offers the group or individual the opportunity to see how their thinking copes with the challenges and frustrations of the grind of day to day parenting. Ask them to listen to a brief presentation on some general types of thinking about difficulties and distortions identified in the research as being associated with a lot of problems in peoples lives including anger management. The challenge is to see if they can identify with any of the following flawed thinking processes:

- **'I must be perfect as a parent'** Probably most, if not all parents, indulge to some degree in 'perfectionist' type thinking. This is around having high expectations of themselves as parents. They should be the perfect parent, who must do well in every aspect of it and win approval of those around them including their children? They must excel as parents, create and experience wonderful relationships with their children and be able to handle anything that their children throws at them. However, what can happen, if parents cling onto such 'perfectionist' thinking. Being unable to live up to these high expectations may lead to the growth of a negative view of self and a sense of being worthless. They then start to run themselves down, saying they cannot cope and are useless! This may well generate depressive feelings and a sense of helplessness as well as anger related difficulties.

- **'My children must always treat me well'** Some parents will have unrealistic expectations of their children, and may believe that their children should treat them well all the time. They may think that their children should act in certain ways, and in particular, their children should never act in a bad manner towards them as parents. Some of these parents may even see their children's behaviour as catastrophic and horrible and get to the stage where they feel they can't stand it any more. It may go further, and because their child or children are behaving as they 'shouldn't' or 'mustn't', that they become undeserving of forgiveness. They may believe that there must be something wrong or even bad about their children when they behave in ways that they don't like. Such thinking may be coming from the expectations they have placed on themselves as parents and the intensity of their reaction to their children is a result of their own devastated aspirations. Parents thinking in these ways may grow to view everything as bleak, and they may experience a growing sense of not being able to manage the demands that their children put on them.

- **'Parenting should be easy'** Finally in this category, parents may be thinking that they don't deserve to experience difficulties and serious problems as parents. They have not faced up to the real challenge of parenting and that it is hard work. Consequently, they have exhausted their ability to tolerate frustration and have convinced themselves that they are at the end of their tether and need to explode. They will experience a strong sense of failure and there may be a sense of things getting worse with the individual increasingly being unable to do anything about them.

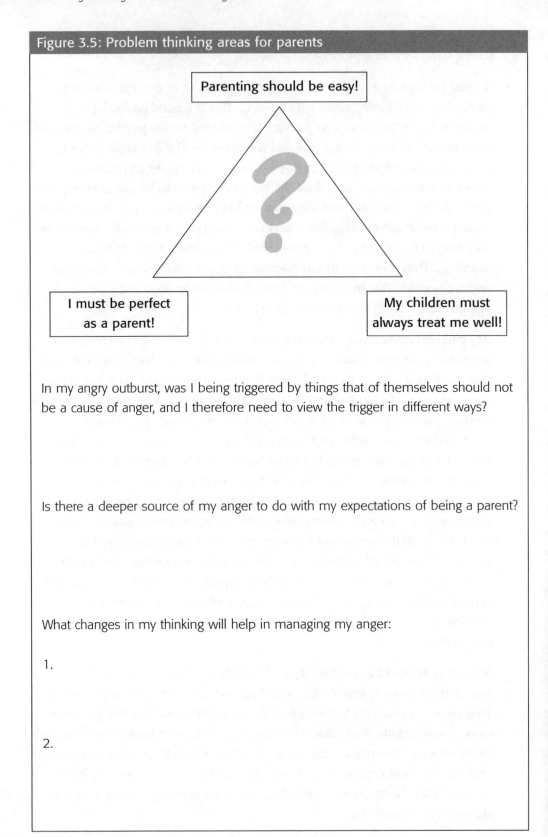

Figure 3.5: Problem thinking areas for parents

Parenting should be easy!

I must be perfect
as a parent!

My children must
always treat me well!

In my angry outburst, was I being triggered by things that of themselves should not be a cause of anger, and I therefore need to view the trigger in different ways?

Is there a deeper source of my anger to do with my expectations of being a parent?

What changes in my thinking will help in managing my anger:

1.

2.

Reflect briefly with the group that these and other similar types of thinking can be present within us all to varying degrees. We all need to keep reflecting on how we see things. 'Maintaining unrealistic expectations and conclusions is like driving a car with one foot on the accelerator and one foot on the brake' (Golden, 2003: 134). If anyone can get a sense of being caught up in some of this type of thinking then they may have found an important source of their anger, rage and aggressive behaviour.

Ask each person or the individual to think about the three general areas mentioned. Three points in the room or three different chairs can be used to represent the problem thinking areas as indicated in Figure 3.5. Participants should proceed to the point where they feel they can see links to their thinking. Using a group round, ask each person to identify the area of their thinking that may need to be explored and challenged more.

3.5: Challenging and changing bad thinking

Presentation and individual work

In this section, the challenge is for each participant to try to apply the work they have just done to the example of one their own angry outbursts which they began to explore in the previous session. Ask them to take a few moments to recall the example, but this time try to put most of the focus on what they were thinking as the situation developed. The challenge is to be really specific as to the thinking processes that went on in relation to their example of badly managed anger. This is important as it will only be through being clear about what their thinking actually entailed that they will be able to identify any of the problematic or 'stinking' thinking that may have been going on.

Acknowledge that this will not be easy. We are often so busy and active in meeting the demands of life that we are not aware of such inner talk going on. The challenge for participants is to really try to turn up the volume on what was actually going on mentally within themselves as the situation unfolded. They may well have been going on internal automatic pilot and will need to work hard to try to bring to awareness the key unrealistic thoughts that lay behind their angry outburst. Nevertheless, remind participants that the vast bulk of the literature on anger stresses that poor thinking is a significant cause of anger related problems. This places an onus on each participant to do this hard personal work. This will not be the end of the story but for now it is a critical starting point.

Give participants enough time to work individually in silence to capture their thinking, to identify a weakness in their thinking and to decide a different way of thinking about the situation that would have had the impact of cooling and lessening their anger arousal. Ask them to try to latch on to one of the key forms of irrationality mentioned in 3.4 to see if they can relate to them. If they can stop believing in one of these areas it may lead to different outcomes and also possibly carry over positively into other areas of their thinking. Figure 3.5 may be used as a resource and handout for those who wish to work on paper and record their new reframed thinking. (There is also the option for participants if they completed and kept Figure 2.8 from the previous session, to refer back to it to see the relevance of their learning in this session).

At the end of the individual work, ask each person to contribute an example of a positive change in their thinking in relation to their anger example. Affirm all contributions and accept those that are unable to present their example yet. Acknowledge that it can be really difficult at first, and point out that there is further material to cover which may help people get there and encourage them to stay with it.

Hopefully, some of the group will have gained some insights into their inner thinking world and how this affected their handling of a difficult situation, pushing themselves up the moving stair too quickly towards a crisis and the abusive behaviour! They also need to recognise that their way of thinking will have become habitual and that they have developed a deep pattern that will be difficult to quickly change. The real challenge will be to try to put their new insights and learning into practice, and to progress. They will need to keep thinking hard about their reactions to situations and put themselves through such exercises **many times, vigorously, strongly and powerfully!**

Finally, the facilitators should also watch out for unrealistic expectations from participants who, for example, are indicating that by making a change in their thinking they would suddenly feel great about a situation which had previously driven them into a raging fury! The participant's view can be acknowledged and there may be a case where an individual experiences a transforming moment of insight, but it should be gently pointed out that such an event is an unlikely occurrence.

3.6: Taking care of yourself and closure

As a lead in to this session, point out to the individual or group that the way they think is also related to their physical condition. If they are very tired or very agitated they will perceive things differently than if they are calm and relaxed. This short relaxation exercise is aimed at trying to help them keep their physiological arousal level within reasonable limits day in, day out, so that when something agitating or provoking occurs, their base line is not so high that they immediately shoot to a dangerously high level. In this session, the emphasis will be on calm natural breathing but will also introduce a thinking (cognitive) element which is just about saying a soothing word or phrase to oneself and developing a more passive attitude and learning to relax.

Give the individual or participants a moment or two to make themselves comfortable in their seat or to lie down if they prefer. Appropriate music can be put on and the following script can be used:

'Now you are going to take some time to practise relaxation techniques. In whichever position you have chosen, make sure that you are comfortable. Close your eyes and with the mouth closed take one deep breath in through the nostrils...then, exhale slowly, through the nostrils. Continue to breathe in and out through the nostrils at your own natural rate for five breaths.

Now on each exhalation, mentally repeat the word 'calm' to yourself. Continue this practice for few breaths.

The next part of the exercise is to develop a passive attitude. Mentally repeat to yourself 'nothing matters'. Continue to repeat this for five minutes. As thoughts come into your head, try to mentally set them to the side. Try not to judge or analyse the thoughts – let them come in and go out – it doesn't matter what they are.

Take note of noises inside and outside the room. Try to let them fade so that there is no particular sound that you are aware of. Stay with this practice.

Be aware of your quiet breathing, in and out through the nostrils and the mind becoming passive. Try to feel calmness. Let nothing else matter. Stay with this practice for five minutes.

When the practice is complete, I will tell you that I am going to count from five backwards to one. When I get to one, stretch your arms and legs, yawn and sigh, begin to open your eyes slowly.

Five ... four ... three ... two ... one ...

Bring your awareness back to your position in the room.

Now that you have completed the exercise, know that this is a state that you can go to at any time. Try to make this time available for this practice every day.

Closure
(See end of Session 1, page 42.)

Session 4

Escalating Emotions

All honest emotions are positive emotions.

Pert, 1997: 193

4.1 Welcome, outline, objectives and check in

The objectives of the session are that you will:
- Increase awareness of the nature and impact of your emotions.
- Understand emotional hi-jacking.
- Begin to work at managing your emotional arousal.
- Learn about managing your stress.

4.2 Exploring emotions

4.3 'Put down Pat' and the 'emotional hijack'

Break

4.4 Drawing your anger

4.5 Reducing intense feelings of anger

4.6 Taking care of yourself and closure

Facilitators' Guidance for Session 4

4.1: Welcome, outline, objectives and check in

Welcome participants and display the session title, objectives and outline. Begin the session by explaining that the focus will be on the emotions or feelings point of the triangle of behaviour. Emotions are a normal natural part of life and the session will be about exploring and managing them. The first and second objectives are about encouraging participants to think further about their emotional life and how they manage this area. The session will encourage participants to look into their own emotional worlds to try to get some sense of how this connects to their difficulties with anger as parents. The third objective is specifically aimed at allowing participants to process and seek to influence the emotional arousal parts of their anger. It will do this through a challenging personal exercise that participants will be asked to complete towards the end of the session. As in all sessions, the final objective relates to assisting people in learning stress management strategies and working at their overall life balance. Check that the group or individual understands the objectives and briefly run through the content of the session.

Before preceding with these themes, participants will be encouraged to check in to the session. Each will have a minute or two to address their anger diary and make a general comment as to how they feel about their anger (see guidance pages 25-26 and 44).

4.2: Exploring emotions

Presentation, exercise and individual work

Begin this section by reminding participants that the emphasis will be on the emotional point of the triangle of behaviour. Present Figure 4.1 which is a simple representation of how the brain tends to operate in responding to the situations it encounters. The analogy of an air traffic controller can be used to explain how the brain functions. In most situations, this controller part of the brain tends to send the information it is getting to the thinking part of the brain. That is why it is so critical for people to look at their thinking – just as they began to in the last session – to see how it may inflame or arouse their emotional responses inappropriately. Whilst it is critical that participants continue to monitor their thinking and beliefs that lead to their emotional arousal, it is not just as simple as that. As Figure 4.1 shows, there is a 'thinking' brain and an 'emotional' brain. If an emotional response is required, then the signals are sent to that part of the brain to allow this to happen. This is where we begin starting to explore the emotions.

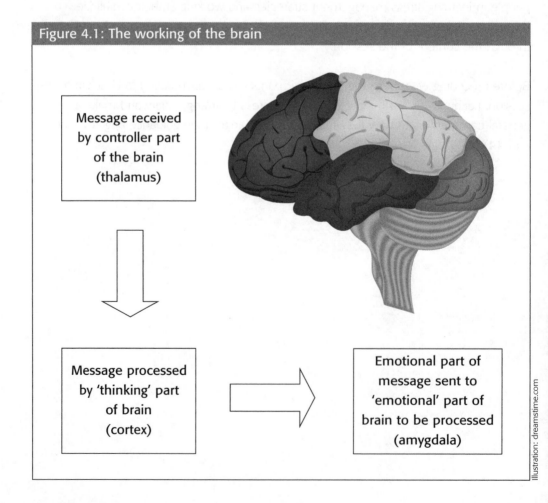

Figure 4.1: The working of the brain

Message received by controller part of the brain (thalamus)

Message processed by 'thinking' part of brain (cortex)

Emotional part of message sent to 'emotional' part of brain to be processed (amygdala)

Illustration: dreamstime.com

Proceed by asking the group to think about all the emotions that they are aware of. This can be done either as a discussion or, if it suits the group, by using a flip chart. (Some parents may have a limited repertoire of labels for not only their own feelings, but those of their children.) Try to ensure as full a range of emotions are outlined as possible relating to the four basic emotions identified in Figure 4.2 which can be used as a resource (see Appendix 3 at the end of this book for list of some emotions).

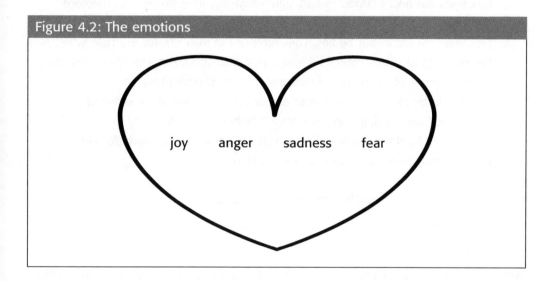

Figure 4.2: The emotions

joy   anger   sadness   fear

Ask the group to reflect on the range of emotions they experience and how they manage these. Some emotions are obviously more pleasant than others. Try to develop a wide ranging discussion on the nature, complexity and messiness of the emotional side of life. Some of the main points that should be made and need to be covered are outlined in Figure 4.3 which again can be used as a resource. This is about increasing their awareness of their own emotional life, the stream of feeling that is a constant presence in every person, and how these emotions shape what they perceive, think and do. Before moving on, ask the individual or use a group round to address the following:

1. Identify an emotion that they find difficult to deal with other than anger.

2. What connection, if any, does it have to their difficulties with anger?

Theory/evidence base

As with many of the areas that this programme attempts to cover, there is a vast body of literature on the subject of emotions. It is not possible to do justice to all the complexities. The emotions are central to our experience as human beings and, like our finger prints, they are what distinguishes us from other people. They are many and varied but it is generally agreed that there are a small group of core emotions, of which anger is one. The challenge for us is to manage these emotions as best we can.

Figure 4.3: Exploring emotions

1. Emotions or feelings are natural, normal experiences which everyone encounters. They are a positive part of being human, and are part and parcel of our social experience.
2. Emotions are sources of energy and power. They get us to do things.
3. Emotions are neither good or bad, right or wrong, they simply are. They are there for a reason. They are what makes us human.
4. Emotions are felt in our bodies. They are not like instincts, for example when the pupils in our eyes contract if a light is shone into them. However, they are something we all experience. Emotions, though, can be prevented.
5. We should try to stay in touch with all our emotions and get a sense of where they are coming from and what is behind them. If we try to ignore, suppress or bottle up feelings this can cause a build up of psychological pressure that needs to escape sooner or later.

We bury our emotions alive!

'When emotions are too muted they create dullness and distance; when out of control, too extreme and persistent, they become pathological, as in immobilising depression, overwhelming anxiety, raging anger, manic agitation' (Goleman, 1996: 56). It is important, therefore, to be able to both identify and become more aware of how our emotions may impact on us and relate to each other. 'Making sense of and managing anger is, in part, based on recognising the influence of other emotions related to our anger' (Golden, 2003: 130).

The air traffic controller analogy used earlier in the session, refers to the part of the brain known as the thalamus, which is the reception point for information. Information that is received by the brain comes from all the senses, but mainly by vision. It is processed firstly by the thalamus, and then sent to the thinking part of the brain, the cortex, which works out the best response. If an emotional response is required then a message is sent to the emotional part of the brain, the amygdala, which then decides the type of emotional response to make.

These two parts of the brain, the logical or rational, and the mammalian or emotional, have also been referred to as the two memory systems – one for ordinary facts and one for emotionally charged ones (Goleman, 1996: 21). Furthermore, it does appear that in terms of evolution the emotional brain evolved before the more rational one 'The fact that the thinking brain grew from the emotional reveals much about the relationship of thought to feelings, there was an emotional brain long before there was a rational one' (Goleman, 1996: 10). As another source puts it, 'The body and mind are not separate, but really are one system co-ordinated by the molecules of emotion' (Pert, 1997: 285). The point is that more research from the field of neuroscience is emerging into the complex nature of the relationship between, and the role of the emotions, in our thinking. Studies into the brain and the emotions are revealing the intricacies and mystery of the processes of human behaviour. There is continuing controversy about the primacy of emotional or rational reactions in how human beings respond to situations that they encounter (Goleman, 2004). This issue is addressed further in the following evidence and theory base section.

In this session, the complexity of the relationship between thinking and emotion is opened up and the causal relationship between our thinking and our emotional management that was put forward earlier, is further refined. Without losing sight of the importance of self-awareness and critical thinking, the onus here is on participants to work at emotional issues and develop their emotional intelligence within a complex, socially interactive world. The challenge is to help them begin to integrate this with, and layer onto, the cognitive work covered next.

4.3: 'Put down Pat' and the emotional hijack

Presentation, discussion and individual work

Ask the group to listen to the following story about a young child called Pat. Pat could be a male, Patrick or a female, Patricia: each person can decide for themselves who they think Pat is.

> *As a young child, Pat was teased mercilessly by a parent. She or he was subjected to jokes that had a cruel edge and that often had the effect of mocking and humiliating him or her, particularly in front of other family members and friends. When Pat became upset, this delighted the parent who would mock and tease all the more. As a result, Pat grew up as a young person clearly establishing within her or his emotional storage system the possibility that powerful people will humiliate and hurt. Not surprisingly, this has made it difficult for Pat as an adult to deal with the range of problems and difficulties that life presents. Pat even finds it very difficult to take a good natured tease or joke and often responds with immediate anger.*

Either in pairs or as a group work through questions 1-3 in Figure 4.4. If working in pairs, each pair could take a different emotion and then feed back to the bigger group.

Figure 4.4: Put down Pat and dealing with difficult emotions

1. In what ways may Pat experience anxiety and how difficult will this be for Pat to manage? How will this relate to Pat's experience and expression of anger?

2. In what ways may Pat experience depression and how difficult will this be for Pat to manage? How will this relate to Pat's experience and expression of anger?

3. In what ways may Pat experience shame and how difficult will this be for Pat to manage? How will this relate to Pat's experience and expression of anger?

Dealing with a difficult emotion that I experience:

Finish this part of the session by allowing participants to reflect on an emotion that they feel is causing them difficulty. Figure 4.4 can be used as resource for this personal exercise.

The emotional hijack

Explain to the group that the example of Pat, a person who clearly has suffered emotional abuse opens up the idea of how emotional reactions can come before the thinking processes talked about in the previous session. The key point to be made is that, when a person with Pat's previous experiences encounters certain events they may have an immediate emotional impact. As Figure 4.5 shows, they may actually bypass or short circuit the 'thinking' part of the brain and go straight to the emotional part in what is known as the emotional hijack. In terms of the triangle of behaviour, we are starting with the emotions and going straight into the actions before we are able to think about what we are doing. We are straight up the escalator into the 'ancient' part of the brain which is the one needed to deal with threat, be it physical, psychological or emotional. An emotional response does not tend to be as accurate as a thought out one; indeed the more powerful the emotion, the less precise the response. It will tend to be immediate but sloppy and a knee-jerk, automatic response is triggered, usually following a fight or flight model where in a crisis there is no time to think carefully about options, and the body short circuits to take the necessary action. So, for Pat, could it be that a harmless joke or jibe may be so psychologically threatening that it triggers this hijacking of the emotional part of the brain?

Ask participants to reflect on their own anger and how it erupts. In what ways do they feel they are sometimes hijacked. Do they have a sense that the emotional brain has taken over, they are not thinking straight or not at all, and they are straight into reacting before they know it?

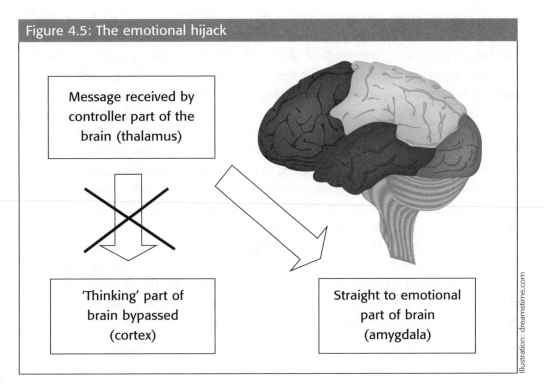

Figure 4.5: The emotional hijack

Message received by controller part of the brain (thalamus)

'Thinking' part of brain bypassed (cortex)

Straight to emotional part of brain (amygdala)

Illustration: dreamstime.com

Theory/evidence base

This session, with the example of Pat, has shown that it is not always thoughts first and then feelings, unlike the ideas covered in Session 3. There are times when, in response to external stimuli, emotions precede intellectual awareness. 'Feelings and thoughts are as inseparable as two sides of the same coin' (Meehan, 2000: 9). 'Some emotional reactions and emotional memories can be formed without any conscious, cognitive participation at all' (Goleman, 1997: 18). As another source puts it 'We often feel without thinking and the most damaging family transactions flow from emotional responses that bypass thinking' (Bradshaw, 1996: 51).

The first half of this element considers the links between anger and other emotions. There is some debate in the literature around anger as a primary or secondary emotion and how it relates to other emotions. Using the example of 'Put down Pat' the session seeks to offer the opportunity to participants to consider their own experiences with other difficult emotions. Are they experiencing anxiety – constantly worrying about issues in their lives? Is there an issue with depression – have they experienced long lasting and constant negative events that have impacted on them? Are there issues around the difficult emotion of shame for anyone? As with Pat, and as a result of being humiliated, have they experiences of the intense and profound feeling of shame, a global reaction based on an assessment of one's whole self as being flawed. It is also the case that some of the literature suggests that shame is the driving force for anger and aggression in males (Kivel, 1992).

The second part of the element introduces the concept of the 'emotional hijack'. The 'theory' of the emotional hijack is shared with participants in this element as well as the two following elements, drawing their anger and reducing emotional arousal. These elements are aimed at helping participants try to connect to this messy emotional material in a more experiential, less intellectual way. People's emotions can have a 'mind' of their own, one which can hold views quite independently from their rational minds. The emotional hijack takes the person to crisis point, – either fuelling it with further distorted thinking or by shooting straight to it because of the intensity of the emotional charge. The person then begins to listen to the 'beast brain' screaming in his or her head. When this is happening, it is babble and is not rationale. The power of emotion will overwhelm rationality. The person cannot stay neutral. The body is being given the command to flood with adrenaline – it is preparing itself to rip someone's face off or to run away. The person in this position cannot hope to think or speak their way out of situations because all of the neurons are firing off in the ancient beast part of the brain and none of the neurons are in the rationale part. This is when the red mist comes down, and the person has lost it! It will be impossible to get the voice to be quiet! At best they may get the volume to turn down.

Break

4.4: Drawing your anger

Presentation and exercise

Begin this sequence by explaining that, when someone is in the midst of an episode of aroused anger, it is not something that they can rationally step back from and explain. They are caught up in the maelstrom of messy emotions swishing about inside them with all sorts of physiological reactions as they saw on the body map. One way of trying to get some sort of access is to use the medium of art. Stress to the individual or group this is not about being artistic or demonstrating skills in drawing or painting, its just trying to capture some of the essence of the outburst of anger and what it actually felt like for the person. To reinforce the point, ask the individual or participants to use the hand that they don't usually write with. Ask each participant to reflect on an occasion when they felt their anger was extremely intense, as bad as it ever has been for them as a parent. (It is better, but not essential, that they choose the example they have already been processing in previous sessions). Then allow a good ten to fifteen minutes for the exercise and a little time for participants to process what they have put down in their drawing. The drawings will speak for themselves, but participants may wish to reflect on, and analyse them further, in relation to some of the material covered on the programme. For example, does the drawing represent their anger at a point when they feel an emotional hijack has triggered them immediately up into a crisis point? Or does it depict something that built up as a result of their thinking about a particular situation and their growing sense of being treated badly, unfairly, disrespectfully, etc and how this type of thinking led to their emotional arousal?

Theory/evidence base

This type of drawing exercise is designed to offer another approach in helping people think about their emotional life and their anger in particular. It can help make more real and tangible some of the ideas around the emotions that are being considered in the session. As one commentator has said, it can prove to be 'an easy, valuable and practical technique which transforms inner forces into visible shapes and creates conditions in which these visible shapes can then be transformed into ordinary words and understanding' (Benson, 1996: 217).

4.5: Reducing intense feelings of anger

Presentation and individual exercise

In this sequence participants will have the opportunity to see if it is possible to reduce significant levels of emotional arousal. To begin, give participants a minute or two on their own to identify a situation with one of their children in which they became extremely angry (it may be the situation they have just drawn or the example they used in previous sessions). Then ask them to engage as much as they can in the following exercise.

- Suggest that this exercise may work better if they close their eyes as they will be working with intense personal information.

- Continue by asking each person to remember the negative situation or event in detail. Can they get a sense again of the intense feelings of anger and rage that they experienced. Let them erupt within themselves again with their full intensity – try to fully experience them for a few moments.

- Whilst still experiencing the negative emotions, ask each person to try really hard to try to change their feelings.

- Urge them to get in touch with their gut level feelings of anger and push themselves to change – to experience different and less intense, more healthy feelings – for example being disappointed instead of devastated, irritated instead of enraged, annoyed instead of furious etc.

- Can they turn down the heat and, however slightly, reduce their emotional intensity just by focusing on it?

- Encourage participants to concentrate and try to trace what they have done.

- Can they also get a sense of some change to their thinking, some new or more rational or sensible thoughts that can create and control their feelings?

Give participants a moment to 'come back' and debrief the exercise with them. Although it is not real, participants may have got a sense of struggling with and being able to get some control of their escalating emotions. Each person needs to reflect on the degree to which they were able to stay just with their emotions or when their thinking processes were present. Thinking, feeling, and doing are not neatly separated discrete things but a messy fusion that is difficult to untangle. The triangle of behaviour which is used throughout the programme represents the connection in a somewhat simplistic way. This could be presented again to participants to let them reflect once more on how it relates to the example of their anger that they have been reflecting on (see Figure 1.7). If any of the participants have continued to work with the example of their mismanaged anger selected in Session 2, there is also the option for them to refer back to Figure 2.8 and to see the relevance of their learning from this session.

4.6: Taking care of yourself and closure

Inform the group or individual that the session will finish with a visualisation exercise. Participants should get themselves comfortable, sit upright, and be relaxed, not rigid. Allow them a few moments to compose themselves. Tell them that the exercise will last no more than five minutes during which time they should keep their eyes closed. Ask them to try to stay with the practice to the end of the exercise. The following script may be used:

Close your eyes. Imagine that you are at the top of a staircase. This staircase will lead you to a place of perfect tranquillity. A beautiful garden.

Visualise the stair case before you. See yourself on the top stair. Know that you are about to go down the stairs, one at a time. Mentally, begin to count backwards:

10   You are leaving the day's activity and hassle behind.
9   Allow sounds around you to fade into the distance so that you are unaware of any sound in particular.
8   With the mouth closed, become aware of breathing in and out through the nostrils.
7   Note any tension that you may be holding and then allow your muscles and limbs to become relaxed.
6   Allow the muscles of the face and head to relax. Allow the teeth to slightly part and the jaw to loosen. Draw the shoulders down.
5   With each out breath feel that you are breathing out the remains of any tension, worry or anxiety – give it all to the out breath.
4   As you start to feel calm, be aware of a sense of stillness.
3   Your breathing is light and your body heavy.
2   Your are at peace as you go down to your special place.
1   You have arrived at the garden.

Walk to your special seat that has been left for you. Look around you. Take in the scene. Notice the colour, the shapes, the sounds, the smell. Bask in the warmth and comfort of it all. Breathe in the soothing fragrance of the place. Be still...be present... just be...

Rest for a while in this deep inner peace. Give thanks for this place, this still centre. And knowing that you can return to it at any time, chose now to take with you the memory and feeling and experience of its gentle calm. Move slowly towards the staircase. Count your journey back, staying with the scent and bringing its peace and deep relaxation with you as you go back up.

1   2   3   4   5   6   7   8   9............10

When you reach 10 you are once again back where you started. Rest for a moment on your chair, then, in your own time, wriggle your toes and fingers, open your eyes and gently come back into the present, refreshed and energised. Without rush or hassle, come back into the here and now as we finish the session.

Closure
(See end of Session 1, page 42.)

Session 5

Children and Anger

Children are entitled to be treated humanely, in the same way as adults expect to be treated.

Iwaniec

5.1   Welcome, outline, objectives and check in

The objectives of the session are that you will:

- Increase your understanding of how badly managed parental anger may affect the development of your children.
- Increase your understanding of children's anger.
- Develop clear plans for responding to your child's anger.
- Learn about managing your stress.

5.2   Parental anger and children's development

5.3   Parenting styles and managing anger

Break

5.4   Accepting and understanding your child's anger

5.5   Coping with your child's anger

5.6   Taking care of yourself and closure

Facilitators' Guidance for Session 5

5.1: Welcome, outline, objectives and check in

Welcome participants. Display the session title, objectives and outline. Begin by pointing out that they are now beginning the second half of the course. The core material on anger, what it is, how it is experienced and expressed, the stages of an angry episode, the harm mismanaged anger can do and the importance of peoples thinking, feelings and actions in contributing to poor anger management has now been covered. They need to hold onto the concept of the 'Triangle of Behaviour' and should now be working at changes they need to make in relation to their thinking, feelings and actions (put up Figure 1.7 to remind people). This is the basis upon which they should be working at change in relation to managing their anger, and monitoring and reflecting on it in their anger diary during the second half of the programme.

Explain that the remaining sessions will aim to build upon this process and will include additional material which may be relevant to participants' anger to further assist in the process of change. This particular session looks at childhood and anger. The first objective is to increase participants' understanding of how unmanaged parental anger may impact negatively on children during the different stages of their development. The second objective is about the difficulties children may have with their own anger, the reasons for this and how they may be helped to handle it. This leads into the third objective which is the development of a clear plan for each participant to respond to their own children's anger outbursts. This may well involve participants managing their own resultant anger. As usual, the final objective centres on improving stress management. Check that the group or individual understands the objectives and briefly run through the content of the session.

Before proceeding with these areas, participants will be offered the opportunity to briefly check in to the session. Each will have a minute or two to address their anger diary and make a general comment as to how they feel about their anger (see guidance, pages 25-26 and 44).

5.2: Parental anger and children's development

Presentation and exercise

Begin this element by pointing out that all human beings go through a series of developmental stages from the beginning to the end of their lives. They have to successfully complete particular tasks in each stage, i.e. physical, psychological and emotional, to allow them to move on to the next stage and increase their chances of having a reasonably happy life. The task for participants is to briefly consider these childhood and adolescent stages and to reflect on the following question in relation to each of these periods:

> *What do you feel would be the main effects of mismanaged parental anger on the child or young person at this stage?*

(Figure 5.1 may be used as a resource for this exercise).

Stage 1: Infancy (0-2 years) – Basic trust versus Basic mistrust

This is the earliest stage of development and is where the core issue and basic task is to achieve trust in the world and people. Infants are absolutely helpless and vulnerable. The messages they receive from being loved, nurtured, cared about and how those in positions of power treat them will stay with them for life. This stage is also about exploratory and developmental behaviours and from only a few months old they start to explore the world around them. This exploratory and learning behaviour will blossom if the child feels they can trust the people around them. The child needs to feel securely 'attached' to someone in order to fully develop as a person.

Put the question to the group or individual.

> *What do you feel would be the main effects of mismanaged parental anger on the new born infant?*

List or otherwise record main effects.

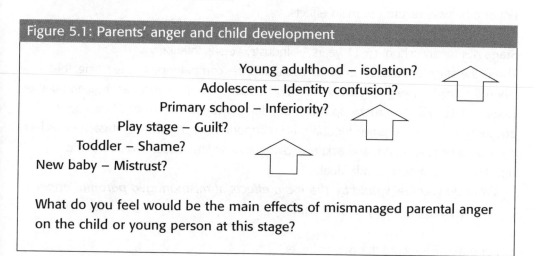

Figure 5.1: Parents' anger and child development

Young adulthood – isolation?
Adolescent – Identity confusion?
Primary school – Inferiority?
Play stage – Guilt?
Toddler – Shame?
New baby – Mistrust?

What do you feel would be the main effects of mismanaged parental anger on the child or young person at this stage?

Stage 2: Toddlers (2-3 years) – Autonomy versus Shame and doubt
This is the 'no stage'. The central issue is about autonomy. The child is learning to think
and trying to develop their own will and get what they want. Its not just about learning
to walk and stand up in a physical sense, but about being able to stand up for
themselves and being able to do whatever they want! They will want to do many new
things but may not have the skills to do so and can easily become frustrated. They will
not yet be emotionally able to handle complex emotions. This will cause a fuse to blow
and break the circuit with a tantrum. 'The ability of children to pick the worst times, the
most embarrassing moments, to display the mother and father of a tantrum is the
common experience of many parents' (Faupel et al., 1998: 80). 'Toddlers choose
exactly what will get your goat, because deep down they are wanting to be stopped'
(Biddulph, 1998: 51). The challenge is to try to achieve an appropriate level of
guidance and firmness. Put the question to the group or individual.
> *What do you feel would be the main effects of mismanaged parental anger*
> *on the toddler?*

List or otherwise record main effects.

Stage 3: Play age (3-5 years) – Initiative versus Guilt
This is the high energy stage when children begin to master the three skills of
language, movement and imagination (Linn et al., 1988). The child's playfulness,
curiosity and initiative continues to develop and the degree to which they can continue
to do so depends on the critical factor of managing guilt (Erikson, 1959). This stage is
when the child is learning to be one of the human race and needs to be supported
and encouraged. Put the question to the group or individual.
> *What do you feel would be the main effects of mismanaged parental anger*
> *on the young playful child?*

List or otherwise record the main effects.

Stage 4: Primary school (5-11 years) – Industry versus Inferiority
This is the stage of industry, of building confidence, competence and learning. It is
when the child is navigating the world of school, friends and life generally, learning the
give and take skills that make up much of adult life (Biddulph, 1998). Once again,
encouragement and positive feedback is so important. Recognising that each of us has
our own talents and gifts, and acknowledging and valuing these, is vital. Put the
question to the group or individual.
> *What do you feel would be the main effects of mismanaged parental anger*
> *on the young primary school child?*

List or otherwise record the main effects.

Stage 5: Adolescents (teenagers) – Identity versus Identity confusion
This stage involves making the transition from childhood to adulthood. The adolescent will move between being very much of a child to being very much of an adult. 'The teenager moves forward like the tide – in waves, in and out' (Bidulph, 1998: 107). They frequently escape to the front of a mirror hoping there's a better way to put oneself together. Each new acne blemish is scrutinised and the identity questions are asked, 'Who am I? What am I doing here? What am I going to become? 'It will be difficult to be tolerant if deep down you are not quite sure...that you will ever grow together again and be attractive, that you will be able to master yourself, that you really know who you are' (Erikson, 1959: 53). Adolescence is a period of life that is mistake prone by design, when intellectual capacities and powers of reasoning are still developing, and young people learn from doing and making mistakes. Put the question to the group or individual:

What do you feel would be the main effects of mismanaged parental anger on the adolescent?

List or otherwise record the main effects.

Stage 6: Young adulthood (18-35) – Intimacy versus Isolation (optional)
This may be an issue for some participants, particularly older parents, given that the trend within most western societies is that children stay longer in the family home before moving to independence, with the tensions and conflicts that this may cause. There may also be issues of continuing anger towards a child even after they have moved out of the family home. If appropriate, put the question to the group or individual.

What do you feel would be the main effects of mismanaged parental anger on the young adult?

List or otherwise record the main effects.

Individual input or group round
Ask the participants to take a few moments to consider their own situation and in particular, if there is anything that has just been covered that would help them manage their own anger with their children. To do this each person could reflect quietly on the following:

1. Is there a particular stage of development of my children that I have found difficult and in what ways could I change how I handle things.

2. Does any of this relate to my example of badly managed anger that I have been working on in previous sessions and what new thinking or new ways of dealing with my feelings or new actions would I use if dealing with the situation again.

Try to encourage each person to come up with at least one new insight.

Theory/evidence base

This session is mainly based on the work of Erik Erikson who promoted the notion that there are stages of life, from infancy through to advanced age and that each stage is associated with specific psychological struggles that shape a major aspect of our personalities. He believes that there are eight distinct stages in human development and that in each stage we have particular tasks to achieve. If we do not master the task at a particular stage it is much harder for us to tackle the next one. As another commentator has put it 'Each stage marks a crisis. Each crisis is a time of heightened vulnerability as well as a time of potential growth' (Bradshaw, 1996: 162-3). Erikson's model has been challenged, particularly in terms of the identity and intimacy stages in that it does not fit with the experiences of women, who, it has been argued, address intimacy and relationship issues before or alongside issues of identity (Carter and McGoldrick, 1989). Nevertheless, and accepting these qualifications, I believe the model remains helpful and powerful in understanding human development. At the same time, I have included perspectives from other commentators in this area. Additional information and ideas on each of the stages is included below. This may assist facilitators in the discussions which develop, although in my experience it is likely that participants pick up on the main issues themselves.

For **new born infants** in situations where there is excessive parental anger present, there is the danger that their need for love and affection will not be met. The experience of emotional and physical neglect and abuse may leave them with a suspiciousness and hostility which is very hard to shift. 'The failure to establish basic trust can have physical, emotional, social and spiritual consequences for later life' (Linn et al.,1988: 37). On one level, it may slow down the child's development, since it is only as their trust builds that they will feel confident to be able to move into more exploratory learning behaviours. It is clear that traumatic early experiences of maltreatment may have a very disruptive and long-term impact on brain development and on the child's processing of experiences and general functioning. Of course, exposure at any age to abusive and violent behaviour can seriously delay development, but 'early exposure may create more severe disruptions by affecting the subsequent chain of development tasks' (Rossman, 2001, 58). In terms of how experiencing abusive violent behaviour might leave a person in relation to their emotions, the literature suggests a link to later hostility and anger. This appears to stem from an absence of trust in the basic goodness of others and centres around the belief that others are generally mean, selfish and undependable (Williams and Williams, 1994).

As children move into the **toddler stage** then the struggle is between being over-permissive or over controlling. Shame and doubt may develop as the child chooses their own will and experiences the disappointment of their parents for not living up to their expectations. This is the period when the soft love needed for the new baby needs to continue alongside some firmness and clarity if the child is making the wrong choice. If parents are constantly saying 'no', then the child may be reluctant to make their own choices. It is crucial that children are able to begin to develop a sense of will, of being in control and of making their own choices. This is the stage that helps build resilience, a sense of self that fosters both physical and emotional health later in life. Excessive mismanaged parental anger will shatter this.

The **play stage** raises the fundamental developmental issue of how the child manages the tension between taking the initiative, experimenting and the guilt that they will experience in terms of the controls and reactions from the carers or parents. If anger continually leads to the child being constantly chastised as a 'bad boy' or 'bad girl', their sensitivity may be shattered and they may end up with deep guilt and self-hatred. They may find it difficult to distinguish between their behaviour being 'bad' or themselves being 'bad'. Excessive anger, aggression and punishments may exacerbate this problem. Signs of the child's unhealthy guilt and self – hatred will vary. They may become excessively angry at themselves or at others, particularly at their parents.

In the **primary school stage** children who do not experience encouragement and positive feedback or who struggle within competitive families and educational structures can be seen as poor performers and may begin to experience feelings of inferiority and have associated difficulties. Once again, mismanaged anger can reek havoc in relation to this developmental area.

In relation to the **adolescent phase**, it is clear that with some adolescents, but by no means all, a wide range of negative behaviours may be identified by their parents. A 'me first', assuming the worse, blaming others (particularly parents) and minimising the consequences of their actions type of thinking and behaviour can develop. These are behaviours that most people probably all use to varying degrees but can be more extreme and pronounced in adolescents when moving towards maturity (Goldstein et al., 1998). Some teenagers may be volatile and boundary breaking. They may show intense anger. Indeed, often teenagers are terrified when they become so angry that they lose control. Negative parental anger may provoke and exacerbate some of the above problems.

Although not a frequent area of consideration for this programme, there is growing evidence that relationship difficulties between parents and **older adult children** may be spilling over into outbursts of inappropriate anger. 'In America, many grown sons today don't want to give up the comforts of their more prosperous parents' generation to go out into the world and struggle. Commonly, they don't see any need to pull up roots until they're 30 or much beyond' (Sheehy, 1996: 56).

5.3: **Parenting styles and managing anger**

Presentation, group exercises and discussion – individual work

Inform the participants that in this session, they will be further exploring their style of parenting and will have the opportunity to see if they can apply any of the information received in terms of dealing with the difficulties they experience in managing their anger.

As a lead into this section, emphasise the following points:

1. This is not a parenting course and will not cover a wide range of issues in relation to their abilities as parents.

2. Always remember that the most important things are their motivation and commitment to the parenting role. If that is absent (and the fact that they are here is a sign of commitment) then working on anger management almost becomes irrelevant. However there are parents who do not fully commit to their children, who do not take on their responsibilities and by their actions or lack of them are insensitive, rejecting or are unavailable for their children. Even worse there are parents where there are significant levels of insecurity, avoidance, disorganisation or violence and the potential for serious emotional difficulties for children emerges. Much more significant intervention is required than an eight session anger management course.

3. Of course, there is no such thing as 'perfect parents', and most of us get by as best as we can. 'Good families – even great families – are off track 90 per cent of the time' (Covey, 1999: 9). The approach taken on this programme is that the participants are the people who know their children best. They are their child's inner compass and they don't need experts to tell them what to do, let alone to tell them that they don't know their own child. It is within such a spirit that the material is offered.

Following on from the above points ask the group to imagine a line across the room to represent a continuum of their parenting styles. This can be drawn or made real in some way if preferred as in Figure 5.2. On one end of the line are those parents who are very passive, appear to be a little unsure about putting down limits to behaviour or who are unable to assert their authority. They may have a 'whatever makes you happy attitude' and may not be really involved to the point that they are almost neglectful to their children. This goes right to the other extreme where we have parents who are very authoritarian and can be rigid and strict with very strong beliefs. Involvement with the child may be more about issuing orders and being firm, with little interest in listening.

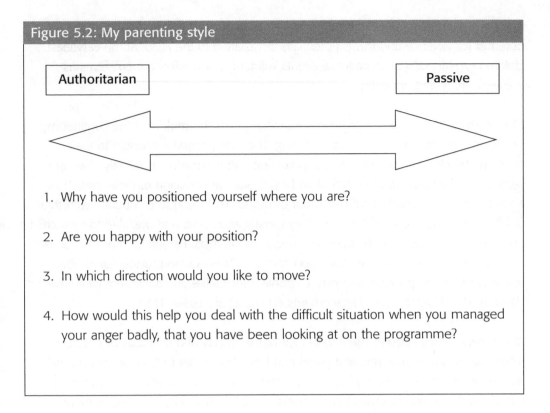

Figure 5.2: My parenting style

Authoritarian

Passive

1. Why have you positioned yourself where you are?

2. Are you happy with your position?

3. In which direction would you like to move?

4. How would this help you deal with the difficult situation when you managed your anger badly, that you have been looking at on the programme?

Ask the group members to position themselves on the line and then give each person the opportunity to address the questions in Figure 5.2. Participants may need a little time to work at Questions 3 and 4. Continue to encourage them to recognise the choice they have in either staying with old ways that haven't worked or trying to move towards new thinking, new ways of dealing with feelings or the taking of new actions. If in group mode, encourage other participants to make suggestions that may help individuals move forward.

Evidence/theory base
The session has the potential to open up wider parenting issues, although there will not be the opportunity to dwell on these for too long. The literature identifies differing parenting styles across the continuum in Figure 5.2 (Calder and Hackett, 2003).

On the authoritarian end, behaviours such as the overuse of punishment, shouting and screaming at the child, physical punishments and intense anger may be prevalent. At the other extreme, there may be a range of permissive and neglectful styles of parenting. These include being frequently unavailable, either emotionally or physically, giving in to a child's tantrums, ignoring misbehaviour, not responding to expressions of a child's needs, not giving structure or taking responsibility etc. Where there are significant levels of insecurity, avoidance or disorganisation then the potential for serious emotional difficulties for children emerges. At both ends of the continuum there is the potential for violence and this is potentially devastating to the child. At the very least, children experiencing such negative events will tend to experience themselves as helpless, angry and unworthy.

Most parents hope to find a position somewhere near the middle of the continuum in providing authoritative and secure parenting. They are generally available to their children and children experience their parenting and themselves positively. They are sensitive and attuned to the physical and psychological condition of their child. They accept their child regardless of behaviour or mood. They tend to co-operate with their child's needs and accomplishments. They remain accessible and available to their child, not obsessed or absorbed by their own needs or interests. Parents do not have to be perfect in each of these areas, but 'good enough'. Parents who provide reasonably warm, sensitive, responsive, interested, flexible, predictable and consistent care have children who develop secure attachments (Howe et al., 1999: 155).

Attachment theory stresses the importance of the quality and character of children's relationships with their carers and peers and how this relates to their developmental well-being on all levels, be it physically, psychologically, emotionally or behaviourally. It is about the profound emotional relationship between a baby and one or more parents or caretakers (Bowlby, 1979). Put more simply, if attachment issues are sorted out and a child feels secure and loved, then developmental and exploratory behaviours will happen and the child can begin to move forward positively into their lives. This is why it is so important that parents strive to work towards the secure authoritative style of parenting outlined above.

Break

5.4: Accepting and understanding your child's anger

Presentation, exercise and discussion

Begin this element of the session by explaining that the first half has been about considering some ideas around parenting and children's development to help participants manage their own anger better. In this second part of the session, the challenge is to work at improving the ability as a parent to help their child manage anger. To begin, ask the group or individual to list the things that they do or say which they know are likely to make their children angry. Record the list and keep for later. This can be reasonably light hearted and may contain 'trivial' through to more 'serious' behaviours but process in a non-judgemental way and just allow the examples to stand.

Move on by asking each person to look at their own attitudes towards their children's anger. Following on from the first part of the session, participants should be able to accept their children's anger as normal. They need to explore how prepared they are to accept their children's rights to both experience and express their anger. Encourage some brief discussion on this issue, and including:

- Have they ever told their child to go to their room when angry?

- Have they ever stopped their child expressing their anger?

- Ask them to think about a time when they were angry as a child. What did their parents or adults do?

Discuss in the group and record some of the main points before moving on.

Point out that there is another side to the coin, which is that for some parents, there may be a fear about addressing this anger and helping their child learn to manage it. 'We no longer want our children to grow up in fear of our anger, but we now live in fear of theirs' (Doherty, 2000: 14). This is what will be examined now, beginning with the anger of young toddlers, the tantrums!

Tantrums

Begin by pointing out that it is important to recognise that sometimes children can learn to use emotions in order to get what they want. This does not just apply to anger but to other emotions such as sulking or shyness. 'The child thus learns the emotion 'most likely to succeed" (Biddulph, 1998: 63). For the purposes of this programme the emotion focus will be on anger and in particular tantrums. Tantrums are learned by accident. The first time a tantrum overwhelms a child of two years who is finding it difficult to handle frustration or take 'no' for an answer, they are simply swept away with their own fury and sense of injustice. Whilst it might help defuse some of the pent-up tension and rage and bring a sense of relief, the main motivation and energy that may keep tantrums going is the effect on big people! Parents may be embarrassed, frightened, uptight or whatever, and sometimes for the sake of peace may give them what they want. 'Thus tantrums, as an anger racket, sometimes become ingrained' (Biddulph, 1998: 64).

Figure 5.3: Tantrums

1. **Never let it pay off!**

2. **Ignore or physically contain the child!**

3. **Follow up in big way!**

4. **In future get in first!**

5. **Plan better!**

It is vital, therefore, to find ways to deal with tantrums. Work through the guidance points in Figure 5.3. Participants need to try to put into practice some of the ideas outlined in the figure without being physically abusive or threatening to their child. They need to continually address and hold their young child to account for the behaviour and help them see that it will not provide them with solutions to their frustrations.

Dealing with the tantrums of the 'terrible twos' is just one aspect of parents' roles in taking on the responsibility of helping their children with their anger as they grow up. It doesn't get any easier to cope with as the child gets older. It is always difficult to deal with any other person's anger and this equally and perhaps applies more so to the anger of our own child. 'It is extremely uncomfortable to witness any child expressing anger through tantrums or physical aggression' (Golden, 2003: 270).

Following on from the ideas about how young children learn to have tantrums, ask the individual or the group to explore why older children also need help in managing their anger. Note and record the points made by group members. The list below and Figure 5.4 indicate points that should be covered in the discussion if they are not raised by group members:

- Children do not naturally know how to deal with anger, and, whilst it is a natural emotion, anger controls must be taught and modelled to children.

- Related to the above point is the fact that children have fewer mental resources, specifically in relation to parts of the brain that we like to think of as being rational or reasoning. To do the sort of reflective self-awareness talked about in the last session takes a good twenty years to fully develop, and key parts of the brain are not completely mature until early adulthood.

- Consequently, given the above points, the strategies that children use are based predominantly on emotionality rather than mature logic and reviewing.

- Children may be so dependent that they suppress their anger.

- Developing a toleration of frustration requires skills in a consistent and dependable environment and takes time.

- Similarly, impulse control takes time to learn.

So, accepting the need for children to learn to cope with and be helped in this area, in addition to the parenting and developmental issues talked about earlier, the role for the parent in helping their child cope is apparent and vital. This is what we will look at next.

Figure 5.4: Children's anger

- **Becoming a racket?**

- **Need to learn how to manage it**

- **Fewer mental resources**

- **Emotional rather than logical**

- **Too dependent to show their anger?**

- **Learning to deal with frustration and controlling impulses takes time**

- **How understanding am I of my child's anger?**

Evidence/theory base

One angry child probably resembles another in terms of their physiological response. However, the way in which each handles their anger and controls their feelings of rage will vary and be related to their upbringing and personal traits. There may also be connections back to the material on developmental stages and how obstacles or tensions may be leading to a child's anger. Each stage brings its own challenges, tensions and frustrations, which may be threatening and spark off anger. 'Although there can be innumerable types of things that children become angry about, there do seem to be issues which are characteristic of certain ages' (Faupel et al., 1998: 80).

There is also a significant and growing body of literature on the changing emotional picture for children. Over the last century there have been dramatic improvements across a wide range of social, economic and political areas and a recognition of peoples rights. However, there has also been a shadow side to this picture, particularly if one looks deeper into young peoples' emotional and spiritual experiences. Concerns about the emotional health or emotional intelligence of young people have been raised and, one commentator, referring to the American experience, claimed that children are, on average, 'growing more lonely and depressed, more angry and unruly, more nervous and prone to worry, more impulsive and aggressive' (Goleman, 1998: 11). Another commentator, again overviewing the American experience compared the top disciplinary problems being experienced by school teachers in the 1950s compared with the 1990s. A dramatic shift from such 'problem' areas as talking out of turn, chewing gum, making a noise, running in the halls, cutting in line, dress code breaches and littering, to the problems of drug abuse, alcohol abuse, pregnancy, suicide, rape, robbery and assault was identifed! (Covey, 1997: 17). There is no reason to believe that the situation has improved as we have moved into the new century. Even allowing for the fact that many serious issues may have been hidden from public view in the past, there does appear to have been significant negative trends taking place. Drugs, adolescent suicide (particularly among males) and the plague of AIDS are some of the real dangers faced by our young teenagers. 'Their universe is not a playground for experimentation but a corridor of epidemics they have to dodge before they even reach the door to adulthood' (Sheehy, 1996: 51). If we add in inequality and poverty with families having to struggle to make ends meet – then the pressures on families and young people can be great. 'Below certain standards of 'liveability', no one can raise happy children' (Bidduph, 1998: 87).

5.5: Coping with your child's anger

Presentation, exercise and individual work (role play if appropriate)

Explain that before finishing the session, the challenge is for each participant to plan how to deal with a situation in which their child becomes extremely angry and behaves badly as a result. Before beginning the exercise three key points should be made:

1. Actions talk louder than words, and the power of parents showing that they can manage their own anger cannot be overestimated.

2. Important not to escalate the outburst by getting angry too. This is much easier said than done, as the 'natural' reaction to someone being angry is to become angry in return! Even making a commitment to try to achieve this may be a very significant move forward!

3. Be absolutely clear as to the inappropriateness of the violent response, no matter how out of control, or provocative or dangerous the child's behaviour is. 'If you react to your child's anger by becoming aggressive, you have modelled aggression as a strategy to deal with anger, demonstrated that you have little capacity for control, and communicated that you cannot be trusted' (Golden, 2003: 278).

If working with an individual take him or her carefully through the following problem-solving exercise. With groups, the option of working in pairs can be used. To begin, each person needs to identify the situation in which their child is likely to become very angry and behave badly. The task is then, helped by the other, to work through the exercise in Figure 5.4, which can be read out or used as a resource. Give the following guidance in relation to the five areas:

1. In relation to obtaining information it is important to be clear about the facts, to try to step back and be as objective as possible in terms of describing the situation.

2. For each person to be clear about the purpose of their actions and make their actions fit with what they want to achieve.

3. In relation to ways of dealing with the situation, try to come up with as many ideas or options as possible, before starting to criticise or analyse them. It may be useful to offer silly, obviously inappropriate solutions, or even aggressive solutions. Guilt or embarrassment may hold back participants from presenting aggressive 'solutions' but if these can be offered by the facilitator it will help participants understand more the ineffectiveness of such approaches and also reduce their anxiety about discussing them.

4. In relation to selecting their alternatives ask participants to go through each possible solution and see whether it not it meets what they hope to achieve in the second point.

5. The next point to agree is the approach that they will take and to record this verbally or in writing. Each person needs to be clear as to whether or not the things they intend to do involve actions they will take, changes to the way they will think about the situation or different ways of dealing with their feelings.

Figure 5.5: Planning how to deal with my angry child

1. What is the problem situation I have in dealing with my angry child?

2. What do I want to happen, how do I want to feel when it is all over, how do I want my child to feel?

3. What are the possible ways of dealing with it?

4. Which one will I go for?

5. How will I know if it works?

Allow enough time for each pair to work at both individual's situation and plan. Before each participant finalises their plan ask them to briefly listen to the general points below. These may be decisions they have already got in their plan or may suggest further ideas to them. There are a range of possible options for someone to consider in relation to dealing with an angry child (see Figure 5.5 which can also be given out as a resource). The ideas have been grouped together under ways of thinking, dealing with feelings and acting, once again using the triangle of behaviour idea.

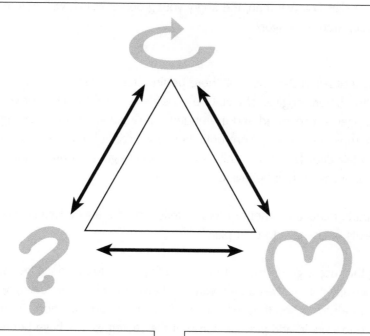

Figure 5.6: Dealing with my angry child

Actions
Stepping back, taking time, modelling positive behaviour, not being sarcastic and critical, staying composed, keeping eye contact, needing to hold the child? Walking away, not shouting. Deep breathing…

Thinking
They're only a child, I will stay calm…I will recognise my child's anger and let them express it…this is a challenge… I can deal with this…

Emotions
Staying calm but not too calm, managing my own anger Recognising other negative feelings such as shame, embarrassment etc.

Thinking

What thoughts may help in facing the difficult situation that will counteract the more normal trigger thoughts towards anger and aggression or avoidance? For example:

- This is a challenge;
- Stay calm;
- They are just a child etc.

Emotions

Will it be possible to get close to the child's anger and not appear too calm and laid back as if it is no big deal? Should they try to demonstrate a level of emotional arousal close to, but slightly lower than, the angry young person? How will they manage their own naturally arousing anger?

Actions

As the angry situation develops will there be time for a moment or two to push the pause button before engaging? Will it be possible to show the child or young person that their anger is recognised and the underlying cause identified? Bawling adolescents out, for example, or goading them until they loose control never works. When will it be possible to talk directly with the child involved and begin to address with them some of the consequences of their behaviour?

Give the participants a moment or two to reflect on the above issues and make any amendments or changes to their plan.

Following this, use a group round to allow each person to identify a key aspect of their plan, particularly if it involves a new way for them of thinking, of dealing with their emotions or a new action they will take in dealing with the situation. The challenge will be to strive to work in and practise some of the strategies that have been identified and explored today.

Role play option

Following on from the group round, the option of a role play could be considered. This will depend on the nature and preferred learning style of the group or individual, but playing out one of the scenarios to try to demonstrate how to deal with the angry child can be an extremely useful learning strategy and should be tried if at all feasible. A facilitator could play the role of the angry child or the child's parent may wish to take it on. Clearly, the role play will have to be carefully managed, but also a 'light touch' needs to be used in not putting anyone under too much pressure. It should be brief and allow the participant, having worked through their problem solving exercises and identified specific ways that they would try to handle their child's anger, to 'practise' some of these in an experiential way. (Appendix 5 provides further guidance on setting up and running role plays).

Theory/evidence base

It is important to recognise parents' own insights into their children's anger. 'Any attempt to help your child better manage and express his anger requires your understanding of how he currently does so' (Golden, 2003: 70). Parents need to use their knowledge and experience of their child's anger outbursts. It is also the case that in relation to their children's anger, the reaction of some parents may be to 'rush in and do something to take it away or make things better' (Lerner, 1989: 151). They need to try to be able to listen to their children's thoughts and feelings, to take responsibility for their own decisions and not base them on their child's state of emotionality. They also need to take their responsibility for setting clear rules about behaviour and enforcing them.

It may be, that on occasion, the child's level of arousal may be so extreme that it will not be possible to reason with them. If the child is already well into the crisis stage and is 'completely unable to make rational judgements or to demonstrate any empathy with others' (Faupel, Herrick and Sharp, 1998: 11) then will it be possible to walk away? What can be done? Holding the child, or having them placed somewhere safe may have to be considered. On the other hand, will it be necessary, and possible, to walk away and allow the young person to walk away?

Ultimately, the session is about trying to help each participant develop 'independent problem – solving skills based on critical, mature, and clear thinking to enable the best solution to his or her circumstances. Problem solving approaches encourages people to think and learn' (Iwaniec, 1997: 338-9).

5.6: Taking care of yourself and closure

Explain to participants that the following exercise is a simple, but effective, muscular relaxation technique. It is best to do the exercise on the floor but it can be practised in a chair. Playing soft, relaxing music in the background can be helpful to this session. Give a moment or two for participants to get ready and then take them through the following script:

- Sit or lie down quietly with the back straight and the arms resting on top of the thighs if sitting or the arms alongside the body with the backs of the hands on the floor. Allow the fingers to gently curl.

- Allow the body to settle with feet apart. Allow the feet to fall away from each other if lying on the floor.

- Keeping the mouth closed, inhale and exhale through the nostrils. Allow the stomach to rise on the inhalation and fall on the exhalation. Concentrate on establishing this slow relaxed breathing pattern for about five minutes.

- To relax the muscles:
  - Tense the whole of the right foot, release and let go.
  - Tense the whole of the right leg, release and let go.
  - Tense the whole of the left foot, release and let go.
  - Tense the whole of the left leg, release and let go.
  - Clench the right fist as tight as you can, release and let go.
  - Tense the whole of the right arm, release and let go.
  - Clench the left fist as tight as you can, release and let go.
  - Tense the whole of the left arm, release and let go.
  - Tense the shoulders by bringing them up towards the ears, hold the tension, release and let go, bringing the shoulders well down.
  - Tense the head and face by tightening the forehead, closing the eyes tightly and clenching the teeth. Then release and let go all tension out of the face and head and have the teeth slightly apart in the mouth.
  - Feel all tension draining from the body. If you aware of tension in any part of the body, release it and let it go.

- Take your awareness back to the breathing and become aware of any changes in the breathing pattern – the length and depth of each breath.

- If any thoughts are rising, do not try to stop or judge them, acknowledge them, then let them go. Allow the mind to settle and become quiet.

- Allow the body to enjoy this state of relaxation.

- Enjoy the stillness of the mind, the calmness of the body.

- When the relaxation is completed, stretch the arms up and over the head and the legs and feet away from the body. Yawn, sigh and fully stretch the whole body.

- Open the eyes slowly.

- Stand up slowly, and let the arms hang alongside the body.

Closure
(See end of Session 1, page 42.)

Session 6

Gender, Life Experiences and Parental Anger

Your bad experiences can make you special.

Bidulph

6.1 Welcome, outline, objectives and check in

The objectives of the session are that you will:

- Increase the understanding of your anger as a man or a woman.
- Consider the impact of past experiences on your anger.
- Apply this new understanding to managing your parental anger.
- Learn about managing your stress.

6.2 Men, women and anger

6.3 Dealing with your parental anger as a woman or a man.

Break

6.4 Traumatic life experiences and parental anger (1)

6.5 Traumatic life experiences and parental anger (2)

6.6 Taking care of yourself and closure

Facilitators' Guidance for Session 6

6.1: Welcome, outline, objectives and check in

Welcome participants. Display the session title, objectives and outline. Begin by pointing out that there are two themes to this session, the first about gender issues and how significant these are in terms of helping people manage their anger as parents, and the second deals with previous life experiences, particularly of violence and trauma (see evidence and theory base below).

Point out that the first objective is to help participants reflect on whether there is any relationship between being a woman or a man, and their respective anger. The challenge for participants is to explore the extent that they feel this may be true for themselves. This will lead on to the more difficult issues of why this may be the case and what they can do about it in terms of managing anger better as a parent. Emphasise that the session is not about attacking one gender over another. The vision is to try to help both men and women advance and fulfil their full potential as parents. By the end of the work participants should feel a balanced view has been presented. The second objective presents the challenge of asking participants to think and reflect on whether any past experiences of violence or trauma is impacting on their ability to manage their anger. Stress that this will be handled sensitively and no one will be asked to share anything they are uncomfortable with. The third objective is to offer participants the opportunity to address either the gender issues or the violence related issues, (or both), and show how they are able to identify and make the required relevant changes in improving how they manage their parental anger. Emphasise that the approach will not be on looking inward and going back into the past. If that is required, it needs to be addressed in another setting. The focus in this session will remain on the present and on participants social functioning, particularly on a practical, problem solving approach in terms of improving their anger management as parents. As in the other sessions, the final objective is about helping participants to learn relaxation and stress reducing strategies.

Before proceeding into these areas, participants will be offered the opportunity to briefly check in to the session. Each person will have a minute or two to address their anger diary and make a general comment on how they feel about their anger (see pages 25-26 and 44).

Evidence/theory base
Facilitators will need to have thought through how they are going to present and deliver this session. There will need to be a degree of flexibility and creativity, given the

different combinations of possible participants. The session may be with an individual female, an individual male, a group comprised exclusively or mainly of either males or females. The guidance will primarily be aimed at those occasions when the programme is being delivered to a group made up of roughly equal numbers of both sexes, with suggestions made in relation to different approaches for the other possible combinations mentioned above.

This session involves tackling one of the most contentious and contested issues in social science, that is, gender. Argument rages across the academic, research, political and religious worlds on issues to do with gender differences and similarities. Consequently, the session also has the potential to be the most 'difficult' for the facilitators in the sense that it may open up divisive gender issues and politics. The approach is to try to steer a way through this field, recognising the strength of individual participants views and feelings while trying to keep people focused on how the material can help them manage their own anger as a man or a woman but more importantly as a parent! Similarly, sensitivity will also be required from the facilitators in dealing with the issues of violence and various traumas which some participants may have experienced.

6.2: Men, women and anger

Presentation, exercise and individual work

Begin by making the general point that, this programme takes the view that there are differences between men and women which affect every aspect of their lives. Any of the parents in the group who have male and female children will probably identify with this. Across all cultures there has been a recognition that men and women have different natures. Not only has this been, and continues to be, the perspective of major religions it is also reflected across a range of areas including neuroscience, genetics, psychology, ethnography and biology. However, point out that not everyone agrees with this, and there is no requirement for them to do so. To help them explore further some of the issues for themselves as a woman or a man, take them through the following three exercises:

1. There are two alternatives for the first exercise. The first is collage work. Get the group or individual to produce collages of how they see men and women. This can be done in various combinations, for example, in a mixed gender group the men could do a 'man's collage' and the women a 'woman's collage' or vice versa! Keep it light hearted and 'fun'. (Please note that significant work is required by facilitators in preparing for this exercise. It is necessary to have gathered up a large number of gender related pictures and images to allow participants to select from). Give the individual or group about 10 minutes to produce their work. Put the finished work up on a wall, and they should begin to bring out, at a general level, some of the different expectations that society places on men and women. 'Every culture has its gender images' (Sammon, 1997: 67).

   Or

   Alternatively, divide the group into males and females and ask each sub group to list approximately 10 things that they feel identify themselves as men or women respectively. Each group or individual to work in relation to their own gender. Record and display the lists. Briefly discuss what they say about the expectations of men and women.

2. The second exercise is a group reflection and discussion on the results of two pieces of social research. Explain that the first experiment looked at how an infant's distress was interpreted differently by observing adults who did not know whether the infant was a girl or a boy. The experiment found that if the observers thought the child was a girl they tended to regard the distress as fear, whereas if they thought that the child was a boy they were more likely to rate the distress as anger! (Fausto-Stirling, 1992). Ask the group or individual to reflect on why this may be,

and particularly how it may lead to differences in how girls or boys may deal with their anger.

Move onto the second piece of research which involved asking school children 'If you had one wish what would it be?' When the findings were analysed the main conclusion related to gender. There was a significant relationship between wishes associated with power and boys, and an even stronger relationship between wishes associated with relationships and girls. (Newman, 2004). (Hopefully, some linkage can be made to the collage or gender lists around the key issue that there may be something in the way society expects girls and boys to behave which may be influencing the observers' perceptions). If this is the case, discuss how much further will such expectations actually lead to differences in how girls and boys learn to manage their anger?

3. Ask the group to participate in one further exercise. They are to explore the language used within our society to refer to men and women who are angry, particularly if it is with a member of the opposite sex. If working with a mixed group, break the group according to sex and ask the female sub-group to think about and record the terms used to describe a woman who is angry with a man. Similarly with the men, ask them to list the terms that are used to describe a man who is angry with a woman. Give permission, but only for this part of the session, for the use of abusive language if such terms are felt to be in common usage to describe either angry men or women. (If working with single gender group or with an individual then either ask them to complete the entire task or work alongside them in doing it together.) Depending on the levels of literacy, and the approach being used within the programme, have the group (or individual) write down or record verbally the respective lists. To try and make the exercise safer and encourage people to participate, stress that it is not the terms that they themselves use to describe someone of the opposite sex who is angry with them (although of course they may well do), but rather it is the terms that they are aware of being used within society.

Compare the two lists which may look something like those in Figure 6.1.

Draw from the group or individual as to what strikes them about the lists. It would be anticipated that there would be differences in how women's and men's anger is viewed generally by society. It would also be expected that there are more negative, trivialising and derogatory terms to describe women's anger. It may be an exaggeration, but is there something in the view that there does not appear to be one unflattering term to describe men who vent their anger on women? (Lerner, 1989).

Figure 6.1: Angry men and angry women

Terms used to describe a woman who is angry with a man	Terms used to describe a man who is angry with a woman
bitch	bastard
nag	raging
shrew	going off on one
witch	cracked up
man hater	psycho
castrator	wanker

Following the three exercises, which should have begun to bring out key points, briefly present the notion that for both women and men there may be pressures arising from how society and the prevailing culture tends to view them which can cause problems. Take the participants through the messages in Figure 6.2.

Figure 6.2: What messages have you received?

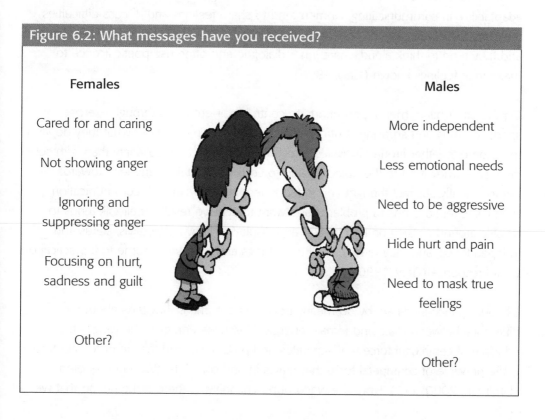

Females

Cared for and caring

Not showing anger

Ignoring and suppressing anger

Focusing on hurt, sadness and guilt

Other?

Males

More independent

Less emotional needs

Need to be aggressive

Hide hurt and pain

Need to mask true feelings

Other?

Theory/evidence base

The material in this section refers to elements 6.2 and 6.3. A selection of literature on gender issues will be summarised and presented below. It will not be possible to do justice to all the various complex and conflicting ideological viewpoints and perspectives, particularly around the more contentious area of trying to explain why differences exist. The aim is to briefly outline the main gender differences from the literature and relate this to emotional and anger management issues.

Oversimplifying it, and in the words of one commentator, 'women tend to be stronger in competencies based on empathy and social skills, with men doing better in those based on self-regulation' (Goleman, 1998: 240). This view is born out by experts in vocational training. 'On average, women are more interested in dealing with people and men with things. Vocational tests also show that boys are more interested in 'realistic,' 'theoretical,' and 'investigative,' pursuits, and girls more interested in 'artistic' and 'social' pursuits' (Pinker, 2002: 351).

Taking the above ideas further and into the world of social relationships and emotions, the literature continues to identify different strategies that men and women use for dealing with their emotions. (Cutrona, 2001). Firstly, in relation to women, they more frequently report direct expression of their feelings, through talking to another person or writing about their emotions. They lean towards feeling, intuition, empathy and adaptability. In communicating, women tend to share feelings and discuss difficulties, their talk will revolve around sharing similar experiences, creating intimacy and rapport and they tend to think aloud, share inner dialogue and often use poetic licence to make their feelings known (Gray, 1996).

On the other hand, men report efforts to control their emotions through exercise, sports, drinking and smoking (Cutrona, 2001). They are more about what they do, and they come together around activities, which mean more about solidarity than with self-disclosure. They tend to the objective and to compartmentalise, and lean towards predominantly abstract thought and independent creativity. In their communication men will offer solutions to problems and want to achieve results, their talk tends to revolve around passing on information and displaying knowledge, skills, status and independence, and they tend to mull over things and then try to come to a practical or useful response (Gray, 1996).

Of course, such ideas are by no means new. Chinese philosophy talks about the difference between male and female energy, 'Masculine energy is the yang – the principle of centrifugal force that separates and pulls away, and the yin or female force is the principle of centripetal force that draws in and connects' (Welwood quoted in Hardiman, 2000: 111). From the world of psychoanalysis, there is the notion that we are all androgynous having both a masculine and feminine side. Women have their masculine side (animus) and men have their femine side (anima). We may not be aware of these subordinate sexual identities but they are there (Jung, 1973). There are feminine and masculine characteristics. However, there are not exclusive feminine or masculine traits, the traits are primarily human ones, 'all powers that are present in masculine nature are also present in feminine nature' (Borden, 2003: 72). No-one has a purely feminine or masculine nature. What tends to differentiate and distinguish the feminine and the masculine is the relative priority among certain traits and tasks which have been outlined above.

Leaving aside the ongoing controversies as to the degree to which the above differences are built into each of us as a man or a woman or arise from the cultural context, the relationship between culture and men and women's anger remains significant. The fact remains, that although there is a sense that things may be changing, much of the literature still puts forward the notion that, to varying degrees, society still basically views little girls as in need of more care because they are little girls and also because they will need to care for others in the future. Little boys, on the other hand, should be loved because they are able to achieve. From this starting point, all sorts of issues may arise for girls, who are not expected to become angry and show such emotions and for boys who are expected to get angry and achieve things.

Taking men first, some research suggests that 'even from the first moments of life, little boys are seen by parents as far more alert and independent and by implication as having fewer emotional needs than infant girls. Ironically, when little boys are themselves studied it appears that they are in fact more needy, cry for longer periods on average, and experience higher anxiety levels faster when left alone.' (Hardiman, 2000: 37). However, because of prevailing perceptions, there will be some boys who are raised to mask their real feelings and present an image of strength, bravado, and self-confidence. They may be supported in expressing and acting out their anger and even encouraged to aggressively express it. Some boys and men may tend to take more risks than women. Some may be less self-critical. Some may demonstrate less sensitivity. It is also clear that although men have as much latent ability for empathy as women, some appear to have less motivation to be empathic. This appearance of being socially insensitive may have more to do with the image they wish to convey than with the empathic ability they possess. More significantly, however, is the fact that, as some men grow up, they may tend to minimise, ignore, deny or suppress their feelings of fear, uncertainty, loneliness or neediness. Some may find themselves unable to acknowledge or discuss real hurt or vulnerability and sometimes do not accept their needs for connection, recognition, respect and love. This will all play out then in terms of how some men experience and manage their anger. Furthermore, the extent of violence, addictions and suicide in our communities and the fact that a significant proportion of this comes from men is a testimony to the negative influences operating on men. The epidemic of fatherlessness among families in the Western world has been well documented, and even for those fathers who are physically present, a number of these are emotionally absent. Some fathers, although well meaning and benign, remain emotionally distant, preoccupied, ignorant of children's needs and uncommunicative. Others become 'brutal, toxic and destructive' (Hardiman, 2000: 113).

With regard to women, societal expectations on girls may see some of them grow up learning to be more focused on their hurt, sadness, and guilt than on anger. Some are discouraged from displaying anger and it is not taken seriously. They are taught to ignore and suppress their anger. Interestingly 'women experience basic emotions more intensely, except perhaps anger' (Pinker, 2002: 345). As a result, anger may often be expressed indirectly. As one commentator has put it, 'Most women have little practice in expressing their anger in a controlled direct and effective fashion' (Lerner, 1989: 95). This is further compounded for some women in that they experience higher levels of anger in the home than men which may be to do with the pressure that they are under, particularly if working mothers. Research has identified women as experiencing high levels of anger, particularly within the domestic context, and this has been related to the fact that women are still far more likely than men to be responsible for household chores and childcare, so the pressures on their home life are far greater (BAAM, 2005).

Of course, the ongoing controversy still remains as to the degree in whether all the above differences can be explained by the culture. It is also the case that the cultural and societal picture is constantly changing and there may be new trends emerging which will impact on both men and women's anger management. Each participant should have the chance to consider material on gender differences, which is summarised in Figure 6.4 in a clear straightforward way, along with further material from the literature. The challenge for the participants in this and the subsequent element, is to come to their own conclusions through discussion and individual reflection as to how their experiences as male or female may be relevant in managing their parental anger.

6.3: Dealing with your parental anger as a woman or a man

Presentation, individual work and group round

Emphasise that, as mothers and fathers, it is important for participants to have some insight into how their anger and the difficulties with it may be related to their experiences of being male and female. At this point, the challenge is for each participant to think about the messages they have received in growing up as a girl or boy into adulthood and how these may be playing out in terms of managing their anger as parents.

It may help if they revisit the example of their badly managed anger that they have been focusing on in previous sessions and take a few moments to look at it from the perspective of gender. Get the participants to recall the example, and then ask them to reflect on the following questions:

- Was their mismanaged anger anything to do with their gender and their expectations in relation to this?

- Was there any issue in relation to the gender of the child and their expectations of that?

- Do they have any expectations about their roles and relationships that they have developed and which may need to be looked at and challenged?

- How can these be changed?

- What new thinking or mindset do they need to work towards in terms of how they understand their gender in the way they will deal with their anger?

- What will help their emotional pain?

- What actions can they take to improve their situation?

Figure 6.3 on page 126 can be used on display or as an individual resource to assist participants in doing their personal work. Using a group round, encourage each participant to share at least one insight, change or new approach that they will bring to managing their parental anger which they feel results from being more aware of gender issues.

Before leaving this section, it should be emphasised once again that the programme wishes to affirm and support both men and women in the task of parenting and the key points in Figure 6.4 should be briefly made.

- **Different does not mean unequal:** The fear, of course, is that difference implies unequal, and the point has to be stressed that difference means strength and that these differences should not be viewed as limitations.

Figure 6.3: Dealing with my anger as woman or a man

Either in relation to my example of mismanaged anger or generally,
what changes would I make?

New actions

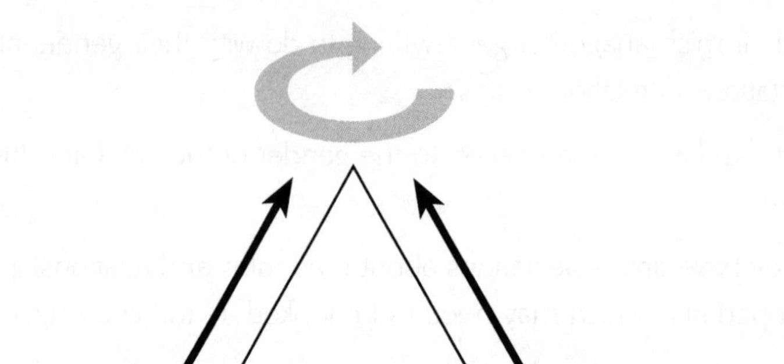

New thinking

**New ways of dealing
with my feelings**

- **It is dangerous to generalise:** Point out that there is no sex difference yet discovered that applies to 'every last man compared with every last woman, so generalisations about either sex will always be untrue of many individuals' (Pinker, 2002: 340). Even in areas where there is a suggestion that one gender may be better, for example women and emotional skills, other research into differences at later points in life has shown that that 'some men will still be better than most women' (Goleman, 1998: 322).

- **Differences are slight for most people:** Differences are slight for most people, they are only tendencies and don't apply to every individual. (Biddulph, 1998). As another authority points out, whenever large groups like men and women are compared on any psychological dimension, there are far more similarities between the groups than differences

- **Each person is a unique individual human being:** Stress that the approach taken by this programme is that no woman is only a woman and no man is only a man. Everyone is different. Each person has a unique individuality and a common human nature. Each has their own individual talents and capacities, be they artistic, scientific, technical, intellectual or otherwise.

- **Both women and men have the potential to be equally good as parents.** Finally, this needs to be stressed to challenge the beliefs 'so widely held that men are by nature less sensitive than mothers to their children and less deeply attached to them' (Burgess, 1997: 98). For example, and in relation to the scope of this programme, 'Parenting styles do not, overall, differ significantly and within couples they tend to converge' (Burgess, 1997: 185).

Stress that participants do not have to accept what they have heard, but it represents the view taken by the programme. It is based upon the idea that there are some differences, but they are complimentary and both genders are equally equipped to provide positive parenting and meet the challenges of life.

Figure 6.4: Men and women
• **Different but equal**
• **Don't generalise**
• **Slight differences for most**
• **Each person is a unique human being**
• **Both women and men have the potential to be equally good as parents**

Break

6.4: Traumatic life experiences and parental anger (1)

Presentation and individual work

Begin this element by explaining to participants that there is an extensive body of research material which shows how anger related problems have been linked to various traumatic experiences including military conflict, situations involving bereavement or serious personal injury, and being a victim of violent crime or domestic violence. Acknowledge that there may be some of the participants for whom this is a real issue. They may have been a victim of such behaviour and they need to take a little while to consider these issues. Stress that no one will be expected to share details of any matter which is still causing them distress and upset. They will not be asked to pick over old wounds or hurts. The thrust of the programme is about addressing and trying to improve current and future behaviour. To this end, the issue is whether or not there are negative events from their past that may still be impacting on their anger management and whether they need to do anything about them.

Explain to participants that there can be emotional consequences from such experiences that they may or may not have been able to resolve. They need to acknowledge and begin to accept that, as a result of such violence, it is normal to experience emotional chaos, pain and confusion, which can be intense and ongoing. This might also play out for them in finding it more difficult to manage their anger. They may not have had the opportunity, or been able to work at, dealing with these feelings and coming to terms with the shock and violence they experienced. Ask participants to take a few moments, on their own, to quietly reflect on whether any of their past negative experiences is making it hard for them to manage their anger with their children at times. There is no need for anyone to share any of this material.

If anyone was to experience a strong emotional reaction, this needs to be addressed. The person's pain and hurt should be acknowledged but at the same time every effort made to avoid working through their abusive episode with them either individually or in the group. Within a group, it may also be necessary to briefly address any associated anxiety from other group members. The distressed person should be encouraged to stay with the session to the end and reassured that they will then be offered immediate support. Time can then be spent allowing them to talk about their difficulties, offering empathy, understanding and emotional support, but making it clear that a therapeutic service cannot be offered. To this end, a list of local and accessible supportive counselling resources needs to be kept by programme providers which can be made available to the person.

It is also important to point out that just because people have had difficult past experiences, it does not stop them working at changing their behaviour in the here and now, working at their problems and identifying solutions to better handling their anger with their children. For some, this type of work may also begin to help in dealing with some bad past experiences. It is also the case that not everyone will automatically be trapped forever by their past experiences. Indeed, there may be those who have been able not only to get through bad experiences, but that they have found that these experiences have helped them towards learning, growth and an understanding of other peoples difficulties. It will not be possible for everyone. It may well be a long and arduous struggle. But sometimes, bad experiences can make people special.

Explain to participants that in the next element, they will be asked to take this issue forward a little more but before that, the issue of domestic violence needs to be covered. Using Figure 6.5, point out that if they are the victims of ongoing domestic violence within their family, this may well continue to contribute significantly to anger related parenting problems and needs to be addressed and dealt with. The key point should also be made that if there is any participant who is perpetrating domestic violence within their relationships, they will need to do much deeper work. Domestic violence and abuse is much more than an anger management issue! This particular programme will **not** be able to make positive inroads into domestic violence and it would be misleading and dangerous to claim that it could do so. However, information on domestic violence services should be available and accessible if required by any participant at the end of the session. (It should be accepted and acknowledged that, for some, domestic or any forms of violence may not be an issue).

Figure 6.5: Anger and domestic violence

Domestic violence is more than bad anger management and should be treated much more seriously.

A child who witnesses violence against their parent is also a victim of that violence.

The highest responsibility we will ever have on this earth is parenting and the greatest thing you will ever do for your children is to treat their mother or their father with respect.

Covey, 2000: 75

Theory/evidence base

It is vital to give a clear message that domestic violence is not an anger management problem and needs to be taken more seriously. Teaching anger management techniques to someone who uses domestic violence may, in fact, increase the risk to the victim of such violence as a false sense of security and safety may be created (Heery, 2000).

Domestic violence is just one of a series of possible traumatic experiences that some participants may have experienced. For others it may be serious accidents, violent community conflict, para-militarism, racism, criminal behaviour or sexual abuse. The list is endless. The key is the relationship between anger and the trauma experienced. Anger has long been identified as being a component of traumatic reactions. 'Anger and trauma have an intriguing relationship' (Novaco and Chemtob, 1998: 167). Studies into domestic violence survivors highlight anger along with fear and pain as the key effects. In particular, there is the difficulty of experiencing so much anger against someone but not being able to express it directly because of the fear of the consequences. What then happens to this anger? (Goodman and Fallon, 1995).

It is critical to recognise the emotional chaos, disorder and confusion which will accompany serious traumatic events in anyone's life (Gibson, 1991). For those who have experienced trauma, the ability to integrate their emotional experiences can be overwhelmed. If help has not been obtained, or the natural emotional responses ignored and unresolved, then a pool of feelings with associated behavioural symptoms may remain. The challenge is to balance the recognition and acceptance of such issues with the fact that the programme will not provide a therapeutic response to these difficult situations. Rather it will be trying to help participants recognise, whether, and to what degree, such negative occurrences may still be playing out in relation to their anger as parents and if they can address this or need to seek further help. There is an element of risk in opening up such material with people. There may be issues of denial, repression or suppression playing out particularly for those parents who may have memories and experiences of being abused and have never been able to resolve these (Acton, 1997). Sensitivity and understanding may be required in applying the facilitator guidance above.

6.5: Traumatic life experiences and parental anger (2)

Presentation, individual work and group round

Give participants the opportunity to decide what they want to do with the material they have reflected on privately in the previous element. Display Figure 6.6 on page 132 to help them think this through. Get them to work through the questions and finish with a group round in which each person can say whether or not there has been or is a trauma playing out for them, without disclosing what it is. Whatever stage they are at in recovery from this, can they identify at least one significant change, in terms of how they think about it, how they handle their feelings in relation to it or something concrete they could do which would help them achieve the goal of better managing their anger as a parent.

Figure 6.6: Life experiences and anger

Are there some bad past life experiences that I know are still causing problems for my anger as a parent?

What do I need to do in terms of my past experiences to help me manage my anger better as a parent?

New actions

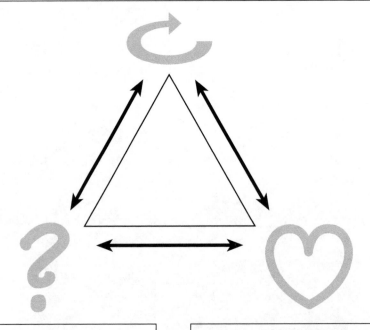

New thinking

New ways of dealing with my feelings

6.6: Taking care of yourself and closure

Prepare the individual or group for another relaxation exercise and take them through the following script:

Sit or lie in a comfortable position. Close your eyes. Breathe in through the nostrils and out through the nostrils for several rounds of breathing. Allow the breath to naturally slow down and become light.

1. Concentrate on the right side of the body only. Be aware of the right side of the body only.

2. As each part of the body is mentioned, take your awareness to that part. Without moving the part, acknowledge any tension, release it, and let it go.

3. Starting on the right side of the body, take your attention to the toes of the right foot, top of the foot, sole of the foot, heel, inner ankle, outer ankle, shin, calf, front of the knee, back of the knee, front of the thigh, back of the thigh, groin, hip, side of the waist, side of the chest, front of the shoulder, back of the shoulder, armpit, front of the upper arm, back of the upper arm, inner elbow, outer elbow, front of the lower arm, back of the lower arm, front of the wrist, back of the wrist, back of the hand, fingers lightly curled, palm of the hand. The whole of the right side of the body. Keep your concentration with the right side of the body. Allow it to become heavy, letting any tension go. Keep concentrating on the right side of the body only for a few moments.

4. Take your awareness to the left side of the body. Acknowledge how the right side of the body feels compared to the left side. Concentrate on the left side of the body only. Be aware of the left side of the body only.

5. As each part of the body is mentioned, take your awareness to that part. Without moving the part, acknowledge any tension, release it, and let it go.

6. Take your attention to the toes of the left foot, top of the foot, sole of the foot, heel, inner ankle, outer ankle, shin, calf, front of the knee, back of the knee, front of the thigh, back of the thigh, groin, hip, side of the waist, side of the chest, front of the shoulder, back of the shoulder, armpit, front of the upper arm, back of the upper arm, inner elbow, outer elbow, front of the lower arm, back of the lower arm, front of the wrist, back of the wrist, back of the hand, fingers lightly curled, palm of the hand. The whole of the left side of the body. Keep your concentration with the left side of the body. Allow it to become heavy, letting any tension go. Keep concentrating on the left side of the body only for a few moments.

7. Now, take your attention to the back of the neck, back of the head, top of the head, the temples, the brow, the bridge of the nose, right side of the nose, left side of the nose, right check, left cheek, upper lip, lower lip, allow the teeth to slightly part and the tongue to rest behind the lower teeth, the chin, the throat, front of the chest, abdomen.

8. Take your attention to the whole body together. Allow the whole body to become heavy and totally relaxed. Stay with this practice for several minutes.

9. Bring your awareness back to your position in the room. Allow the breath to slightly deepen. Begin to make small movements with the fingers and toes. Take the body to full stretch with the hands behind the head and the legs out straight. Rub the palms of the hands together to create an inner heat. Cup the hands over the eyes and then open the eyes to the heat. Draw the hand lengthwise over the face.

10. Move from your position in your own time.'

Closure
(See end of Session 1, page 42.)

Session 7

Conflict, Power and Anger Management

Holding our ground! Not giving in to our children, but not giving up on them either.

Covey, 1999

7.1   Welcome, outline, objectives and check in

The objectives of the session are that you will:
- Explore your natural response to conflict.
- Increase understanding of more positive ways of handling conflict with your children.
- Practise conflict management skills.
- Learn about managing your stress.

7.2   Fight or flight: who wins – who loses?

7.3   Understanding and listening

Break

7.4   Being understood and 'I' messages

7.5   Practising conflict handling skills

7.6   Caring for yourself and closure

Facilitators' Guidance for Session 7

7.1: Welcome, outline, objectives and check in

Welcome participants. Display the session title, objectives and outline. Begin by informing the group that in this session the focus will be on themes of power and conflict within the parent child relationship. Conflict is a normal, and for some, persistent part of family life. Parents need to accept a major part of the responsibility for the way conflict is handled with their children. This session is aimed at helping participants reflect on, and, if necessary, make some improvements in how they are handling their conflict situations. The first objective is to increase their understanding of the different approaches to conflict and in particular what tends to be their own approach – their default position. The second objective is to increase understanding of the processes that occur in a conflict situation and of ways of behaving that have been shown to help de-escalate situations. The third objective is for participants to practise some of these learnable skills. They also need to think about how power is used in these difficult interactions. As in all sessions, the final objective relates to assisting people in learning stress management strategies and working at their overall life balance.

Before proceeding into these areas, participants will be offered the opportunity to briefly check in to the session. Each person will have a minute or two to address their anger diary and make a general comment as to how they feel about their anger (see guidance, pages 25-26 and 44).

7.2: Fight or flight: who wins – who loses?

Presentation, exercises and discussion

Handling conflict

Begin this element by asking the individual or participants to take part in a short exercise. Point out that its purpose will become clear later. The main 'rule' for the exercise is that there is to be no talking and no physical contact. Ask the person or the group to stand up and to listen. Explain that the facilitator is going to stand a little distance away from them, and they are to imagine that the facilitator is someone that they are in conflict with. Each person is to try to get a sense that the facilitator represents something that is really annoying and provoking them.

In their own time, each of them should show by their movement, posture, and stance (still without any speech) how they would normally handle this conflict. Stress again that there is to be no physical contact with the facilitator representing conflict nor with any object in the room. Give each person a few moments to act out their 'style, and ask them to briefly say why they have positioned themselves as they have. Thank them for their participation and get them to sit down.

Naturally, with an individual there will only be that person's interaction, but with a group there should be a range of approaches presented. There may be those who are direct and threatening and rush straight up to the facilitator, closing down personal space and 'eyeballing' him and her. Others may be more tentative and cautious in their approach. Some, perhaps may turn away and show more passive and avoidance behaviours. After each person has spoken about their own actions, a few minutes can be spent discussing the exercise, using some or all of the following questions:

- Why were some more direct and aggressive than others?

- How automatic was the response?

- What about different types of conflict?

- What role does power have in how potential conflicts would be handled?

Use Figure 7.1 to present some of the ideas that have come out in the discussion to explain the flight or fight responses. These are the normal, almost natural reactions to conflict. Remind participants of the body reactions to being angered that were covered in Session 2. These are similar when experiencing conflict and the body short circuits its thinking processes in order to deal as quickly as possible with the conflict, either through fight or flight.

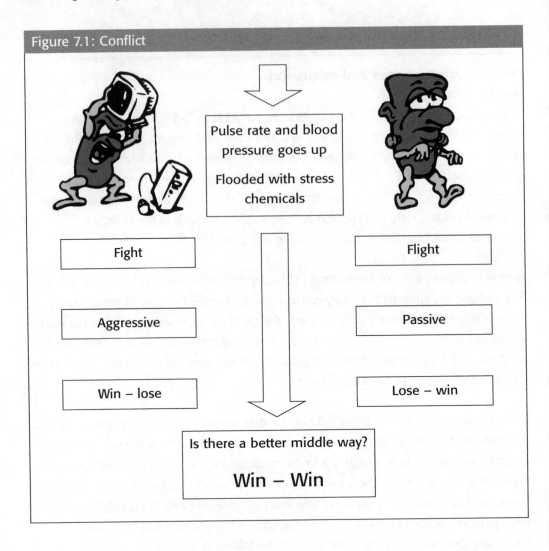

Figure 7.1: Conflict

Pulse rate and blood pressure goes up

Flooded with stress chemicals

Fight	Flight
Aggressive	Passive
Win – lose	Lose – win

Is there a better middle way?

Win – Win

As Figure 7.1 shows, a more modern way of way of looking at these two ancient modes of fight or flight is win – lose or lose – win. Ask the individual or group to reflect for a few moments on how useful such approaches are in handling conflict with their children. A bigger and stronger parent going for consistent win – lose outcomes will probably get their way but what will be the consequences for their children and their relationship?. What happens when their child becomes a teenager? As indicated in a previous sessions, if regularly going for win – lose is accompanied by displays of anger and aggression, this may significantly damage the parent's relationship with their child and their own mental, emotional and physical health.

The other side of the coin is where the parent leans more towards lose-win, takes the path of least resistance and the children usually have their own way. The parent may be more popular in the short term but where will this end up? Even though the parent appears to be passive, the anger is likely to still be there and keeping it in will not work either. The same internal stress reactions will continue with the accompanying bad effects on health. Eventually, as with the pressure cooker, there may well be an explosion of aggression.

Win – win

Continue by explaining to participants that the challenge for this session is to try to find a middle way between fight and flight. Figure 7.1 shows the middle road through difficult conflict and the idea of working towards a win – win approach, where both parties to the conflict are getting something out of it! If appropriate, the win – win idea can be demonstrated in a light hearted way. Ask if the individual or one of the participants would agree to take part in a friendly arm wrestling competition. To win a 'prize' each person has to try to put the other person's hand down, and each time they do this, they win a prize. Start the game, and after 'struggling' through a turn or two, ask the person what way they could play the 'game' so that both they and the facilitator could more easily win a lot of prizes? Very quickly it is clear that by taking turns about to let each person win and moving their arms back and forward both participants can win. This is the essence of win – win. The big question for participants is how far can they take this idea in ongoing and difficult conflicts with their children?

Parental responsibility and power issues

Explain to participants that this raises the issue of their duties, responsibilities and power with their children. How much power do they have, how should and how do they use it? The responsibility on them as parents in managing both their own anger and helping their children learn how to handle their anger remains. They need to find ways to do this that will not abuse nor ignore the influence and authority that they have. This may also mean, that at times, it will appear difficult to find win – win approaches to conflict. Present three key ideas that parents need to think about to see how far they can go for win – win type solutions (Figure 7.2 can be used as a resource):

1. Of course, some issues are too important for compromise and there will be times when parents have to make what appears to be a win – lose decision with a child. For example, insisting that they get immunised, or don't play out in a dark street, or that they have to go to school and so on. This needs to be done in respectful ways. It is vital that parents are clear about what is important. 'Parenting is not about being popular and giving in to every child's whim and desire. Its about making decisions that truly are win – win – however they may appear to the child at the time' (Covey, 1999).

2. On the other hand, there may be situations which appear lose – win for the parent, but may in fact be the best way. Where the issue is not that critical to

the parent, but it is important to the child, by letting the child have their way the parent is saying that because it is important to their child it is important to them. Parents need to be more concerned about the health of the relationship with their child than with winning arguments. The importance is not with who is right but with what is right. There may also be issues with the developmental stage of the child. For example, it is not unusual for young children around six or seven to exaggerate a lot as part of their developmental process. Parents need to be sensitive to this and not overreact and head into conflict. Development occurs one step at a time. Natural processes cannot be forced.

3. Finally, there will be issues in relation to discipline and punishment. The first question is whether the behaviour is serious enough that it has to be addressed. Sometimes it is better to ignore behaviour rather than confront and reinforce it. If 'punishment' is required can more empowering ways be found to deal with this, remembering the importance of the big picture of the relationship. For example, ask participants to think about the difference between sending their child to their room for a whole evening or sending them there until they are ready to apologise or make a positive change to their behaviour and bring the punishment to an end earlier.

Figure 7.2: Power, parenting and win – win

1. The importance of issue may appear to be win – lose but is really win – win.

2. Always remember the relationship: lose – win may really be win – win!

3. Punishment or discipline can be win – win!

Theory/evidence base

In short, when facing a significant emotionally arousing conflict the 'brain's crisis response still follows the ancient strategy – it heightens sensory acuity, stops complex thought and triggers the knee jerk automatic response' (Goleman, 1995: 75). This will normally take the person into the fight or flight mode, which is similar to the anger outburst material covered in Session 2. In this session, the emphasis is on helping participants to try to find a way to manage this difficult process without always going into fight or flight. The research has indicated some gender issues which may be important to be aware of in helping women and men progress in this work. At a general level, there is evidence that shows the inability of some people to deal constructively with conflict – further evidence shows that this can be more of an issue for men particularly within family relationships. Some men have a tendency to either withdraw from conflict or avoid the issue altogether. However, they eventually respond in a confrontational manner. This avoidance – confrontation pattern can be extremely damaging in dealing with conflict. (McKeown, 2001). Once the person has gone into fight mode, and again this may resonate more with a man, but not necessarily, he will experience increased pulse rate, blood pressure and a testosterone surge. There will be a release of stress chemicals that create a feeling of being on edge and ready to lash out. Other research suggests that, because of higher activity levels, hormones, neurotransmitters, or some yet undiscovered biological force, it may take less stimulation to push the average male over the aggression threshold than it does the average female (Kilmartin, 1994). There is also some evidence to show that people who intend to be generally more hostile, including women, 'may well be at higher risk of dying as a result of too many unnecessary fight or flight responses' (Williams and Williams, 1994: 68). Alternatively, moving into flight mode, withdrawal, stonewalling and experiencing repeated negative thoughts and feelings in relation to the conflict has also been associated with a variety of health problems. There is always the danger of the eventual explosion of pent up anger and rage. 'Parents who injure their children are very often from this category: shy, timid parents who finally blow up after a lot of simmering' (Biddulph, 1998: 73).

7.3: Understanding and listening

Presentation, individual work and exercise

Begin this sequence by indicating that the remainder of the session will focus on trying to help participants make real the win – win type approach in handling conflict with their children. This can only happen by finding ways to improve communication with their children during times of conflict. This is the core issue for all sorts of conflict situations in the world. Point out that differences in understanding are common within families and relationships. In fact, most of the real pain within families is to do with misunderstanding. A lot of difficulties are not to do with bad intent but just with the difficulties of trying to really understand each other. Relationships with children need to be built on a foundation of understanding. Therefore, when arguing for win – win in conflict with children, the starting point needs to be looking at how well parents understand and listen to them.

To this end, ask participants to try to imagine how they would reply to the following statement if it was made to them by their children:

> *You promised that you would let me go to the disco, you always tell me lies! I can't believe a single word you say, you hate my friends and you don't trust me, I'm old enough to go. You know I won't drink or anything, you don't let me do any thing I might enjoy, you're always spoiling my fun, I hate you...*

Ask participants to write down or memorise their responses. They do not have to share these, but ask them to keep them in mind as they listen to replies made by other parents. Rather than just reading out the different responses below, a good way to bring the material to life is for the facilitators to act these out and let the group experience the differences and draw their own conclusions.

- You can't be trusted, remember what you did the last time with that cheeky bitch, you are too easily led astray and are too young to be going out with that crowd…

- I don't think it's a good idea. I think you should wait until you're a bit older to go to discos. I think also you should maybe be going out with friends your own age…

- Why do you want to go there for? Do you not think you are too young for those places? What will happen if you don't get in? What will your so called friends do then…

- What are you saying? Do you want to have a night out with your friends because it's too boring for you in the house or are you wanting to go with that crowd because it makes you feel big…

Briefly ask for feedback from the group on how they think the young person may be feeling after each response. In particular, do they think that the young person has felt they have been listened to?

When each response has been considered, point out that some of the research into family life and conflict, and other organisations for that matter, suggests that the quality of listening, most of the time, tends to leave the person feeling that they haven't been heard. Using Figure 7.3, point out that rather than being truly listened to, the young person has been judged, advised, questioned or analysed. Then model one further approach in which the parent shows that the child has been listened to:

- You're annoyed because you're not trusted by me, you feel that you should be allowed to go to this disco, you're angry about this situation, you feel I'm not being fair…

Each person can now be asked to think about their own response and how much judgement, advice, questioning and analysis it contained, or how much true listening they tried to show. If participants wish, they can briefly share and discuss.

Figure 7.3: Listening

1. **Did we judge?**

2. **Did we give advice?**

3. **Did we question?**

4. **Did we try to work out what was being said?**

There may be nothing wrong with the any of the above, but we weren't really listening to understand!

Move on by stressing to the group the importance of listening not only to words but also to emotions. It will be difficult to overstate this. They should be aiming to genuinely listen to their children, particularly in situations of conflict. It will not solve the conflict but it is the basis upon which trying to find a middle win – win type solution needs to rest. To conclude this element, work through the following points and again Figure 7.4 can be used as a resource.

Figure 7.4: Genuine listening

1. Being listened to and feeling understood is the emotional and psychological equivalent of getting air!

2. It's about WILL power not SKILL power!

3. 'The faithful translator'

4. Try to listen even when the going gets tough!

---

1. Next to physical survival, psychological survival is what matters most to people. Being listened to and feeling understood is the emotional and psychological equivalent of getting air! When someone is gasping for the air of being understood nothing else matters. This is what is meant by seeking to understand and is what parents need to try to commit themselves to. Genuine listening gives a parent valuable information about how their child is feeling, helping them to understand their child's views and how they differ, and shows that they are concerned and taking their child's concerns seriously.

2. Reassure the participants that listening is not something that is highly skilled. The technique and skill in listening is just the tip of the iceberg. The great mass of the iceberg, the bit under the water, which is hidden, is a deep and sincere desire to try to understand. In other words we can do it if we really want to.

3. So, how does a parent do it? One of the best ways to learn to listen fully is for the parent to simply think of themselves as a translator. Ask participants to think about what translators have to do between the heads of state of different countries when they meet. They have to really listen hard. They can't pretend to listen, or listen selectively, (as all parents probably do from time to time), they have to really commit to the hard work of listening. Parents have to work at this, particularly in situations with the potential for conflict. Like the translators, they then have to show that they have heard and understood what has been said. For parents, they also need to listen to the emotional message and to remember that 90 per cent of an emotional message is non-verbal. Therefore, they need to not only listen with their ears but with their eyes and heart, and to try to show that they understand their child's feelings.

4. Finally, this will not be easy, particularly if a parent is trying to do it when being verbally 'attacked' by their child. Indeed it will be very difficult but the first task is to

try and get a sense of where the child is coming from and this may mean having to ignore the nasty words and behaviours in order to try to hear the message. The challenge is not to ignore, putdown, or react as if being attacked. Of course, if the child's behaviour is out of control and violent then action may have to be taken to hold or put the child somewhere where they cannot do themselves harm, but as stressed in previous sessions never, never fight physically.

Break

7.4: Being understood and 'I' messages

Presentation and exercise

In trying to find win – win ways through conflict it is not enough for parents just to improve their commitment to understanding their children and their needs. Parents also need to be able to communicate their point of view or position. Point out that this will be the focus in this element of the session. Ask the group to think back to their own childhood and try to remember some of the negative statements that were made to them by their parents, carers or teachers. List these up on a board. There should be a long list of negative, condemnatory 'you' statements. Briefly process the impact and effects of these criticisms or put downs. These criticisms will probably have been experienced by the group as deeply disrespectful and may also have contributed to seriously damaged relationships. Some of the effects may have been so wounding and intimidating that they will have left a legacy of emotional pain with some of the group.

Emphasise the point that parents need to find ways not to repeat such statements to their own children. However, they also need to find a way to allow their views and feelings to be understood and, as parents, be able to state their own views and give necessary feedback to their children. In conflict, there will be times where there is a need to confront and challenge, to be firm, frank, open and honest about parents' own needs, feeling and views of others. Present or share with the group Figure 7.5 which outlines the key importance of using 'I' messages in trying to remain respectful and gentle but at the same time staying faithful to one's own needs.

The importance of 'I' statements is that those making them are able to state clearly and take responsibility for what they really feel and think. Point out to participants that it is always important to remember that when they are giving feedback to their children, they are sharing their perceptions and the way they see the world. It is about knowing when to 'give 'I' messages with respect and tact, – sometimes even with forcefulness and sharpness' (Covey, 1999: 235). Of course, there remains a need to be careful that a nasty or manipulative 'you' message is not hidden within the 'I' message. For example, 'I feel you are a lazy, good for nothing waste of space etc'. Parents need to keep asking themselves how what they say will be helpful to their child.

As discussed earlier the issue may be of such importance that parents are going to have to hold the line. This may mean having continually to repeat oneself, along with repeated refusals, requests or assertions. They have to try to keep the refusals soft and not escalate matters with the child. Be selective in what to respond to in terms of staying with the factual content. Try to keep what is being said brief and to the point whilst staying calm. At the end of the day, as the quote at the beginning of the session indicated, it will sometimes be about not giving in to our children, but in a way that is also about not giving up on them either.

Figure 7.5: 'I' messages

Can we think of ways of using 'I' messages instead of hypnotic put downs when talking with our kids? (Biddulph, 1998)

Holding our ground! Not giving in to our children, but not giving up on them either. (Covey, 1999)

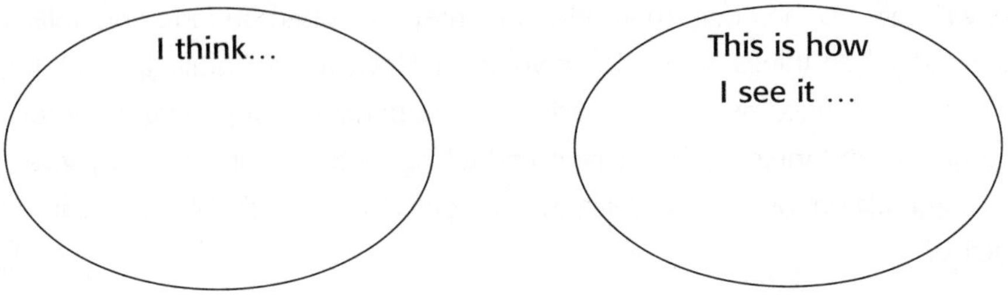

I think...

This is how I see it ...

Evidence/theory base

How children develop resilience in dealing with difficulties in life can be related to their self-image. This self-image may well be negatively influenced by constant condemnatory comments and put downs from parents and carers. The way children are criticised might influence their tendency to be optimistic or pessimistic in their thinking, and this can be important in terms of their emotional health and development. This is one of the reasons for trying to encourage participants to look at their use of negative 'you' statements.

The psychological literature emphasises the importance of an awareness of our own feelings. There is a real danger that through lack of awareness, we will sometimes project, unknowingly, our own feelings onto another. 'I' statements can help us focus more on ourselves and what is going on within us. The seedbed for anger and conflict to run out of control is a culture or tradition of people not being able to say what they really think and feel, a culture in which anger is suppressed and conflict is quickly glossed over (Hart, 2000). It is important that parents try to express their feelings in conflict as early as possible and not let situations develop. If sometimes people may be aware, but don't face up to their feelings or try to express them in other ways, then the danger is that they are being false, into posturing or they are being hypocritical (Covey, 1997).

7.5: Practising conflict handling skills

Presentation and individual work (option for role play)

In this penultimate sequence, participants are given the opportunity to practise handling a conflict. Remind them once more that conflict is a normal part of family life that may continually threaten to tear apart relationships. They need to practise and so get a sense of trying to steer their way through the aggressive or passive unhelpful extremes. Stress to the group that there is no correct formula or precise way of doing this. All families will develop their own methods. They may well often be loud and volatile explosions and then things will settle down again. However, hopefully through this exercise, they may become more conscious of the principles of putting an emphasis on trying to understand their child's position and taking more care in how they give feedback. In addition, other de-escalation and conflict resolution skills may come out in the practice.

The individual or group can choose the example outlined in element 7.3 as a conflict scenario, or the option of someone bringing their own example of a conflict situation they are experiencing can be considered. (Detailed guidance on running the role play is laid out in Appendix 5).

Affirm all efforts within role play scenarios and make links to the material covered. Allow other issues to be processed through group discussion.

Each participant should try to identify specific examples of changes in their thinking, ways of dealing with their feelings or new actions that they will endeavour to take in handling conflict with their children. More time can be spent in problem solving and solution finding with participants if the option of the role play has not been used. Figure 7.6 can be used for participants to note down new ideas or changes in their approaches to conflict with their children. A group round will allow each person to indicate one significant piece of new learning for themselves in terms of how they will handle conflict with their children.

Conclude this element with one final thought on conflict. Difficult conflicts will continue to erupt in most families from time to time. It may not always be possible to sort these out without erupting into aggression and the causing of deep hurt, despite the approaches covered in the session. At the end of the day, families also need to try to build a pattern in handling their conflicts which, after the anger, hurt and guilt; allows for apology, reconciliation and forgiveness (Dominian, 2005). This is not easy but is necessary.

Figure 7.6: Handling conflict

Actions
Really listening, making 'I' statements, sitting down, breathing…

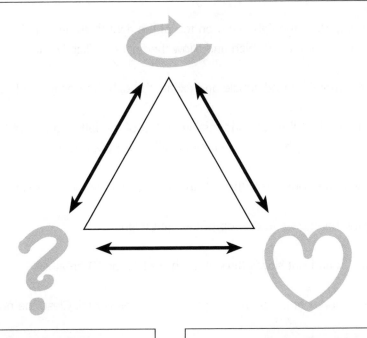

New thinking
Can we get to win – win?
What does my child want or need?
This will pass, steady as she goes,
roll with the punches, someday
we'll laugh at this…

New ways of dealing with feelings
Accepting my feelings, focusing
and staying with them,
managing the arousal.

7.6: Taking care of yourself and closure

Inform participants that the final element will once again be a relaxation breathing exercise and the following script can be used:

This practice should be completed in a sitting position, either on the floor or in a chair. It is not suitable for a lying down position.

1. Make sure that the body is in a steady, upright position.

2. Close your eyes.

3. Rest the back of the right hand on top of the right thigh and the back of the left hand on top of the left thigh and allow the fingers to lightly curl.

4. With the mouth closed, inhale and exhale through the nostrils for five full breaths.

5. With the back of the left hand resting on top of the left thigh, place the index finger of the right hand on the right nostril. Close the nostril.

6. Breathe in and out slowly through the left nostril only for 10 breaths.

7. Bring the hand back to the top of the right thigh.

8. Breathe in and out slowly through both nostrils for 10 breaths.

9. Place the index finger of the left hand on the left nostril. Close the nostril.

10. Breathe in and out slowly through the right nostril only for 10 breaths.

11. Bring the hand back to the top of the left thigh.

12. Breathe in and out slowly through both nostrils for 10 breaths.

13. Bring your awareness back to your position in the room and open your eyes slowly.

Closure
(See end of Session 1, page 42.)

Session 8
Learning and Moving on

> *Experts can explain everything in the objective world to us, yet we understand our own lives less and less.*
>
> Vaclac Havel

8.1 Welcome, outline, objectives and check in

The objectives of the session are that you will:
- Review your learning achieved on the programme.
- Reflect on lifestyle and life balance issues and identify changes you wish to make.
- Make a plan to help you to continue to manage your anger as a parent.
- Evaluate the programme.

8.2 Reviewing the learning

8.3 Applying the learning

Break

8.4 Life balance

8.5 Revisiting change and planning for the future

8.6 Evaluation, celebration and closure

Facilitators' Guidance for Session 8

8.1: Welcome, outline, objectives and check in

Welcome participants and display the session title, objectives and outline. This final session is about reviewing and consolidating the learning and looking towards planning for the future. Hopefully, the time, effort and commitment that has been put in by the participants will have helped increase their own awareness and understanding of how to manage this area of their lives. The first objective is to look back over the programme, review and try to identify the key learning that has been achieved. The second objective is to reflect on the 'caring for yourself' sessions which have been completed, to explore wider lifestyle and life balance issues and identify what changes may be needed to help, directly or indirectly, with their management of anger. The third objective will follow up on the issues raised in the first two, and will aim at planning how to go forward to ensure that learning is maintained, built on and leads to real change. The final objective is to allow participants to evaluate the programme, how helpful they have found it and make suggestions for improvements.

Before proceeding with these areas, participants will be offered the final opportunity to briefly check in to the session. Each will have a minute or two to address their anger diary and make a general comment as to how they feel about their anger (see guidance, pages 25-26 and 44).

8.2: Reviewing the learning

Presentation and individual work

Point out to participants that a lot of material has been covered during the previous seven sessions. The challenge for them now is to become more aware of how this material is influencing and helping them handle stressful, anger inducing interactions with their children. Before reviewing the course, ask participants to bring to mind the main example of their mismanaged parental anger that they have been working at during the programme. They should try to keep a particular example in mind as they are taken through a brief re-run of the programme. This can be done, for each session, as follows:

1. Briefly outline the key points from the session (see below).

2. Facilitate a short discussion on the relevant question from Figure 8.1.

3. Allow a little time for quiet reflection, during which participants should try to answer the question and identify at least one concrete thing that represents their learning from this session. It can be anything as long as they feel it would help them to handle their example of mismanaged anger in a better way.

4. Finally, suggest that participants can note any ideas they have on their own individual triangle template (Figure 8.2) if it helps them. They should place the idea into the relevant box as to whether it is to do with changes in their thinking, feelings or new actions. So, for example, someone who feels they have learnt to think more about the developmental needs of their six year old son will put that in the thinking box.

Session 1 was about choice, responsibility and the challenge of change. It asked the group to think about how things were for them in terms of their management of anger as parents, how they would like things to be and how they were going to get across this gap. It asked them to explore their motivation and commitment to the change programme, the possible hindrances they would face in making progress and their responsibility for their own behaviour. Discuss question 1 on Figure 8.1 and take participants through the guidance in points 3 and 4 above.

In **Session 2**, the work was on trying to understand anger as a normal, natural emotion which everyone experiences to varying degrees, and finding the difficult balance between expressing it too aggressively or manipulatively and suppressing it. Both the aggressive expression or suppression of anger is not helpful and can lead to health problems. The session also covered the stages and process involved in an angry outburst, beginning with the trigger and moving up to the explosion. It also examined another gap; that is, the space between the situation which triggers people is anger and their response – their inner world. Refer to question 2 on Figure 8.1 and take participants through the guidance in points 3 and 4 above.

> ## Figure 8.1: How is my learning helping me
>
> How is my learning helping me to:
>
> 1. Take more responsibility and choice?
>
> 2. Accept and express my anger in a better way?
>
> 3. Make changes in my thinking, mindset, beliefs etc?
>
> 4. Deal with how I feel?
>
> 5. Understand the effect of unmanaged anger on my child's development and helping with their anger?
>
> 6. See how any of my past experiences as a female or male, or of violence, have affected my anger?
>
> 7. Handle problems and conflict in a better way?

Session 3 was about thinking, mindsets, beliefs and perspectives about parenting. What motivates parents and what are their expectations? The session explored whether there is a danger that some parents expect too much of themselves; or believe that it should not be too difficult; or that their children should never be nasty to them. Top triggers were also identified. Refer to question 3 on Figure 8.1 and take participants through the guidance in points 3 and 4 above.

Session 4 looked at emotional life and how emotions can become suppressed, hidden, disturbed or distressed. Remind the group of 'Put down Pat' and the emotional hijacking in Session 4.3. Refer to question 4 on Figure 8.1 and take participants through the guidance in points 3 and 4 above.

Session 5 looked at the stages of childhood, how excessive and badly managed parental anger can adversely affect childrens' development and also how children need to learn to manage their own anger. It also explored ideas around authoritarian or passive parenting, dealing with tantrums and ways of dealing with an angry child. Refer to question 5 on Figure 8.1 and take participants through the guidance in points 3 and 4 above.

Session 6 explored how the two areas of either gender or past traumatic experiences may relate to the way people manage their anger. It considered the different messages that some girls and boys receive about their feelings and how they show their anger. It also acknowledged the devastating impact of violence or trauma on people and how this can leave them with feelings of extreme anger. Refer to question 6 on Figure 8.1 and take participants through the guidance in points 3 and 4 above.

Session 7, the last session, focused on the challenging area of conflict with children and trying to find the difficult middle win-win path between the aggressive or avoidant extremes. The importance of communication with children, seeking to understand them, and giving clear and positive messages was stressed. Refer to question 7 on Figure 8.1 and take participants through the guidance in points 3 and 4 above.

Conclude by pointing out that each participant will have some examples of what is now different in their thinking, managing their feelings and actions which they believe will help them deal with the type of situation in mind, and which previously resulted in mismanaging their anger. Using a group round, ask each participant to share one of the more significant pieces of learning for themselves from the programme. Use Figure 8.2 on page 156.

Evidence/theory base

The challenge of the programme has been to encourage participants, through an adult learning process, to look closely at the inner world of their thoughts, emotions and actions. They needed to identify a change in their thinking, different ways of seeking to manage their emotional arousal or negativity or some new actions in managing their anger. Each person should have some sense of change, and this will be different and personal for each. For example, there may be those who are experiencing a change in their internal disposition, that is, in their thinking and feeling. This leads to, or is reflected by, observable actions in relation to more positive behaviours. Alternatively, there may be those who try out some of the ideas or suggestions from the programme, and find that this will help them in making some progress. 'Sometimes new perspectives lead to action. At other times action generates new perspectives' (Egan, 1995: 173). The fundamental approach of the programme needs to be kept in mind. At its core has been a facilitative and challenging process aimed at encouraging participants to try as hard as possible to clarify what they see to be happening within their relationships with their children. From that they have been able to work at problem solving and solution finding approaches.

Figure 8.2: My learning?

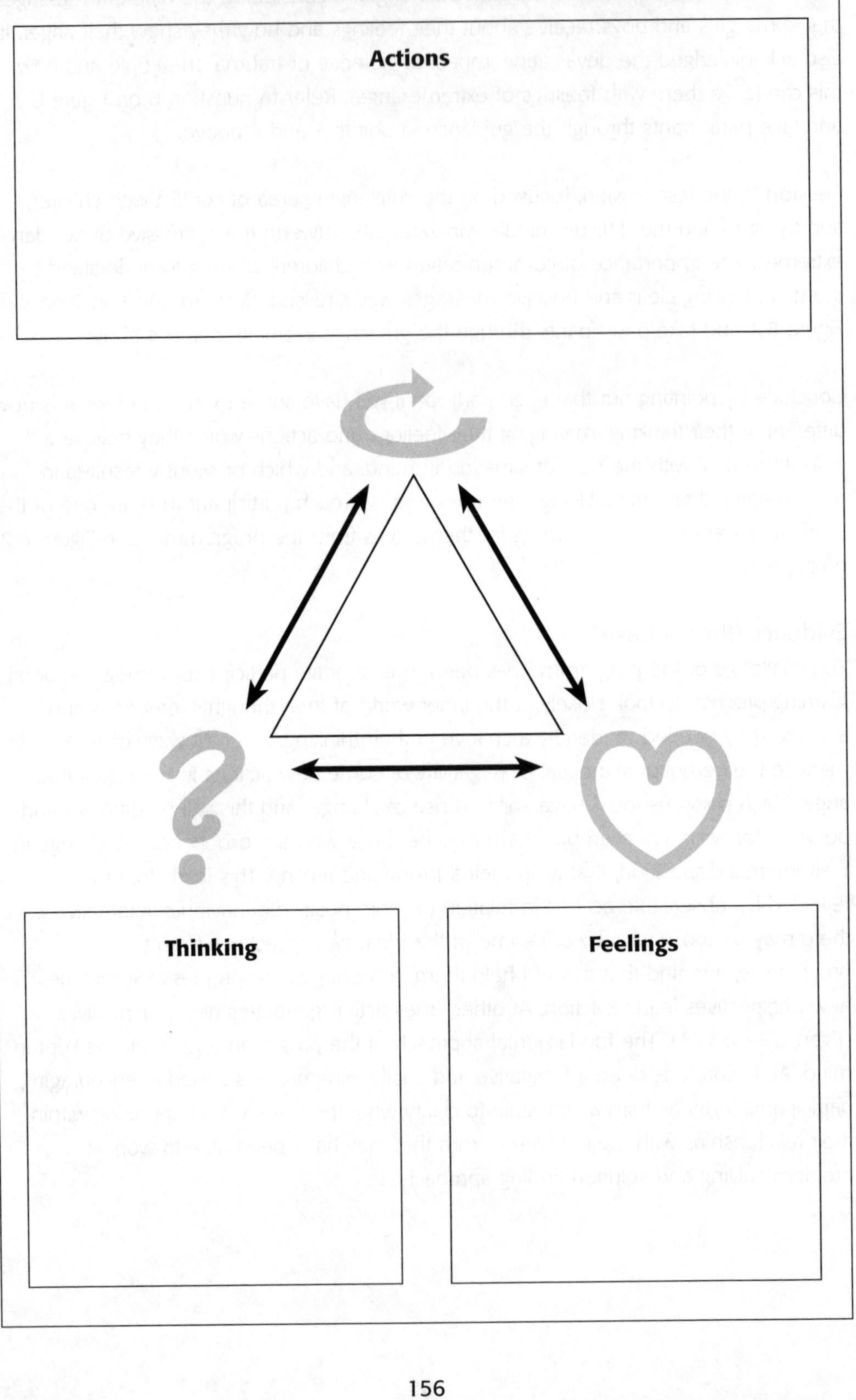

Actions

Thinking

Feelings

8.3: Applying the learning

Individual work and discussion (option for role play)

Explain that in this element, participants are going to apply the learning they have gained using the example of mismanaged anger they identified earlier in the programme. The opportunity for some participants to act out their scenarios demonstrating new interpersonal skills should be considered (see Appendix 5 for further guidance on this). Alternatively, following on from the previous element, each participant should take a few moments to identify their key learning in relation to their particular example and how they could have put this into practice.

It is important to look forward and to encourage participants to explore how they can use their learning to deal with the difficulties they are sure to face. They may feel worried that they are going to lose their tempers again and slip back into the behaviour they have been trying to change. Offer each person the opportunity to work through the points on Figure 8.3 and share in a group round. After each person has given their example, ask for any feedback, suggestions, ideas or comments from the rest of the group.

Figure 8.3: Can I see it coming?

What would be the situation if I were to mismanage my anger with my children again?

What might happen?

When?

Where?

What mood might I be in?

What might the effects be on:
– My children?
– Myself?
– Other family members?

What do I need to do to try to stop this happening?

Break

8.4: Life balance

Presentation and individual work

Draw a triangle on a flip chart and ask the group to think once more about the three points as actions, thoughts, and feelings. Affirm the progress they have made in each of these areas as they have worked on the programme. Ask them to go further to see these three points in a bigger way, that is, as the body, mind and heart, and what makes them human beings. They need to see these things as human gifts and strengths for which they have both the responsibility and the potential to develop. Ask them to consider each in turn.

Beginning with the gift of their bodies and physical abilities, how well are they looking after themselves physically? It will only be through a proper diet, sufficient exercise, adequate sleep and managing stress that a balanced lifestyle can be developed. Are they unbalanced because they are too stressed, spending too much of their time doing physical things, particularly work related? Perhaps they are facing circumstances where they have to work long hours in order to make ends meet or to maintain a reasonable standard of living, or because they chose to. Someone who is enslaved to work may tend to be tired, tense, moody or withdrawn. On the other hand they may be doing little physical activity, particularly exercise, or abusing their bodies through alcohol or drugs.

What about their minds and the human gift of mental intelligence? Are they committing themselves to developing their mental faculties, by reading and study, cultivating their self-awareness or learning new skills. Reflect with the group how much time they are able to devote to this aspect of themselves. (The fact that they have made a commitment to this personal development work is a good example of making progress in this area).

Then there is the heart and the human gift of emotional intelligence. Inform participants that research is telling us that this is even more important than mental intelligence in predicting success and happiness in life. This refers to relationships and with social life – how people get on with others. Ask participants if they have enough time to build positive relationships, both within their families and further afield. For example, much recent research suggests that parents spend half the time with their children than they did twenty years ago. Within some families there is a sense of a time famine, too much to do and too little time to do it. Of course, there are other ways of sustaining the social and emotional part of their lives through giving service, listening to and co-operating with others. Ask participants to reflect on how much of their time do they spend working at and maintaining positive relationships with others, both personally and within their communities.

At this point draw a circle round the triangle and explain that this refers to a final, and in the view of some, the central and most fundamental human gift, which is spiritual intelligence. This is the belief system in something greater and outside human life, the transcendent, something that guides and directs the other intelligences. It gives meaning to people's lives and makes change more possible. It is about integrity and being true to ones highest values and conscience. It is also about prayer and spiritual practices that give a sense of meaning to our existence. Acknowledge and accept that some participants may not believe in a spiritual domain, and indeed this is reflected in some of the literature as well.

Ask participants to reflect on these four human gifts and intelligences. The challenge is to work towards a lifestyle in which they can develop each of them to their full potential. Figure 8.4 on page 160 can be used as a resource. Ask each participant to identify at least one change that they could make to their lives to develop in any of these areas.

To conclude this element, stress that participants' progress, or lack of it, in each of these areas will be closely related to managing their anger. They can get into a vicious circle, where, if they neglect themselves, they will find their anger getting worse which in turn will further damage their physical, mental, emotional and spiritual health. The opposite will be a positive and benign circle where significant improvement in any of these areas will help in managing their anger. As they begin to manage their anger better, their physical, mental, emotional and spiritual lives will improve.

Evidence/theory base

This material applies not only to this life balance element but also to the 'Taking care of yourself' elements at the end of each previous session. Taken together, they aim to provide the opportunity for participants to consider issues to do with their own life balance and the pressures they are under and to experience a range of exercises aimed at helping them deal with negative stress in their lives. The seven previous 'Taking care of yourself' sessions focused on the physical and mental techniques of stress management. They have given participants a flavour of some of the things they can do to relax themselves. This is important in relation to what is known about stress as outlined below. However, in this element a more 'whole person' approach is taken in encouraging participants to address wider lifestyle issues to manage the pressures and stress they experience and in accepting the interrelationships of body, mind, heart and spirit. It also seeks to encourage participants to take responsibility for their overall well-being to see how this may help as much with anger as the learning of specific anger management techniques. For example, it is now widely accepted in medical circles that 'at least two thirds of all diseases are caused by lifestyle choices that people make' (Covey, 2004: 336). These relate to diet, smoking, abusing the body through

Figure 8.4: Human gifts and life balance

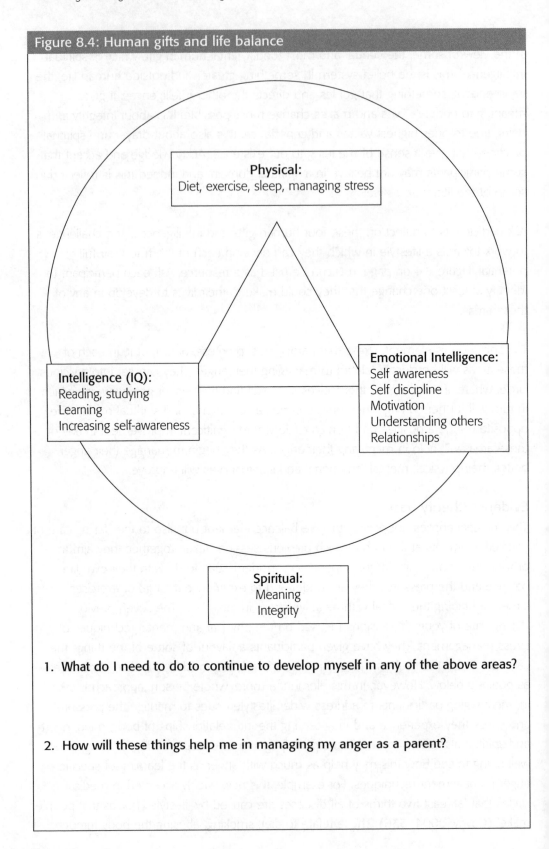

Physical:
Diet, exercise, sleep, managing stress

Intelligence (IQ):
Reading, studying
Learning
Increasing self-awareness

Emotional Intelligence:
Self awareness
Self discipline
Motivation
Understanding others
Relationships

Spiritual:
Meaning
Integrity

1. What do I need to do to continue to develop myself in any of the above areas?

2. How will these things help me in managing my anger as a parent?

drug and alcohol misuse, lack of physical exercise, burning the candle at both ends and so on. As is outlined below, the choices that a person makes in this area of their lives will have an impact in terms of managing stress and anger.

It is important to remember that stress in itself is not harmful. On the contrary it is a natural and wonderful condition of life. On the one hand, the adrenalin rush it gives is exhilarating and can bring out the best in people. The concept of 'eustress' comes from the positive tension between where a person is now and where they want to go – something meaningful that inspires or drives them – as in being a parent. Research has shown how eustress braces the immune system and increases longevity and enjoyment in life. In short, people shouldn't avoid stress if it's the right kind of stress (Covey, 2004).

On the other hand, stress may be the spice of life but it can also be the kiss of death. This usually refers to the other type of stress, distress. This results from too many difficult pressures in life arising from people's circumstances, the experiences they have gone through, and in the choices they make. Excessive and prolonged stress produces copious amounts of stress hormones called cortisols. These chemicals clog up our cells, generate a lack of well-being and a general feeling of tiredness associated with irritability and aggressiveness. It is not a sudden, dramatic thing, but is a process that develops and is cumulative. It is understandable why it is called the silent killer. Stress hormones can impair our immune system, leaving us vulnerable to a host of illnesses.

There is also significant research to show that there is an association between difficulties with stress and anger problems. 'Stress is the fuel of anger' (McKay, Rogers and McKay, 1989: 03). There is a two way relationship between tension and anger. Physical tension creates stress, which may predispose a person to anger. Anger then causes additional body tension so it becomes easy to get locked into a vicious cycle of stress and anger. It is not just a physiological vicious cycle. In addition, mental health will be affected, not only as a consequence of physical problems but at a deeper level. As another source has said 'Our ability for rational thinking disappears when we lose our tempers' (Faupel, Herrick and Sharp, 1998: 28). People who are constantly angry tend to become more inflexible and rigid in how they look at and deal with situations and people. For some there will be a severe deterioration in their mental health, and not surprisingly this may spread into the emotional and social areas of people's lives. 'Damage to personal relationships is one of the most common costs of anger, and probably the worst' (Ellis and Tafrate, 1997: 11). Social support systems can weaken because of chronic anger leading to isolation and loneliness which, as in a vicious circle, can be associated with a broad range of illnesses. Finally, for some, this may go right through into the deeper spiritual level into their very core and sense of purpose and reason for living.

8.5: Revisiting change and planning for the future

Begin this penultimate element by asking participants to think of the flight of an aeroplane. It has just left point A and its destination is point B. Draw the two points on a flipchart with a line between them, to show the route the plane should take. Point out that during the actual flight wind, rain, turbulence, air traffic, human error and other factors all act on the plane. These move it slightly in different directions so that for most of the time the plane is not on the proper flight course, and in fact it is often going in a different direction. When people are struggling with change they can be off track just like the plane, and often be going in the wrong direction. Illustrate this on the flipchart with a squiggly line, showing the 'real' route of the plane – up and down, backward and forward, until it eventually reaches its destination. The point is that during a flight a pilot receives constant feedback from radar, ground control, other planes, etc. These tell the plane that it is off track and adjustments can be made to get back on the right path. The absolute crucial fact is that the destination is known so mistakes can be corrected.

Suggest to participants that this is a good image to have about change. Life and change is a bit like the aeroplane. People are constantly going off track and they need to keep trying to get back. This is particularly so with something like anger. A person can only get back on track if they are clear about the destination. The destination is what parents really want in their lives and in particular what they want with their children. Most parents know deep down that it is their relationships with their children that are really important to them. This is the incentive to getting back on track. It's the old story, when a person is on their death bed it will be these things that they consider most important. Remind participants of the first session when they explored their motivation and the cycle of change. It is natural to have slip ups, set backs and relapses.

The other critical point to be made at this point to participants is, that as well as their gifts of the four intelligences, physical, mental, emotional and spiritual, which they have just looked at, they also have the powerful gift of choice. Some participants are likely to have faced, or be facing, very difficult circumstances, such as having to deal with past violence, discrimination, limited incomes, etc. The vision of the programme is to challenge the notion that these disadvantages will determine how things will be for that participant and shape the way they will behave. They are not the whole story. By doing this work, each participant is showing that they have the power to choose to be the type of parent they want to be with their children.

Ask participants to draw together their learning so far and to complete a plan or strategy that they feel will help them to make positive changes. They need to be specific and identify the things they are going to do that will help them achieve the goal of managing their anger better with their children. Earlier, they will have identified in the triangle of behaviour their learning and change areas in relation to their thinking, feelings and actions. There may also be issues arising from their life balance element. Each participant should have some time to work at organising and prioritising what they are going to do, using Figure 8.5 as a resource.

Evidence/theory base

It is important not to have unrealistic expectations of what people can achieve. Whilst for some people, real, dramatic change may be beginning to take place, this is unlikely to be the case for others. As with most things in life, it is extremely difficult to change long established and ingrained patterns of behaviour, and in particular with anger. It is a challenging emotion to master. 'It is no wonder, then, that to learn to handle our anger is a complex task which usually cannot be completed before adulthood, or even mid-life, and which often is never completed' (Peck, 1980: 67). Nevertheless, over the eight sessions, and with commitment and motivation, seeking solutions and new ways of dealing with situations, and beginning to see some positive outcomes, there may be a sense of real change for some participants.

The difficulties with change may also relate to biological, psychological and social factors experienced by participants. Of course, such factors cannot just be swept aside, particularly for parents having to raise children in situations of deprivation and poverty. These issues will be addressed further in Part 3 of the manual. The approach taken on the programme is to challenge those perspectives that see a person's choices and behaviour as being largely a product of genetic make-up or their psycho-social experiences. 'Such deterministic maps give a skewed picture of our own deep inner nature, and it denies our fundamental power to choose' (Covey, 1999: 349).

Figure 8.5: My plan for change

My most important change:

Other changes:

My reasons for these are:

The steps I will take:

The ways other people can help me are:

Some things that could interfere might be:

I will know my plan is working when:

8.6: Evaluation, celebration and closure

Genuinely affirm the difficult personal work that participants have been prepared to do on the programme. Ask them if they would be prepared to give feedback as to how they have found the programme. It is useful, if working with a group, to have a general discussion first about the programme, and then record feedback on a flip chart under headings:

- Things participants liked or found helpful about the programme.

- Things that they didn't like or didn't find helpful.

- Any ideas or suggestions about improving the programme.

This can also be done in a similar way with someone who has done the programme individually.

Ask participants if they would also be prepared to give individual post programme feedback at the end of the session or within a short period and also if they would agree to completing follow-up evaluation in six months time (see Part 3 and Appendix 6).

Finally, try to mark the end of the programme in a way which celebrates the work of the individual or the group. Recognise in some sort of ritual way that it is an ending and express thanks and appreciation to those who have participated. Thank them for their openness and honesty and for the undoubted contribution that they will have made to the facilitators' own learning and the development in doing this type of work.

PART THREE

TAKING PAMP FORWARD

> *Below certain standards of 'liveability', no one can raise happy children.*
>
> Biddulph, 1998: 87

Introduction

Ultimately PAMP aims to facilitate a positive learning process for parents struggling with managing their anger in their relationships with their children. In this final section, PAMP's appropriateness, effectiveness and future contribution to this type of work will be considered, and three main issues will be addressed. Firstly, there is the bigger picture of the social and economic situations experienced by many potential participants. This raises questions as to the appropriateness of putting so much energy, enthusiasm and expertise into such a focused project. Secondly, given that a reasonable case can be made for the programme as a useful intervention, then the responsibilities of agencies and individuals to make it an ethical and effective intervention. Finally, how best to take the programme forward and gather an evidence base to sustain its future growth.

The bigger picture

Various commentators in differing contexts have pointed out the dangers of some social work interventions regressing to the individualisation of wider social problems. Structural issues of inequality, discrimination and their ilk are ignored and the onus is put on people to sort out their own problems whatever the circumstances they are experiencing. Can these types of criticisms be fairly put against this programme? Many of its potential participants may face ongoing problems with welfare rights, housing, health problems or financial difficulties. In addition, there may be issues of substance or alcohol abuse, maternal depression or other mental health problems. One study indicated that in some child care teams in Britain, social workers have up to 90 per cent of parents on their caseloads suffering from mental health problems or alcohol or substance misuse difficulties (SCIE, 2003).

Reviewing the current evidence and how best to intervene with families experiencing difficulties, two key conclusions are relevant to this programme. Firstly, there are issues with the way some people parent their children that are not just to do with social and economic circumstances. While environmental stressors are relevant, it has now come to be widely recognised that major factors in the emotional neglect or abuse of children are deficits in child rearing skills. Secondly, there may be other parental problems that need addressing before embarking on working at parenting skills. 'No amount of help, however, is going to be effective if an alcoholic mother is not going to stop drinking, or a depressed mother does not get treatment' (Iwaniec, 2003: 56).

Families in trouble need a multi-disciplinary and multi-dimensional approach. Within that, programmes such as PAMP can have their place. The bottom line is that intervention strategies need to be based on a 'comprehensive holistic assessment, addressing the needs of children as well as parents and the communities they live in; choosing methods, approaches, and services that will provide healing for the child; acceleration of developmental attainments; change of parental attitudes towards the child...as well as helping parents with many difficulties, such as poverty, social isolation, mental-health problems, dysfunctional marital relationships, family violence, substance misuse and so on' (Iwaniec, 2003: 55).

Programme effectiveness and integrity

The points made above do not, on their own, provide a justification for using scarce resources to deliver this programme. As indicated in the foundation section, the research into parenting skills work and anger management is not conclusive and, given the innovative nature of PAMP in combining these two areas there is little previous specific research. The best that can be said is that in its design it has sought to follow closely the literature which indicates that the 'best developed, researched, and evaluated methods are those based on social learning and cognitive or behavioural treatment' (Iwaniec, 1997: 31). Based upon this foundation, there are three elements that need to be considered to ensure that it can be effective and do what it claims to do.

Tight design

This manual seeks to contribute to and enhance the design of the programme. It sets out clearly its underpinning value base as well as its knowledge and skill requirements. Each session is clearly structured to move participants through a process of learning and change. Clear tasks within each session are aligned to meet defined objectives that come together to meet the overall aim of the programme. It is important to have the material in a manual so that the integrity of treatment can be evaluated and replicated, as discussed below. There will always be some tension in using a manual based programme. On the one hand, there may be the danger of being dogmatic about the programme and insisting that it is delivered in precisely the same way to allow for programme integrity, consistency and research. The challenge is to create enough space to allow for creativity and flexibility in how it is delivered to different individuals and groups so that it is grounded in their own realities, communities and cultures, without losing its essential elements. 'We need a balance of clear manual guidelines, possibilities for improvisation and space for individual therapist differences – a difficult task' (Herbert, 2000: 87).

Sound management

The second important element in programme integrity centres on the responsibility of agencies who wish to use PAMP to ensure that the organisational culture and structure is in tune with what is required. Agencies will need to fully recognise the commitment involved, and take the appropriate steps to ensure that they do the following:

- Understand the PAMP programme and promote it properly.
- Procure appropriate funds, equipment and accommodation.
- Manage information about the programme.
- Support facilitators.
- Monitor its delivery.
- Evaluate and improve delivery if required.
- Build partnership and consultancy arrangements with other agencies.

Agencies may also be able to enhance the programme in various innovative and creative ways. For example, building in things like crèches during the sessions, or having social events immediately after the work. Another idea would be to produce resources for the programme such as a short tape of relaxation exercises.

Skilled practitioners

Finally, there is an onus placed on the people who will be tasked with facilitating PAMP. Key issues for maintaining the integrity of the programme include the following

- a commitment to the values of the programme;
- an understanding of the knowledge base; and
- developing skills in relationship building, organising, presenting, facilitating, motivating and group work.

This manual contains a sufficient basis of the above material to allow a committed worker to operate effectively in this area. Considerable patience, skill and support will be required. However, it is important to remember that the programme is specifically targeted at people who are already acknowledging they have a problem and are prepared to address it. It is about providing space and a meaningful opportunity for them to do so. As stated earlier, this type of intervention can be delivered by a wide range of people. It is significant, for example, that the Youth Justice Board in England and Wales has recommended that in terms of who should facilitate managing offending behaviour programmes, staff members' personal skills and qualities should have a higher priority than their qualifications or professional background alone. Research on the quality of staff involved in similar cognitive behavioural programmes concluded that such programmes should be facilitated by those interested in, and committed to, the work (Feilzer et al., 2004). Supportive supervision or co-working arrangements with someone with more experience in this area may assist prospective facilitators increase their confidence and competence.

Evaluation and building the evidence base

At this point, the evidence suggests that PAMP, delivered in a well planned and supported way, has the potential to be helpful to some parents experiencing difficulty. In order for it to survive, it needs to build an evidence base – to clearly test out its claims. It has been piloted both in group and individual delivery mode in N Ireland but on a limited basis. There was generally positive feedback from participants, and they also assisted in refining the manual to what it is now. It is imperative that this is built on. 'Numerous ingenious programmes have been carefully nurtured into existence and steered through to their conclusions, only to disappear – because not one shred of evidence had been gathered about their clientele, their functioning or their effectiveness' (Maguire, 1995: 50).

To this end facilitators of this programme should strive to evaluate empirically the outcomes of the work. It is a valid and important task to commit 'themselves to undertake small-scale, agency-based evaluations of their own practice' (Thyer, 1998: 172). It is only through the gathering of detailed information and feedback from participants and their children that a clearer picture may begin to emerge as to the degree to which the programme is associated with better management of parental anger and the associated benefits to the parent/child relationships. Outcomes research carried out at agency or programme level does not usually require sophisticated experimental designs because the questions being asked are not sophisticated. Basically, they will centre on whether users of the programme felt they were getting better at managing their anger with their children. This 'research' element needs to be built in from the start of the programme. 'Ethical research involves getting the informed consent of those you are going to interview, question, observe or take materials from. It involves reaching an agreement about the uses of the data, and how the analysis will be reported and disseminated'. (Blaxter et al., 2002: 158). In evaluating the early PAMP interventions, I found that when clients were asked about the acceptability of using simple evaluation procedures to help assess the outcomes of practice, they all found such techniques acceptable. Tried and tested questionnaires are provided in Appendix 6 to assist with this process. In some situations, consideration should be given to involving children in the evaluation process. In one sense, they are the primary consumers of the outcomes of this programme. It will often be important to hear the child's view of the progress or lack of it made by their parents who hopefully may have become more consistent and positive rather than harsh and coercive in their parenting (Gould et al., 2004).

A key point is to try and build in an independent element to the gathering of such information. This may involve using a colleague or a different agency. Purchasing independent research can be expensive and whether or not it is possible to negotiate local arrangements with academic institutions or with community development or social care schemes needs to be explored.

Finally, it is important that evaluative material is made as widely available as possible. This will provide a form of quality assurance in that it will lead to critical scrutiny and feedback from others interested in this area of work. It is also the case that locally conducted research is more likely to be perceived as relevant to practice (Newman et al., 2005). Research also has the benefit of reaching people on the ground, and hopefully then the policy makers, which unfortunately does not happen enough with research in social care. Publicising evaluations of practice may also assist others to benefit in terms of developing their own practice initiatives. Ultimately, a commitment to trying to measure and evaluate practice will assist in the ongoing process of theory building and the development of a body of empirical knowledge (Chapman and Hough, 1998).

Conclusion

In coming to the end of this manual, it is my hope that some readers are enthused and motivated to use this material in their important work with parents. It may be a resource that gives additional knowledge or ideas to enhance aspects of their present practice. For those wishing to take forward the entire programme, I can only wish that they find the work as stimulating and enjoyable as I have done. It is a privilege to be involved in helping parents who are committed to improving their relationships with their children. Although everything required is provided in this manual, a range of additional services are also available to support in various ways those who wish to use this programme and details are provided in Appendix 7.

References

Acton, R.G. (1997) *Angry Parents: A Group Psychotherapy Manual for Aggression Management Treatment.* Calgary: Acton House Publishing.

Aubrey, J. (2004) The Roots and Process of Social Action. *Groupwork*, 14: 2.

Averill, J. (1982) *Anger and Aggression: An Essay on Emotion.* New York: Springer-Verlag.

Banks, S. (2001) *Ethics and Values in Social Work.* Basingstoke: Macmillan.

Beck, A. (1999) *Prisoners of Hate: The Cognitive Basis of Anger, Hostility and Violence.* New York: Harper Collins.

Benson, J.F. (1996) *Working More Creatively with Groups.* London: Routlege.

Bergin, E. and Fitzgerald, E. (1994) *Stress and How to Deal with it.* Dublin: SDB Media.

Biddulph, S. (1997) *Raising Boys.* London: Thorsons.

Biddulph, S. (1998) *The Secret of Happy Children.* London: Thorsons.

Biddulph, S. and Bidulph, S. (1998) *More Secrets of Happy Children.* London: Thorsons.

Blaxter, L., Hughes, C. and Tight, M. (2001) *How to Research.* Buckingham: Open University Press.

Borden, S. (2003) *Edith Stein.* London: Continuum.

Bowlby, J. (1979) *The Making and Breaking of Affectional Bonds.* London: Tavistock.

Bradshaw, J. (1996) *The Family: A New Way of Creating Solid Self-Esteem.* Florida: Health Communications.

British Association of Anger Management BAAM (2005) www.angermanage.co.uk

Brown, A. (1992) *Groupwork.* Aldershot: Ashgate.

Burgess, A. (1997) *Fatherhood Reclaimed: The Making of the Modern Father.* London: Vermilion.

Calder, M.C. and Hackett, S. (Eds.) (2003) *Assessment in Childcare: Using and Developing Frameworks for Practice.* Lyme Regis: Russell House Publishing.

Carter, B. and McGoldrick, M. (1989) *The Changing Family Life Cycle.* Harlow: Allyn and Bacon.

Covey, S.R. (1997) *The Seven Habits of Highly Effective People.* London: Simon and Schuster.

Covey, S.R. (1999) *The Seven Habits of Highly Effective Families.* London: Simon and Schuster.

Covey, S.R. (2004) *The 8th Habit: From Effectiveness to Greatness.* London: Simon and Schuster.

Cutrona, C.E. (2000) Social Support Principles for Strengthening Families Messages from the USA. In Canavan, J., Dolan, P. and Pinkerton, J. *Family Support Direction from Diversity*. London: Jessica Kingsley.

Deffenbacher, J.L. (1996) *Ideal Treatment Packages for Adults with Anger Disorders*. In Kassinove, H. (Ed.) *Anger Disorders: Definition, Diagnosis and Treatment*. Pennsylvania: Taylor and Francis.

Dix, T. (1991) The Affective Organisation of Parenting. *Psychological Bulletin*, 110, 3-25.

Doel, M. and Sawdon, C. (1999) *The Essential Groupworker*. London: Jessica Kingsley.

Doherty, W.J. (2000) *Take Back Your Kids: Confident Parenting in Turbulent Times*. USA: Soron Books.

Dominian, J. (2005) *A Guide to Loving*. London: Darton, Longman and Todd.

Dowden, C. and Serin, R. (2001) *Anger Management Programming for Offenders: The Impact of Programmes Performance Measures*. Correctional Service Canada (Retrieved 20th Feb 2005).

Dryden, W.D. (1996) *Overcoming Anger: When Anger Helps and When It Hurts*. London: Sheldon Press.

Eckhart, C.I. and Deffenbacher, J.L. (1996) *Diagnosis of Anger Disorders*. London: Taylor and Francis.

Egan, G. (1995) *The Skilled Helper*. California: Brooks/Cole.

Ellis, A. (2003) *Anger: How to Live With and Without It*. New York: Citadel Press.

Ellis, A. and Tafrate, R.C. (1997) *How to Control Your Anger Before it Controls You*. London: Robert Hale.

Erickson, E. (1959) Identity and the Life Cycle. *Psychological Issues*, 1: 1, 74-6.

Fausto-Sterling, A. (1992) *Myths of Gender: Biological Theories about Women and Men*. New York: Basic Books.

Faupel, D., Herrick, E. and Sharp, P. (1998) *Anger Management: A Practical Guide for Teachers, Parents and Carers*. London: David Fulton.

Feilzer, M. et al. (2004) *The National Evaluation of the Youth Justice Boards Cognitive Behaviour Projects*. Oxford: University of Oxford.

Feldman, P. (1993) *The Psychology of Crime*. Cambridge: Cambridge University Press.

Gibson, M. (1991) *Order for Chaos: Responding to Traumatic Events*. Birmingham: Ventura Press.

Golden, B. (2003) *Healthy Anger*. Oxford: Oxford University Press.

Goldstein, A.P., Glick, B. and Gibbs, J.C. (1998) *Aggression Replacement Training: A Comprehensive Intervention for Aggressive Youth*. Illinois: Research Press.

Goldstein A.P. et al. (2004) *New Perspectives on Aggression Replacement Training: Practice Research and Application*. Chichester: Wiley and Sons.

Goleman, D. (1996) *Emotional Intelligence*. London: Bloomsbury.

Goleman, D. (1998) *Working with Emotional Intelligence*. London: Bloomsbury.

Goleman, D. (2004) *Destructive Emotions and How We Can Overcome Them*. London: Bloomsbury.

Goodman, M.S. and Fallon, B.C. (1995) *Pattern Changing for Abused Women*. London: Sage.

Gould, N., Gould, H. and Brewin, M. (2004) Using Repertory Grid Technique with Gray. In Gray, J. (1996) *Mars and Venus Together Forever*. London: Vermilion.

Participants in Parenting Programme – A Pilot Study *Practice*, 16: 3.

Hart, (2000) Anger: How to Deal with it. *Reality*, January 2000.

Hardiman, M. (2000) *Ordinary Heroes: A Future for Men*. Dublin: New Leaf.

Herbert, M. (2000) Children in Control: Helping Parents to Restore the Balance. In Canavan, J., Dolan, P. and Pinkerton, J. *Family Support: Direction from Diversity*. London: Jessica Kingsley.

Heery, G. (2000) *Preventing Violence in Relationships*. London: Jessica Kingsley.

Howarth, J. and Morrison, T. (2001) Assessment of Parental Motivation to Change. In Howarth, J. *The Childs World*. London: Jessica Kingsley.

Howe, D. et al. (1999) *Attachment Theory, Child Maltreatment and Family Support*. Basingstoke: Macmillan.

Iwaniec, D. (1997) Evaluating Parent Training for Emotionally-abusive and Neglectful Parents: Comparing Individual versus Individual and Group Intervention, *Research on Social Work Practice*, 7: 3, 329-49.

Iwaniec, D. (2003) Identifying and Dealing with Emotional Abuse and Neglect, *Child Care in Practice*, Vol 9:1.

Jones, S. (2002) *Developing a Learning Culture*. London: McGraw-Hill.

Jung, C. (1973) *Letters, Vol 1*. Princeton NJ: Princeton University Press.

Kassinove, H. (Ed.) (1996) *Anger Disorders: Definition, Diagnosis and Treatment*. London: Taylor and Francis.

Kilmartin, C.T. (1994) *The Masculine Self*. Toronto: Maxwell Macmillan.

Kivel, P. (1992) *Men's Work: How to Stop the Violence that Tears Our Lives Apart*. Minnesota: Hazelden.

Knowles, M.S. (1984) *The Adult Learner – A Neglected Species*. Houston: Gulf Publishing.

Kolb, D.A. (1984) *Experiential Learning: Experiences as the Source of Learning Development*. New Jersey: Prentice Hall.

Linn, M., Fabricant, S. and Linn, D. (1988) *Healing the Eight Stages of Life*. New York: Paulist Press.

McKay, M., Rogers, P.D. and McKay, J. (1989) *When Anger Hurts: Quieting the Storm Within*. New Harbinger Publications.

McKeown, K. (2001) *Intimate Relationships Between Men and Women What are the Problem Areas?* Paper Delivered to Cross Border Seminar Series on Mens Issues. Belfast.

Maguire, J. (Ed.) (1995) *What Works: Reducing Re-offending*. Chichester: John Wiley and Sons.

Maslow, A. (1970) *Motivation and Personality*. 2nd edn. New York: Harper and Row.

Meehan, J. (2000) *Reasons Have Hearts Too*. Allen, Texas: Thomas More Publishing.

Miller, W.R. and Rollnick, S. (2002) *Motivational Interviewing: Preparing People for Change*. New York: The Guildford Press.

Newman, T. (2004) Money, Friends and Muscles: The Wishes of Primary School Children in a South Wales Community. *Research, Policy and Planning*, 22: 3.

Newman, T. et al. (2005) *Evidence Based Social Work: A Guide for the Perplexed*. Lyme Regis: Russell House Publishing.

Nomellini, S. and Katz, R.C. (1983) Effects of Anger Control Training on Abusive Parents. *Cognitive Therapy and Research*, 7, 57-68.

Novaco, R.W. and Chemtob, C.M. (1998) Anger and Trauma: Conceptualisation, Assessment and Treatment. In Follette, V.M., Ruzek, J.I. and Abueg, F.R. *Cognitive Behavioural Therapies for Trauma*. London: Guildford Press.

NSPCC (2005) *Research on Parenting*. London: NSPCC.

Peck, M.S. (1980) *The Road Less Travelled*. London: Arrow.

Pert, C.B. (1997) *The Molecules of Emotion: Why you Feel the Way You Feel*. London: Simon and Schuster.

Pinker, S. (2002) *The Blank Slate*. London: Penguin Books.

Pollack, W. (1998) *Real Boys*. New York: Henry Holt.

Prochaska, J.O., DiClimente, C.C. and Norcross, J.C. (1992) In Search of How People Change: Applications to Addictive Behaviours. *American Psychologist*, 47: 9, 1104-14.

Rogers, C. (1988) *Freedom to Learn for the Eighties*. Columbus OH: Merrill.

Rossman, B. (2001) Longer Term Effects of Children's Exposure to Domestic Violence. In Graham – Bermann, S. and Edleson, J. (Eds.) *Domestic Violence in the Lives of Children: The Future of Research, Intervention, and Social Policy*. Washington, DC: American Psychological Association.

Sammon, S.D. (1997) *Life After Youth: Making Sense of One Man's Journey through the Transition at Mid-Life*. New York: Alba House.

Sheehy, G. (1996) *Mapping Your Life Across Time*. London: HarperColliins.

Thompson, N. (2003) *Promoting Equality*. Houndsmills: Palgrave Macmillan.

Thorpe, M., Edwards, R. and Hanson, A. (1995) *Culture and the Processes of Learning*. London: Open University Press.

Thyer, B.A. (1998) Promoting Evaluation Research on Social Work Practice. In Cheetham, J. and Monsoor, A.F. *The Working of Social Work*. London: Jessica Kingsley.

Williams, R. and Williams, V. (1994) *Anger Kills*. New York: Harper Paperbacks.

Parents' Anger Management
The PAMP Programme

Would you be interested?

- **Do you worry about loosing your temper as a parent?**

- **Have you ever lost control with your children?**

- **Have you ever regretted the way you have acted with your children when angry?**

- **Are you worried that you may do something which could cause physical or emotional harm to your children?**

- **Are you worried about the effects of your behaviour on yourself, your children or family?**

.... will be running an eight session learning programme for interested parents in the autumn. It is open to any parent who feels that they want to be better at managing their anger as a parent. Each session lasts 2 hours.
The programme is intended to be educational, enjoyable, challenging and aimed at giving people the chance to take time out to consider ideas and ways of better managing their anger.

If you would like to find out more about this adult education programme, beginning in the Autumn, please contact

....

Parents' Anger Management: The PAMP Progamme

Purpose: To learn to manage anger as a parent by:

Aims: Increasing awareness of anger, stress and aggression.
Identifying a personal list of main anger arousing situations and circumstances as a parent (my triggers).
Challenging and making changes in thinking in relation to anger arousing situations.
Learning ways to be calm, such as breathing focused relaxation, progressive muscular relaxation, and guided imagery training.
Improving coping skills in dealing with provocative, problem and conflict situations.
Reducing the frequency, intensity and duration of anger as a parent and the use of aggression.

Methods: Discussing, exploring, taking in new information, practising and learning new behaviours, sharing experiences, participating, challenging one's thinking, supporting and striving for positive change.

Programme: Eight structured two hour sessions of work focusing on anger and parenting. An educational, enjoyable, challenging experience, aimed at giving people the chance to take time out to consider ideas and ways of better managing their anger as parents (individually or in a group).

The PAMP programme has been designed in light of what research indicates are the most helpful approaches in assisting people who recognise they have a personal problem with their anger and who want help to begin to address it.

Appendix 2: PAMP Contract

PAMP Contract

1. I understand that **PAMP** is providing an educational service for me and will not be offering medical or psychological diagnosis, prognosis or treatment or counselling services.

2. I will treat all other members of the group and the facilitators with respect.

3. I will attend all sessions on time in an alcohol and drug free state.

4. I agree to maintain the confidentiality of the group.

5. I agree to some of the sessions being observed by another party. (This is for training purposes and to ensure that the programme is being delivered appropriately) (Optional)

6. I understand that if there are child protection issues that are of concern, these will have to be reported to the relevant agencies.

7. I understand that if I disclose specific details of a serious criminal offence, this information will be passed on to the police.

8. I agree to give my opinion on how useful I have found this course both at the end of the course and in six months time.

9. I have read and fully understand the above contract and agree to abide by all the conditions outlined.

Signed:_____   Date:_____

Appendix 3: Some Emotions

Emotions

Unpleasant	pleasant
anger	love
hate	joy
fear	excited
jealousy	happy
rage	well being
anxious	contented
tense	close
frightened	enthusiastic
terrified	relaxed
abandoned	secure
lonely	peaceful
isolated	proud
guilt	serene
boredom	passionate
confused	inspired
disappointed	uninhibited
embarrassed	alert
suspecting	alive
dislike	accepting respect
regret	loving
mixed up	confident
contempt	spontaneous
humiliated	

Appendix 4: PAMP Session Record

PAMP Session Record

Session No:

Name:

Date:

1) Check-in

2)

3)

4)

5)

6) Taking care of myself

Participation:

Action required:

Next session:

Signed:

Appendix 5: Using Role Plays

Using Role Plays

There are three sessions in which the option of role play is suggested during the programme. Firstly, in Session 6, the option of playing out how best to deal with a child's anger outburst can be considered. In Session 7 there is the possibility of playing out a conflict situation. Finally, in Session 8, participants can be offered the chance to show how they would apply their learning to the particular example of their badly managed anger that they have been working on during the course. (Depending on the group or individual and the nature of the learning style and approach, other opportunities to play out various approaches throughout the course can also be considered). The following points and guidance reflect my own experience in trying to facilitate experiential learning, and are offered to facilitators who feel confident and competent in using such methods.

Firstly, initial resistance to role play is common, but with humour and gentle persuasion it can usually be overcome. As with all exercises, stress that no-one is compelled to do a role play, but strive to encourage them to do so. Participants can also withdraw from the role play at any point.

It is better if persons do not play themselves in role. Particularly in group delivery, any person who wishes to bring a personal example situation should agree to play their child and brief someone else to play the parent. If working individually, it may be helpful for the facilitator to play the child and let the client play themselves as the parent. If working in groups, where not everyone will want to act out in front of the group, or there may not be time for every one to do so, consideration should be given to having people form pairs or threesomes to play out scenes. One of the threesome could act as an observer and try to identify particular behaviours and perhaps give some feedback.

If setting up a particular scene or scenario to be played out in front of the group it is better to use fictitious names for the role play and also separate chairs not normally used by participants for the exercise. Give a basic script to each character but do not over define. The main aim will be usually just to illustrate and demonstrate particular skills e.g. non-threatening posture and non-verbal communication, listening, checking out understanding, using I statements etc. Agree with group to use 'freeze' to stop role play, with participants staying still to illustrate non-verbal threatening behaviours, or it may also be possible to suggest and then practise alternative non-violent behaviours.

Another approach that can be considered is the 'hot seat', with several or all of the group each taking turns to work through a conflict situation in the middle of the room. To keep it going, one of the facilitators may act the part of a child who is acting badly or in conflict with the parent, or if one of the groups own problem situations has been selected then the parent could play their own child. This can often help increase parent's empathy to the child's position and behaviour. As in the above there can be an agreement to 'freeze' or stop the role play with participants staying still to illustrate non-verbal threatening behaviours, or it may also be possible to suggest and then practise alternative non-violent behaviours. If anyone gets upset during a role play – give them some attention.

Whenever a role play is finished, it is important to de-role in a clear way, almost to make it a ritual:

1. Get participants to share how they are feeling in role.
2. Ask them to leave their role, return to their own seats and say who they are.
3. Ask if they are comfortable with being themselves again.

It is also important to emphasise that if participants are given permission within the role play to act abusively, that is not the way they would normally behave within the group. Make sure everyone is OK.

Appendix 6: PAMP Evaluation Schedules

PAMP Evaluation (1) (End of programme)

Date: .... Name: ....

Please circle the number which indicates how satisfied you were with each of the following things: 1 = Excellent; 2 = Very Good; 3 = Good; 4 = Just OK; 5 = Poor

Overall level of satisfaction with the main aim of PAMP to help me manage my anger with my children in better ways	1 2 3 4 5
Facilitator's delivery of the course	1 2 3 4 5
The handouts provided	1 2 3 4 5
Information covered in course	1 2 3 4 5
Length of course	1 2 3 4 5
The exercises and activities	1 2 3 4 5
The experience of being on the course	1 2 3 4 5
What you enjoyed most about this course?	
What you enjoyed least about this course?	
What could have been improved?	
Was there any aspect you were interested in that was not covered in the course?	
Any other comments you would like to make?	

Would you agree to being contacted again in six months time to see how helpful you have found the course by then.

Thank you very much!

PAMP Evaluation (2) (Six months after programme)

You completed the PAMP programme approximately six months ago and agreed that I could contact you to get your views about the programme at this point. Would you please take a few moments to complete and return this form.

The purpose of the programme was to help you improve how you managed your anger as a parent.

Since completing the programme which statement most reflects your situation now?

Intensity of my anger as a parent

The intensity of my anger towards my children has:
- reduced significantly
- reduced a little
- stayed the same
- increased a little
- increased significantly

Any comment you wish to make in relation to the strength or intensity of the anger you are experiencing:

When I am angry with my children how long does it last? The duration of my anger has:
- reduced significantly
- reduced a little
- stayed the same
- increased a little
- increased significantly

Any comment you wish to make in relation to the duration or length of time that your anger experiences last:

Expressing my anger: When angry:
- I can say how I am feeling a lot better
- I can say how I am feeling a little better
- there is no change in how I show it
- I still keep some of it in and do not say how I am really feeling
- I keep it all in and hide my true feelings

Any comment you wish to make in relation to how you express your anger:

Anger and aggression: I show my anger towards my children:
- a lot more aggressively
- a little more aggressively
- as before
- less aggressively
- not aggressively at all

Any comment you wish to make in relation to how you are expressing your anger:

Effects on your relationship with your children: My relationship with my children has:
- improved significantly
- improved slightly
- not changed
- got slightly worse
- got a lot worse

Any comment you wish to make about your current relationship with your children:

Overall view from doing the PAMP programme (score between 0 and 10)

0	1	2	3	4	5	6	7	8	9	10

Absolutely no
help at all!

Has helped me
tremendously!

Any further comments you wish to make:

Thank you for taking your time to complete this form. As with the feedback you have already given, it will assist us to continue to improve the programme so that we can offer a useful service to parents.

Finally, if you found that you have made little progress and have concerns about yourself and your children, it is your responsibility to seek further support and guidance. For further help, please feel free to contact: ....

Appendix 7: Supporting PAMP

Supporting PAMP

The author is committed to supporting those wishing to use this programme. To this end a range of support services are available, including:

- Powerpoint presentations of programme figures

- Training programmes to agencies or staff wishing to deliver PAMP

- Consultancy to agencies or workers delivering PAMP

Contact through e-mail at gheary@ntlworld.com or 07951 215952

or

Access can be gained by contacting the Parents Advice Centre in Belfast who assisted in the piloting of the programme and are committed to continuing to provide it as one of their services.

Their contact details are:

Parents Advice Centre
Franklin House
12 Brunswick Street
Belfast BT2 7GE
N Ireland
Tel: 028 9031 0891
e-mail: belfast@pachelp.org
Website: www.pachelp.org

The Best of British Baking

The Best of

British

BAKING

Classic Sweet Treats
and Savory Bakes

MARIE RAYNER

Photography by
Darren Muir

ROCKRIDGE
PRESS

*For my father, who has always
been my biggest fan*

Contents

Introduction

An exciting thing is happening. In recent years, I've noticed a trend of people wanting to make their own baked goods. Whether they have been inspired by *The Great British Bake Off* or simply want to fill their free time, more people are getting into the kitchen, finding a stand mixer, and grabbing a rolling pin. This is a wonderful thing!

I have always been an avid home baker. When my five children were growing up in Canada, I loved to bake cookies and cakes to put in their packed lunches and offer as afterschool snacks. On weekends I would bake them pies, and of course every holiday or special occasion meant baking even more goodies to help make our family celebrations special. I have never relied on store-baked or processed goods—making my own has always been more rewarding to me.

Yet when I moved to Great Britain to work as a personal chef on a manor estate more than 20 years ago, I had never seen such a wonderful variety of baked goods in my life as what greeted me there. Fruited scones, tiffin bars, Eccles cakes, lemon drizzle cake, sausage rolls, iced buns—there was no end to the tantalizing delights that winked at me from the shop windows!

Cupcakes were not just cupcakes; they were fairy cakes! What in the world is a tiffin cake? How could one fail to fall in love with baked goods with such fancy names? I wanted to try them all, and I really wanted to bake them all. I was inspired by great bakers like Mary Berry and James Martin, who made me believe that I, too, could become a great baker.

Over the next 20 years, my baking journey would take me across the length and breadth of not one but four very individual countries in the United Kingdom: England, Scotland, Wales (which together make up Great Britain), and Northern Ireland (not to be confused with the Republic of Ireland, which is a separate country entirely). Each nation places their own unique stamp and flair on the baked goods produced within their various counties.

Perhaps your ancestors, like some of mine, came to North America from the British Isles. You may have a longing to get back to your roots and taste the cakes and goodies that your grandmother used to bake. Some of you may wish to visit Britain and test out some of their "bakes" and cakes. Maybe you have been inspired by watching British baking shows. Whatever your reasons, your love of British baking has brought you here today to learn more and to "get stuck" into some great British baking recipes, so welcome!

I'm happy to bring to your table all of the expertise and a wealth of knowledge gathered during my years of living and baking in Britain. I promise that new great and tasty things are about to come from your kitchen! Dust off your apron and crack open your baking cupboards. You're about to get started on one of the most delicious baking journeys of your life!

CHAPTER 1

British Baking

When I came to Great Britain, I thought there wouldn't be much difference between the baking I had done at home in Canada and what existed there. This was an English-speaking country, after all. Oh, how wrong I was! Toe-may-toe, toe-*mah*-toe!

British Baking 101

Before working in Great Britain, I had always baked with the most basic ingredients. I had no idea that so many varieties of sugar existed, or even flours. Being so close to the European continent meant that the UK was armed with many more choices for ingredients to use in baking than I'd previously known of.

I found there was a proper way of doing things and a definite regional difference between one area and the next. Since the UK comprises four separate countries, it's not surprising that the cakes and baked goods of each one would vary a great deal!

Generally, I found their baked goods to be less sweet than what I was used to in North America—even the bread. There is a considerable difference.

I soon learned to bake by weight, rather than by volume. Baking by weight is a more accurate way of baking, as it leaves no room for error.

British bakers use more natural ingredients and flavors in their baking and far fewer processed products. They rely heavily on the use of dried fruits and fresh dairy products, of which they have some of the best in the world.

Cake mixes and other baking mixes were not available in Britain when I first arrived. This is a change that has occurred only over the last few years. The British like to bake from scratch!

Once you master the basics through the recipes in this book, there is nothing you won't be able to bake and enjoy. This book contains a multitude of fresh, from-scratch, delicious recipes, varying from simple biscuits (what the British call cookies) to sweet or savory breads and everything in between.

Understanding Culture through Food

Like other cultures throughout the world, British baking has been greatly influenced by the cultural history of each area of Britain, as well as the diversity of products and ingredients grown and produced locally.

One way to really get to know a culture is to dig in to what fuels the people's appetites. There is great cultural diversity in Great Britain, and this reveals itself in many of their dishes, with many hearkening back to the days before colonialism.

You will find that most regions in the United Kingdom are sensitive to the regionality of their baked goods, with many having achieved a Protected Designation of Origin, or PDO, which very much pertains to the region, history, country, and area of its origin. In this book, you will find recipes originating from each country in the UK, and, wherever possible, I have taken great care to highlight their history and origin.

Although England, Scotland, Wales, and Northern Ireland are each a part of the UK, they take great pride in their individuality and have their own separate flower symbols, saints, holidays, traditions, and foods by which they identify themselves. There are also three different languages spoken—English, Welsh, and Gaelic—although the majority of people speak English. Differences stem from the variations in culture and history that each separate country brings to the bountiful table that is Britain. Let it be noted that the English are English, Welsh are Welsh, Scots are Scots, and Irish are Irish. They will be very quick to let you know the difference!

ENGLAND

England is the largest and most populated country in the UK and brings a multiplicity of baked goods to the table. There are many regional differences in baking, with each English county bringing its own unique spin. Baking recipes can vary greatly. Its proximity to "the Continent" (as mainland Europe is lovingly referred to) has also influenced its style of baking.

WALES

Wales, to the west of England, brings an entirely different flavor to the menu, with plenty of griddle or stone cakes (cakes baked on a baking stone), simple fruited breads, seed cakes, and honey cakes. Many Welsh share simple values that are reflected in their style of baked goods; beloved recipes have been handed down from generation to generation with great pride. The Welsh are famous for their delicious Bara Brith (page 77), which is a lovely fruit bread that you will find at every tearoom in the country. It is meant to be enjoyed with plenty of fresh Welsh butter and hot tea.

SCOTLAND

Scotland, to the north of England, is a large and diverse country, with plenty of coastline, beautiful highlands, and myriad inland lakes and rivers. The cuisine of Scotland is quite simple but has also been heavily influenced by the French. Mary, Queen of Scots brought with her many of the traditions and flavors of France, having been brought up in the French Court. Scotland also grows some of the finest raspberries and oats to be found in the world. You may not find much in the way of fancy iced buns or cakes heavily laden with buttercream icing coming from their bake shops, but you will find some of the best shortbread biscuits and oat cakes on the planet.

NORTHERN IRELAND

The Irish and Northern Irish diet has long relied heavily on potatoes, and so potatoes show up at most meals, often more than once. Irish potato farls are common breakfast breads, made from leftover potatoes, traditionally baked on a stone griddle or "girdle," and best enjoyed alongside an Ulster Fry. Speaking of bread, nothing can compete with a slice of warm Irish soda bread slathered with fresh Irish butter (try the widely available Kerrygold or Northern Irish brand, Abernethy butter), produced by cows fed on that beautiful green grass.

A Brief Trip through (Baking) History

History has played a large part in the development of baking and baked goods in Great Britain. Many other cultures and peoples have greatly influenced British baking. The Norse invaders, the Normans, the Celts, and the Romans all left their marks on British culture and British baking, with lots of traditional dishes from their homelands adapted to what was grown and available for use in Great Britain. This influence has created a food culture that is diverse and quite unique.

British Baking versus North American Baking

One thing that all four countries in the UK have in common is their use of wholesome and natural ingredients. You will find that their cakes are not as sweet as North American cakes, nor are their biscuits (cookies). They rely a lot on dried and candied fruit and have long benefited from having been a seafaring region with easy access to goods, nuts, and spices from all over the world.

The British love their puddings, and by that I don't mean what North Americans usually understand pudding to be. *Pudding* is a term the British use to describe the dessert course of the meal, not a milky concoction to be eaten with a spoon. To the British, pudding includes a wide variety of cakes, "bakes" (baked goods), and pies.

You will find their cakes and bakes to be quite simple in comparison to those found in North America. If there is frosting at all, it will likely be a glacé, which is more like a glaze. Most cakes are topped only with a dusting of sugar. Jam figures hugely in their bakes and is often used to fill cakes, cookies, and tarts. Raspberry jam is most commonly used, but the British are also fond of marmalade cakes and use apricot jam to glaze many baked goods. Buttercream icings are used to fill and top cakes, such as a coffee and walnut cake.

The Hallmarks of British Baking

Many British desserts are accompanied by jugs of warm custard, which they love to pour over their desserts, be it a lush chocolate gateau or a warm apple crumble. They also enjoy lashings of heavy unsweetened cream poured over the top.

Biscuits in the UK are cookies, and most of them are meant to be dunked in and washed down with hot cups of tea. Flapjacks are not pancakes but chewy oat bars, sometimes filled with nuts and dried fruits, and often topped with chocolate.

British flour for the most part is unbleached and comes in different weights, each meant for different uses. They also have a wide variety of sugars and mainly use butter in their baking. Shortening is not used on a regular basis, although you will sometimes see margarine being called for (but not in this book).

Dried and candied fruits are used far more often than chocolate. When chocolate is used, the British like to use good chocolate with a high cacao count. Sweetened shredded coconut is not to be found at all; it is always desiccated, which is much smaller and drier, and comes both sweetened and unsweetened. Larger shaved pieces of coconut make fabulous decorations for cakes and confections. Ginger is another favorite flavor here. You might see four different kinds being used in one bake: ground, candied, preserved, and fresh!

There are five common kinds of pastry: short crust, rough puff, puff, choux, and hot water. There are variations on these as well. Cakes tend to be dense and buttery, and there is no end to the types of pies on offer, both sweet and savory.

Baking Staples

The following ingredients are the ones you will find used in this book. I have highlighted some ingredients that you may not be familiar with. Wherever possible, I explain their uses and where you can find them. Ingredients suggested for each recipe are the best ones to use for that recipe; proper results cannot be guaranteed otherwise. I also offer suitable substitutions where I can.

Flours

Several flours are available in Britain, each lending its own property to the bake. It is important to use the right kind of flour for each recipe, as to do otherwise can greatly affect the outcome.

All-purpose (also known as plain) flour: This flour is generally used for cakes, biscuits, pastries, or any recipe requiring a flour with a low gluten content. This type of flour is used most in the recipes in this book.

Bread flour: Commonly called strong flour in the UK, this flour has a higher gluten content and is thus best suited for making breads.

Self-rising flour: This is an all-purpose flour with a raising agent added to it. Commonly used for baking cakes in the UK as well as scones, self-rising flour is not always easy to find, so I've included instructions on how to make your own (see page 22).

Whole-wheat flour: This flour has not had the bran or germ removed from it. It comes in both plain and self-rising varieties, and is known as whole-meal flour in the UK.

Cornstarch: This is commonly known as corn flour in the UK.

Sugars

Many bakers choose to use unrefined or less refined sugars in their bakes. There is a subtle difference in flavor, but overall you will have just as much success if you have access to only more refined sugars.

Caster sugar: This sugar is the one most used for baking. With a finer texture than regular granulated sugar, it blends smoothly, producing baked goods with a more even texture. If you are unable to find caster sugar, you can process regular granulated sugar in a food processor to give you finer granules.

Icing sugar: Also known as confectioners' sugar or powdered sugar, this very fine sugar is used for making icings and glazes and for dusting over finished baked goods.

Brown sugar: This comes in both light and dark varieties. It is the same as North American light and dark brown sugar but is referred to in the UK as being soft, so you'll see it in recipes as "soft (light or dark) brown sugar." I think the term *soft* is there because it has a higher moisture content than granulated sugar and is not free-flowing. This is largely due to the inclusion of molasses. The more molasses in the sugar, the browner it will be.

Demerara sugar: This is a less refined sugar than regular granulated sugar. Also known as turbinado sugar, demerara has a much coarser grain and darker color, although not as dark as brown sugar. It is mainly used for dusting the tops of cakes and bakes for a crunchy texture.

Golden syrup, dark treacle, and honey: Golden syrup is unique to the UK. It can be difficult to find in North America except in specialty shops or online. It has an almost caramel-like flavor, with lemon undertones. Golden Eagle Syrup is a suitable substitute. Dark treacle is like molasses but with a somewhat stronger flavor. You can use molasses in its place, although it may not give you quite the same kick as dark treacle. Alternatively, you can purchase it online. Honey is nature's sweetener. It is suggested that you use clear, runny honey, as it dissolves much easier than the creamed variety.

Leaveners

A leavener is something added to a baked good to give it lift or to make it rise. There are only three leaveners used in the recipes in this book, all of which are common and easy to find.

Baking powder

Baking soda

Yeast: I call for fast-acting or regular dried yeast, depending on the recipe.

Fats

Fats add richness, moisture, and flavor to baked goods. Baked goods with added fat taste better and feel better in the mouth. They also have a much nicer texture.

Butter: European butter tends to be less salty and lighter in color than North American butter. If you are able to source European butter, I recommend using it. If you cannot find European butter and need to use North American butter, use a lightly salted variety—or use unsalted butter and add salt as needed to the recipe.

Lard: Lard is a pork fat that has no discernible taste. It works beautifully in pastries. It has a higher melting point than butter or shortening and produces a delectable, flaky result.

Suet: Suet is the hard white fat found on the kidneys and loins of animals, predominantly sheep and cattle. It is a crumbly fat used to make foods such as puddings, pastries, and mincemeat filling. You can find it in specialty shops or online. In a pinch, you can use frozen grated butter or shortening instead, although the finished product may have a slightly different flavor.

Spices and Flavorings

All the spices and flavorings used in this book are fairly simple. For that reason, I highly recommend that you use the freshest and purest spices and flavorings you can access.

Ground cinnamon

Ground ginger

Whole nutmeg: I prefer to grate my own, as it has a much fresher flavor.

Mixed spice: This is a specialty baking spice, similar to pumpkin or apple pie spice. The British use it a lot in their baking. You can easily make your own, which I recommend. Just mix together 1 tablespoon ground cinnamon, 1 teaspoon each ground coriander and ground or grated nutmeg, ½ teaspoon ground ginger, and ¼ teaspoon each ground cloves and ground allspice. Store in an airtight container, out of the light, for up to 6 months.

Pure vanilla extract

Dairy Products and Eggs

Butter: I recommend using European butter, or else lightly salted or unsalted North American butter.

Cream: In the UK we have double cream (equivalent to heavy whipping cream in the US) and single cream (for which you can use half-and-half).

Eggs: All eggs used are large free-range eggs, unless otherwise indicated.

Milk: I use homogenized whole milk.

Add-Ins

These ingredients will be required in some recipes for complete authenticity.

Apricot and raspberry jams

Blanched whole almonds

Candied citrus peel: This can be purchased online and in British supply shops. You can also find it in some grocery stores in the baking section. A recipe for making your own is on page 76.

Candied ginger: This is available online or at specialty shops.

Custard powder: Bird's is the most common brand and can be purchased in some well-stocked grocery stores, British supply shops, or online.

Dried pitted dates

Dried raisins, currants, and sultanas (golden raisins)

Flaked (very thinly sliced) almonds

Glacé cherries: These can be found in the baking section of some grocery stores. If you cannot find them, you can use rinsed and dried maraschino cherries.

Ground almonds: This is often labeled almond meal or almond flour.

Marzipan: This thick almond paste is used to wrap or fill cakes.

Old-fashioned or rolled oats

Walnut halves

How to Select the Proper Tea

What is a good bake without tea? The British love to pair a fresh biscuit or slice of cake with a nice hot cup of tea. It is commonly thought that hot tea can solve all of life's problems. Tea was not actually introduced into Britain until the 1700s, but once it was, it proved to be so popular that the British are now the largest consumers of tea in the world. Once a luxury reserved only for the upper classes, it is now quite affordable for all.

For everyday use, I would recommend a good orange pekoe tea. An English or Irish breakfast tea will serve you very well from morning to midafternoon. Reserve specialty teas such as Earl Grey for occasions such as tea parties, or in the late afternoon for a special pick-me-up.

"High tea," or afternoon teatime, is a bit of a small meal, involving finger sandwiches, small savories such as sausage rolls, and something sweet like a slice of cake, cookie, or tart. It is meant to stave off hunger until dinnertime, which can sometimes be as late as 8:00 or 9:00 p.m. A typical teatime menu using some of the recipes from this book might include Sausage Rolls (page 82), Classic Fruited Scones (page 42) with cream and jam, and a slice of Victoria Sponge Cake (page 60).

In other parts of England, suppertime is also known as teatime, a term merely used to signify the evening meal, which is usually served around 6:00 p.m.

Essential Equipment

You will not need much in the way of complicated or unusual equipment to make most recipes in this book. All baking dishes are metal, unless otherwise specified. Metal pans are more proficient heat conductors and cool down more quickly than glass bakeware. They also cook things more evenly.

Baking scale: Although you can certainly bake using standard measuring cups, baking by weight will give you much more accurate results. There are many good digital scales available that will allow you to measure by weight. Most will allow you to add one ingredient, reset the tare, add the next, and so on.

Measuring cups: These are used to measure dry ingredients; they are usually metal with a handle.

Glass measuring cup: This is used to measure liquid ingredients; Pyrex is the best-known brand.

Measuring spoons: You'll need at least 1 tablespoon, 1 teaspoon, ½ teaspoon, and ¼ teaspoon, although other in-between sizes come in handy.

Wooden spoons

Balloon whisks (large and small)

Silicone spatula

Metal spatula

Round metal cookie cutters in a variety of sizes

Rolling pin

Pastry bag with a variety of tips

Pastry brush

Fine wire sieve: This is useful for sifting ingredients together as well as for dusting icing sugar on top of finished baked goods.

Electric hand mixer

Mixing bowls (small, medium, and large): I recommend glass bowls, which can also be used in the microwave.

Rimmed Swiss roll pan (9-by-13-inch)

Large rimmed baking sheets (18-by-26-inch)

Round cake tins: You'll want two 7-inch and two 8-inch pans; I like the kind with removable bottoms.

Rectangular baking tin (7-by-11-inch)

Deep round cake tin or springform pan (9-inch)

Round pie tin (9-inch)

Round tart tin (9-inch)

Shallow tart tin with 12 cups or 12 individual tart tins

Loaf tin (8-by-4-inch)

Square cake tin (7-inch)

Flat griddle pan or large heavy-bottomed nonstick skillet

Wire cooling racks

Helpful But Not Entirely Necessary

Bench scraper

Citrus juicer

Citrus zester

Metal skewer (for testing cakes)

Nutmeg grater or Microplane

Pastry blender (you can use your fingertips or a fork in most cases)

Stand mixer

Using a Digital Scale

A digital scale is a must in my kitchen. It is invaluable for measuring the smallest to the largest of ingredients. There are some great battery-operated ones now, and options to suit every budget.

Measuring by weight is a much more accurate way of baking, as it leaves no room for error. Although both weight and volume measurements are included with the recipes in this book, you will find that measuring by weight is much easier and quicker, as well as more accurate and precise than by volume. Surprisingly, measuring cups can vary a great deal in size, whereas weight never changes.

If using traditional volume measurements, the proper way to measure dry ingredients is to spoon them into a dry measuring cup, without packing them down, and then level them off using the straight side of a knife. One exception to this method is brown sugar, which in most cases is packed into the cup. With brown sugar, if you can dump it out and it holds its shape, you know you have measured correctly. For wet measurements, use dedicated wet measuring cups, which are generally made of glass and have a pouring spout.

Techniques and Tips

There is a right way and a wrong way to do everything in this world, and that includes baking. It is extremely important to do things the right way for positive and consistent results. Following my tips and techniques can help ensure success every time you bake.

Leavening

Make sure that your yeast, baking powder, and baking soda are well within the use-by date as printed on the package.

There are several kinds of yeast available, including fast-acting yeast, which only needs to be mixed into the flour, and regular dried yeast, which must be proofed first. To proof regular dried yeast, follow the directions on the package.

To test the freshness of your baking powder or soda, add some to water. If it bubbles, it is good to go. Normally, when using baking soda in a recipe, you will need to add something acidic to get a good rise. That is why most soda breads also use buttermilk or sour milk.

Preparing Yeast Bread Dough

Kneading is one of the most important parts of making yeast breads. Kneading helps develop the gluten in the bread, enabling it to rise properly. Do not stint on the time required. A properly kneaded dough should be smooth and elastic without any lumps or dry spots. At this point the dough is usually left to rise until doubled in volume.

Next comes shaping. The proper way to shape a traditional yeast loaf is to tip the dough out onto a lightly floured board or countertop. Using a lightly floured rolling pin, press the dough out into a rectangle. Use only enough flour to keep it from sticking. Roll it up tightly from the long edge, pressing the seam shut on the underside. Next, bring each end of the loaf over to the underside, and pinch the seams closed. You can then place your loaf into the tin or onto the baking sheet, seam-side down and leave it to rise again.

This second rising is (perhaps confusingly) also referred to as proofing. Underproofed or overproofed yeast doughs will not rise properly in baking. To test if your dough is proofed enough, poke your index finger into it. If it springs back right away, the dough needs to rise for a bit longer. If your finger leaves an indentation that springs back slowly, then the dough has proofed enough. If you have overproofed your dough, it will not spring back at all. This means that most of the air bubbles in your dough have collapsed—but not to worry, you can still rescue it. Simply punch down your dough again, reshape, and allow it to proof again.

Mixing Batter

For ideal cakes, it is recommended that all ingredients come to room temperature before beginning, unless specified otherwise. Unsurprisingly, beating by hand will take longer than if beating with an electric mixer. Generally, cake batters should be beaten only long enough for all the ingredients to be combined thoroughly, with no dry streaks or lumps remaining. Overmixing results in a cake that does not rise as tall, with a tough crumb.

For quick breads, it is acceptable to have a few lumps in the mix. For best results, mix only to just combine.

Cutting Butter into Flour

With scones, the fat is rubbed into the flour using your fingertips with a snapping motion. It is important to work quickly so the fat does not melt. As you are rubbing, lift your flour up into air. This helps aerate the flour and gives a nicer rise. Be careful not to overwork your dough. A light touch is your best tool.

With pastry, it is important to keep everything cold so the fat is incorporated into the flour rather than melted into the flour. Cut in the fat using a pastry blender, using an up-and-down motion with a slight twist. Ideally your flour-fat mixture should contain pea-size clumps of fat. If you overhandle the dough, you will have a tough pastry. Keep a small amount of the flour in reserve for when you are rolling it out, so you don't add too much extra flour into the mix, which can result in a drier, tougher pastry.

Rolling Out and Shaping Dough

A light touch is best when working with dough that needs to be rolled or patted out. Resist the urge to over-flour your countertop, rolling pin, or hands. When making scones, try to get as many scones cut from the first cut. Scones made from the scraps and re-rolls will not be as tender. Take care not to stretch your pastry as you are fitting it into a pie tin, as stretched pastry shrinks.

Knowing When Your Bake Is Done

Bread: It should be golden brown on top and sound slightly hollow when tapped on the underside.

Cake: The top should spring back when lightly touched. A toothpick inserted into the center should come out clean.

Cookies: They should look firm and be lightly browned on the bottoms and just around the edges. A finger poke should not leave an indentation.

Pastries: They should be dry, golden brown, and flaky-looking, never doughy or pale.

Pies: The outer ring of the filling in single-crust pies should be firm, with only a slight jiggle in the center. This will firm up as the pie cools. For double-crust pies, the upper crust should be flaky and golden brown, with the filling bubbling up through any air vents. The filling in a meat pie should register 160°F on a probe thermometer.

Where to Begin

Each chapter in this book contains simple, delicious, classic bakes that are guaranteed to get you into the kitchen baking. With handy tips, you can be sure to get the best out of each recipe. Looking for a crisp oat-filled buttery hobnob to dunk into hot tea? You can find this recipe on page 28. Do you enjoy a light flaky scone studded with fruit? Try the Classic Fruited Scone on page 42. Fancy a simple cake to help celebrate a special occasion or just because? Try the lush Victoria Sponge Cake on page 60.

Want a flaky yet savory bake? Perhaps my Sausage Rolls recipe on page 82 will suit you! Can you picture yourself cozying up to a cup of tea and a toasted crumpet in front of the fire this winter? I can! Find my tasty recipe on page 116. I assure you, they are a lot easier to bake than you might think!

Handy Recipe Tips

Ingredient Tips: Additional information on selecting and buying ingredients and working with them.

Technique Tips: Tips for prepping, assembling, and baking more efficiently and successfully.

Variation Tips: Suggestions for adding or changing ingredients to mix things up or try something new with the recipe. Boring stops here!

Now that you are armed to the hilt with everything you need to know, it's time to put on your "pinny" and get into the kitchen. Let the baking begin!

CHAPTER 2

Biscuits and Shortbreads

Viennese Whirls, 22

Digestive Biscuits

I can almost guarantee that you will find a packet of these in the cupboard of every kitchen in the UK. Crisp, buttery, and delicious, they are one of Britain's most popular biscuits, perfect for dunking into a hot cup of tea. *Makes 24*

PREP TIME: 15 minutes **BAKE TIME:** 15 minutes

⅔ cup (100 grams) whole-wheat flour

¼ cup (35 grams) all-purpose flour, plus more for dusting

1 tablespoon rolled oats (not old-fashioned oats)

½ teaspoon baking powder

8 tablespoons (1 stick/110 grams) butter, softened

½ cup (100 grams) soft light brown sugar, packed

1 to 4 tablespoons whole milk

1. Preheat the oven to 375°F/190°C. Line two rimmed baking sheets with parchment paper and set aside.

2. In a bowl, whisk the whole-wheat and all-purpose flours with the oats and baking powder. Set aside.

3. In another bowl, cream the butter and brown sugar by hand until light and fluffy. Stir in the flour and oat mixture and combine well. Begin adding the milk, 1 tablespoon at a time. Add only enough milk to give you a thick dough, suitable for rolling. The dough should not be tacky or crumbly.

4. Tip the dough out onto a lightly floured surface and knead it gently until you have a smooth ball. Try not to overhandle the dough.

5. Using a lightly floured rolling pin, roll the dough out to ⅛ inch thickness. Cut into rounds using a 3-inch cookie cutter. Use a spatula to transfer to the prepared baking sheets. Repeat until all of the dough has been used, reworking and cutting any scraps. Prick each cookie once or twice with the tines of a fork.

6. Bake for 15 minutes, until crisp and golden brown around the edges. Transfer to wire racks to cool completely. Store in an airtight container.

Technique Tip: Try to get as many cookies as you can from the first cuts. Reworked scraps will not be quite as nice as first cuts.

Variation Tip: Baked and cooled cookies can be dipped in melted chocolate for an extra special treat. Melt some semisweet or milk chocolate chips in the microwave according to package directions. Spread a small amount of melted chocolate on top of each cookie with a small offset spatula.

Viennese Whirls

These beautiful, buttery cookies literally melt in your mouth. They are sometimes sandwiched together in pairs around vanilla buttercream icing. I prefer them adorned with a small piece of glacé cherry. Don't skip the chill time—it's essential for best results. *Makes 20*

PREP TIME: 15 minutes, plus 30 minutes to chill **BAKE TIME:** 15 minutes

1 cup (2 sticks/225 grams)
butter

⅔ cup (75 grams) icing
(confectioners')
sugar, sifted

1⅔ cups (225 grams)
self-rising flour (see tip)

⅛ teaspoon
vanilla extract

5 red glacé cherries,
washed, dried, and
quartered

1. Line a rimmed baking sheet with parchment paper and set aside.

2. Using an electric hand mixer, cream the butter and sugar together until well combined and very soft. If not creamed enough, your dough will be too stiff to pipe. Stir in the flour and vanilla.

3. Transfer the dough to a piping bag fitted with a large star nozzle. Pipe the dough into rosettes on the prepared baking sheet, at least 2 inches apart. Place a piece of cherry on top of each.

4. Place the baking sheet in the refrigerator to chill for 30 minutes.

5. Preheat the oven to 350°F/180°C.

6. Bake the chilled cookies for 15 minutes, until firm and just beginning to turn golden around the edges. Transfer to a wire rack to cool completely. Store in an airtight container.

Ingredient Tip: You can easily make your own self-rising flour. Simply add 1½ teaspoons baking powder and ½ teaspoon salt to every 1 cup (140 grams) all-purpose flour needed.

Melting Moments

These crisp cookies have a lovely, almost shortbread-like texture. Rolled in oats and topped with a tiny piece of a glacé cherry, they are wonderful enjoyed with a hot cup of tea. *Makes 16 to 20*

PREP TIME: 15 minutes **BAKE TIME:** 15 to 20 minutes

½ cup (40 grams) rolled oats (not old-fashioned oats)

3 tablespoons butter, softened

5 tablespoons (69 grams) lard

6 tablespoons (72 grams) fine granulated sugar (caster sugar)

1 large free-range egg yolk, slightly beaten

⅛ teaspoon vanilla extract

1 cup plus 1½ tablespoons (150 grams) self-rising flour (see tip on page 22)

4 or 5 glacé cherries, washed, dried, and quartered

1. Preheat the oven to 350°F/180°C. Line a rimmed baking sheet with parchment paper and set aside.

2. Put the oats in a bowl and set aside.

3. In a separate bowl, cream the butter, lard, and sugar together until light and fluffy. Beat in the egg yolk and vanilla.

4. Using a wooden spoon, stir in the flour and incorporate thoroughly. (You may need to use your hands to get in the last bits.)

5. Using your hands, roll the dough into 1-inch balls, then roll each ball in the oats to coat.

6. Place the oat-coated balls on the prepared baking sheet, 2 inches apart. Use your thumb to slightly flatten each ball, and place a piece of cherry in the center of each.

7. Bake for 15 to 20 minutes, until light golden brown. Let cool on the baking sheet for several minutes before transferring to a wire rack to cool completely. Store in an airtight container.

Custard Creams

These crisp biscuits have a beautiful crumbly texture and are sandwiched with a delicious custard-flavored buttercream filling. A food processor is very helpful to make these. You can also make them with an electric mixer, but it will take longer to bring the dough together. *Makes 24*

PREP TIME: 15 minutes, plus 20 minutes to chill **BAKE TIME:** 10 minutes

For the cookies
1⅔ cups (225 grams) all-purpose flour, plus more for dusting

⅓ cup (52 grams) custard powder

¼ cup (30 grams) icing (confectioners') sugar, sifted

¾ cup (1½ sticks/170 grams) butter, diced

½ teaspoon vanilla extract

For the filling
3½ tablespoons butter, softened

1½ cups (200 grams) icing (confectioners') sugar, sifted

2 tablespoons custard powder

1 to 2 tablespoons whole milk (if needed)

To make the cookies

1. Combine the flour, custard powder, and icing sugar in the bowl of a food processor. Pulse to combine.

2. Drop in the diced butter and vanilla. Pulse just until everything begins to come together (12 to 15 pulses). (Alternatively, you can combine all the cookie ingredients in a bowl and beat with an electric mixer until everything comes together.)

3. Tip the dough out onto a large piece of plastic wrap. Bring the dough together into a smooth, flat disk and wrap tightly. Place in the refrigerator to chill for 10 minutes.

4. Line two rimmed baking sheets with parchment paper. Using a lightly floured rolling pin, roll the chilled dough out to ¼ inch thickness. Cut into rounds using a 2-inch cookie cutter. Place on the prepared baking sheets and prick the tops with a fork. Place back in the refrigerator to chill for another 10 minutes.

5. Preheat the oven to 350°F/180°C. Bake the chilled cookies for 10 minutes, just until they begin to color around the edges. Cool on the baking sheets for 5 minutes, then carefully transfer to a wire rack to cool completely.

To make the filling and finish

6. Combine the butter, icing sugar, and custard powder in a bowl and beat with an electric hand mixer until smooth and fluffy. Add a bit of milk if needed, a tablespoon or less at a time, until thick, creamy, and spreadable.

7. Sandwich the cooled cookies together with the buttercream. Store in an airtight container.

Chocolate Bourbon Biscuits

These sugar-dusted rich chocolate biscuits boast a wonderful creamy filling. Contrary to the name, they do not actually contain any bourbon. Traditionally, each individual cookie has 10 holes poked into it with the flat end of a wooden skewer. *Makes 14*

PREP TIME: 15 minutes **BAKE TIME:** 10 minutes

For the cookies
3½ tablespoons butter

¼ cup (50 grams) soft light brown sugar, packed

1 tablespoon golden syrup

¾ cup (105 grams) all-purpose flour, plus more for dusting

3 tablespoons unsweetened cocoa powder, sifted

½ teaspoon baking soda

1 to 2 teaspoons whole milk

2 tablespoons granulated sugar, for sprinkling

For the filling
3½ tablespoons butter, softened

1 cup (130 grams) icing (confectioners') sugar, sifted

1 tablespoon unsweetened cocoa powder

2 teaspoons whole milk

⅛ teaspoon vanilla extract

To make the cookies

1. Preheat the oven to 300°F/150°C. Line a rimmed baking sheet with parchment paper and set aside.

2. In a bowl, cream the butter and brown sugar together with an electric hand mixer until light and fluffy. Beat in the golden syrup until well combined.

3. In another bowl, whisk together the flour, cocoa powder, and baking soda. Sift this mixture into the creamed mixture. Add the milk, a little at a time, until soft, even, and a bit crumbly.

6. Mix the icing sugar with enough milk to make a thick, spread-able glaze. Spread the glaze over the tops of half of the cooled cookies, then place half a piece of cherry in the middle of each. Allow to set.

7. Spread up to 1½ teaspoons of raspberry jam on the remaining cookies, spreading it completely to the edges. Top each with a glazed cookie, glazed-side up.

Technique Tip: The granulated sugar most used for baking in the UK is caster sugar. It is a fine granulated sugar, noted for its ability to melt into bakes without leaving any grit behind. You can easily create your own if your sugar is particularly coarse by pulsing regular granulated sugar in a food processor.

Millionaire's Shortbread Bars

Thought to be a Scottish recipe, these bars boast a crisp and buttery shortbread crust, with a sweet caramel filling and rich chocolate topping. You'll need a food processor for the shortbread base. This is a decadent and very "moreish" bar—that is, irresistible! *Makes 12*

PREP TIME: 15 minutes, plus 1 hour inactive time   **BAKE TIME:** 20 minutes

For the shortbread base
½ cup (1 stick/
    110 grams) butter
1¼ cups (175 grams)
    all-purpose flour, plus
    more for dusting
¼ cup (55 grams) fine
    granulated sugar
    (caster sugar)

For the caramel filling
¾ cup
    (1½ sticks/170 grams)
    butter
½ cup plus
    1½ tablespoons
    (115 grams) fine granu-
    lated sugar (caster sugar)
3 tablespoons
    golden syrup

1 (14-ounce/400 grams)
    can sweetened
    condensed milk (not
    evaporated milk)

For the topping
8 ounces (200 grams)
    semisweet chocolate,
    broken into pieces

1. Preheat the oven to 350°F/180°C. Butter a 9-inch square baking tin and line it with parchment paper, leaving some excess overhang for ease in lifting out the finished bars.

To make the shortbread base

2. Combine the butter, flour, and sugar in the bowl of a food processor. Pulse until the mixture begins to bind together, about 10 pulses. Tip the mixture into the prepared baking tin. Using lightly floured fingertips, press the mixture into the tin evenly, smoothing over the top. Bake for 20 to 25 minutes, until completely set and golden brown around the edges.

To make the caramel filling

3. While the base is baking, combine the butter, sugar, golden syrup, and condensed milk in a medium saucepan. Gently heat over low heat, stirring continuously, until the sugar has completely dissolved and is not gritty.

4. Bring the mixture to a boil, then reduce to a slow simmer. Stir continuously for 6 to 8 minutes, until the mixture becomes very thick and caramel-colored. Pour the caramel over the top of the baked shortbread base. Place in the refrigerator until cold, about 30 minutes.

To make the topping

5. Melt the chocolate in a heat-proof bowl set over a pan of simmering water. Do not allow the bottom of the bowl to touch the water. Stir until completely melted. Pour the melted chocolate evenly over the top of the chilled caramel base, smoothing it out to cover. Return to the refrigerator to chill until solid, 30 to 45 minutes. Once solid, cut into 12 bars to serve. Store any leftovers in the refrigerator.

Peppermint Petticoat Tails

These charming biscuits make the perfect addition to an afternoon tea. They are called petticoat tails because the ruffled edge is said to resemble the ruffles in a lady's petticoat. The addition of peppermint extract makes these a bit more special. You can, of course, leave it out if you prefer. You will need a 9-inch fluted tart tin with a removable bottom for this pretty treat. *Makes 8*

PREP TIME: 15 minutes, plus 30 minutes to chill BAKE TIME: 25 minutes

1 cup plus 2 tablespoons (2¼ sticks/250 grams) butter, softened
½ cup (95 grams) fine granulated sugar (caster sugar)

½ teaspoon peppermint extract
1⅔ cups (250 grams) all-purpose flour, plus more for dusting

⅔ cup (100 grams) cornstarch (corn flour)
½ teaspoon salt
Icing (confectioners') sugar, for dusting

1. Combine the butter, sugar, and peppermint extract in the bowl of a food processor. Pulse together until pale and creamy. (Alternatively, beat with an electric hand mixer until pale and creamy.)

2. Sift together the flour, cornstarch, and salt in a bowl. Tip this mixture into the food processor or mixer and pulse or beat just until the mixture starts to form small clumps.

3. Tip out the dough onto a lightly floured surface and bring the dough together to form a ball. Use a light touch and try not to overwork the dough.

4. Place the ball of dough in a 9-inch fluted tart tin with a removable bottom. Using floured fingers, press the dough to fill the tin as evenly as you can. Use a light touch and try not to really compress the dough.

5. Use the tines of a fork to mark the dough into 8 even wedges, and place the tin in the refrigerator to chill for 30 minutes.

6. Preheat the oven to 350°F/180°C.

7. Place the tart tin on a rimmed baking sheet and bake for 25 minutes, just until it's beginning to turn golden brown around the edges. Remove from the oven and re-mark the edges of the wedges with a fork while still very warm.

8. Cool completely, dust with icing sugar and break into wedges to serve.

Chocolate Tiffin Bars

Chocolate tiffin bars, or tiffin cake as it is also known, is said to be the favorite dessert of Princes William and Harry. There is no real baking involved. They are a quick and easy make for the family without any heating up of the kitchen. Beloved by children, young and old alike, tiffin bars make for great party fare! *Makes 8*

PREP TIME: 10 minutes, plus 1 hour to chill **BAKE TIME:** 15 minutes

7 tablespoons (95 grams) butter
¼ cup golden syrup (in a pinch you can use corn syrup)

3 tablespoons unsweetened cocoa powder, sifted
2 tablespoons soft light brown sugar, packed
1 cup (150 grams) raisins

2½ cups (225 grams) broken digestive biscuits (or broken graham crackers)
8 ounces (225 grams) milk chocolate, melted

1. Generously butter an 8-inch square baking tin, then line with parchment paper, leaving a bit of an overhang. Butter the parchment paper as well. Set aside.

2. Combine the butter, golden syrup, cocoa powder, and brown sugar in a large saucepan. Melt over medium-low heat, stirring constantly, until the sugar no longer feels gritty and everything is well combined. Stir in the raisins.

3. For the best texture, make sure the crumbled biscuits are a mix of sizes, with some larger bits and smaller bits, along with some crumbs. Stir the crumbles into the butter mixture in the pan, mixing everything together until the biscuit pieces are well coated and the raisins are evenly distributed.

4. Tip this mixture into the prepared baking tin. Press into the pan firmly using the bottom of a metal measuring cup. The mixture should be compact.

5. Pour the melted chocolate evenly over the top of the mixture, spreading with an offset spatula to cover the mixture completely.

6. Place in the refrigerator to chill completely, at least an hour.

7. Once set, lift out and cut into squares to serve. Store any leftovers tightly covered in the refrigerator.

Variation Tip: If you like, you can add candied cherries or dried cherries, dried cranberries, or a mix of these along with raisins to make up the same measure of raisins.

Scottish Shortbread

Is there anything on earth more beautiful or delicious than a crumbly short-bread biscuit? I think not! The Scots are immensely proud of their shortbread and quite rightly so. It is important that your butter be the right consistency. It should be soft enough that you can press your finger into the block, leaving a bit of a dent, but not overly so. *Makes 24 to 30 biscuits or 1 (9-by-13-inch) pan*

PREP TIME: 15 minutes, plus 10 minutes to chill **BAKE TIME:** 45 minutes for a full pan

1¼ cups (2½ sticks/280 grams) butter, softened

¾ cup (140 grams) fine granulated sugar (caster sugar), plus more for sprinkling

2 cups (280 grams) all-purpose flour

1 scant cup (140 grams) cornstarch (corn flour)

Pinch salt

1. In a bowl cream together the butter and sugar using an electric hand mixer until pale in color.

2. Sift together the flour, cornstarch, and salt into another bowl. Stir the flour mixture into the creamed butter-sugar mixture until thoroughly combined, without overmixing. Tip the mixture into a 9-by-13-inch metal baking dish.

3. Using floured hands or an offset spatula, lightly press the mixture into an even layer. Place in the refrigerator to chill for 10 minutes.

4. Preheat the oven to 300°F/150°C.

5. Bake the chilled shortbread for 45 to 55 minutes, until set but not colored.

6. Remove from the oven and immediately sprinkle the top abundantly with more sugar, and then cut into squares or bars. Leave to cool in the baking dish for at least 10 minutes before transferring to a wire rack to cool completely. Store in an airtight container.

CHAPTER 3

Scones and Buns

Classic Fruited Scones 42

Honey-Wheat Scones 44

Cheese and Onion Scones 46

Traditional Rock Cakes 48

Fat Rascals 49

Yorkshire Rock Cakes 50

Scottish Oat Cakes 52

Potato Cakes 54

Northern Irish Soda Bread 55

Victoria Scones 56

Honey-Wheat Scones, 44

Classic Fruited Scones

Classic fruited scones are the scones you will see served in just about every tearoom in the UK. They are buttery, tender, and studded with plenty of sticky sultanas, then traditionally served with clotted cream and strawberry jam. There is much debate about which goes on first, the cream or the jam! This decision depends on where your roots lie, but they are delicious no matter which goes on first! *Makes 10*

PREP TIME: 10 minutes **BAKE TIME:** 10 minutes

2½ cups (350 grams) self-rising flour (see tip on page 22), plus more for dusting

1½ teaspoons baking powder

⅓ cup (75 grams) cold butter, cut into bits

2½ tablespoons fine granulated sugar (caster sugar)

½ cup (75 grams) sultanas

2 large free-range eggs

½ to ⅔ cup (120 to 160 mL) whole milk

Demerara sugar, for sprinkling

1. Preheat the oven to 425°F/220°C. Line a rimmed baking sheet with parchment paper and set aside.

2. Sift the flour and baking powder into a bowl, lifting the sieve high above the bowl to get as much air into the flour as you can. Drop the cold butter into the bowl. Using the tips of your fingers and a snapping motion, rub the butter quickly into the flour until the mixture resembles fine dry bread crumbs. Stir in the sugar and sultanas.

3. Beat the eggs in a small bowl. Remove and set aside 2 tablespoons of beaten eggs. Using a fork, beat ½ cup (120 mL) of milk into the remaining beaten eggs. Add the milk mixture to the flour mixture, stirring together with a butter knife. You should have a soft but slightly tacky dough. Add more of the remaining milk if your mixture is too dry. You don't want a gummy, wet mixture, but you also don't want a dry, crumbly mixture.

4. Tip the dough onto a lightly floured surface and knead it gently a few times before patting it out to a round roughly 1 inch thick.

5. Cut into rounds using a 3-inch cookie cutter. Cut using a direct up-and-down motion, without twisting the cutter. Try to get as many cuts as you can from the first cut. Place the scones on the prepared baking sheet as you go. Gather up any scraps, re-pat, and re-cut, until you have 10 scones.

6. Brush the tops with the reserved beaten eggs and sprinkle with a bit of coarse sugar.

7. Bake for 10 minutes, until well risen and golden brown on the tops and bottoms. Scoop onto a wire rack to cool completely. These are best eaten the same day, but you can store leftovers in an airtight container.

Tips for Baking and Enjoying Perfect Scones

→ Keep your butter well chilled so it rubs into the flour mixture, rather than melting into it.

→ Use a light touch when working with the dough. You'll get a much nicer rise and lighter scone if you avoid overworking the dough.

→ Try to get as many scones from the first cutting that you can. Scones cut from reworked and re-patted dough will not be as tender or rise as tall.

→ Do not twist the cutter when cutting out the scones. A sharp up-and-down motion is best. When you twist the cutter, you seal the dough, so the scones rise lopsided in the oven.

→ When brushing the egg on top of the scones, don't let it drip down the sides of the scones. This will also hamper your rise.

→ Unlike baking powder biscuits, most scones are meant to be eaten at room temperature.

→ Clotted cream and jam are really nice accompaniments to scones, but clotted cream is difficult to find in North America. You can use softly whipped cream in its place.

→ Scones go perfectly with a hot cup of tea!

Honey-Wheat Scones

Traditionally, these delightful whole-meal (whole-wheat) flour scones, made often in Northern Ireland, would be sweetened with a good Irish honey. They are baked as a whole round scored into wedges, and then broken apart to eat. Unlike English scones, these are meant to be enjoyed warm with butter. At one time, they would have been baked on an iron "girdle" (griddle) pan over an open fire. *Makes 8*

PREP TIME: 10 minutes **BAKE TIME:** 20 minutes

¾ cup (105 grams) all-purpose flour

¾ cup (105 grams) whole-wheat flour

2 teaspoons baking powder

Pinch salt

⅓ cup (75 grams) butter, softened, plus more for serving

1 tablespoon soft light brown sugar, packed

4 to 5 tablespoons (60 to 80 mL) whole milk

2 tablespoons honey

1. Preheat the oven to 400°F/200°C. Butter a rimmed baking sheet and set aside.

2. Sift the all-purpose flour into a bowl. Whisk in the whole-wheat flour, baking powder, and salt.

3. Drop in the butter and rub it into the flour mixture with your fingertips using a snapping motion until the mixture resembles fine dry bread crumbs. Stir in the brown sugar.

4. Stir the milk and honey together until the honey has totally dissolved. Remove and set aside a tiny bit for glazing the scones. Add just enough of the milk-honey mixture to the flour-butter mixture to make a soft dough, stirring it in with a butter knife.

5. Tip out the dough onto the prepared baking sheet and gently shape into a 7-inch round. With a sharp knife, lightly score the top into 8 wedges without cutting all the way through to the bottom.

6. Bake for 15 to 20 minutes, until dry and set. Remove from the oven and glaze with the reserved milk-honey mixture. Return to the oven for 5 to 10 more minutes, until golden brown.

7. Remove from the oven and break into wedges. Serve warm, split open, with lashings of soft butter. These are best eaten the same day, but you can store leftovers in an airtight container.

Cheese and Onion Scones

Tender and flaky, these savory scones are delicious on their own, spread with butter, or served alongside a bowl of hot soup. They also make a delicious addition to a traditional British ploughman's lunch, which usually consists of sliced cold meat, some cheese, a bit of pickle, and some salad. Simple and delicious. *Makes 12*

PREP TIME: 10 minutes **BAKE TIME:** 15 minutes

2½ cups (350 grams) all-purpose flour, plus more for dusting

1 tablespoon baking powder

½ teaspoon salt

¼ teaspoon dry mustard powder

½ cup (1 stick/110 grams) cold butter, cut into bits

1 cup (120 grams) grated extra-sharp cheddar cheese, divided

2 scallions, trimmed and finely chopped

1 large free-range egg

1 cup (240 mL) whole milk

1. Preheat the oven to 400°F/200°C. Line a rimmed baking sheet with parchment paper and set aside.

2. Sift the flour, baking powder, salt, and mustard powder into a large bowl. Drop the butter in and rub it into the flour mixture with your fingertips using a snapping motion, until the mixture resembles coarse bread crumbs.

3. Add ¾ cup (90 grams) of cheese and the scallions and stir to combine.

4. In another bowl, beat together the egg and milk. Pour over the flour mixture and stir it in with a fork until you get a soft, shaggy mixture.

5. Tip out the dough onto a lightly floured surface and knead gently 8 to 10 times, just to bring the dough together. Pat into a round about ¾ inch thick.

6. Unwrap the rectangle of dough and place it on a sheet of parchment paper. Sprinkle the remaining ¼ cup (15 grams) of oats all over the dough. Place another piece of parchment paper on top. Using a rolling pin, roll the dough out into a rectangle about 10 inches by 12 inches.

7. Cut into 32 rectangles, each about 2½ inches by 1½ inches. Using a spatula, transfer to a rimmed baking sheet, spacing them at least 1 inch apart. Sprinkle with flaked sea salt.

8. Bake for 28 to 30 minutes until golden brown. Transfer to a wire rack to cool completely. Store in an airtight container.

Potato Cakes

These traditional savory cakes are proof that what the Northern Irish manage to bake up with potatoes with is always delicious. They are wonderful whether served for breakfast, tea, or supper. Who knew leftover mash could taste so good? *Makes 6*

PREP TIME: 10 minutes **BAKE TIME:** 15 minutes

6 tablespoons (80 grams) cold mashed potatoes

¾ cup (105 grams) all-purpose flour, plus more for dusting

¼ cup (50 grams) lard

Pinch salt

Whole milk, as needed

Butter, for serving

1. Preheat the oven to 400°F/200°C. Butter a rimmed baking sheet and set aside.

2. Mix the potatoes and flour together in a bowl. Rub in the lard with your fingertips until the mixture resembles coarse meal. Mix in the salt and just enough milk to produce a soft, pliable dough.

3. Tip out the dough onto a floured surface. Roll or pat into a round about ½ inch thick. Cut into rounds using a 2½-inch cutter. Place on the prepared baking sheet.

4. Bake for 15 to 20 minutes, until golden brown. Serve immediately, with plenty of butter for spreading on the warm cakes. These are best eaten on the same day, but leftovers can be stored in an airtight container for up to 2 days.

Ingredient Tip: Resist any urge to swap the lard for another fat. Lard works best for this recipe.

Northern Irish Soda Bread

There's nothing quite as comforting as a slice of warm homemade Irish soda bread or farls fresh from the griddle and slathered with plenty of fresh butter and jam. It is also excellent with soups or stews. Here's the quick and easy recipe that's a mainstay in most Northern Irish homes.
Makes 1 (8-inch round) loaf

PREP TIME: 15 minutes **BAKE TIME:** 25 minutes

3¼ cups (450 grams) all-purpose flour, plus more for dusting

1 teaspoon salt

1 teaspoon baking powder

1 teaspoon fine granulated sugar (caster sugar) (optional)

1¾ cups (420 mL) buttermilk, divided (you may not need it all)

1. Preheat the oven to 425°F/220°C. Lightly butter a rimmed baking sheet and set aside.

2. Sift the flour, salt, and baking powder into a bowl. Whisk in the sugar, if using. Make a well in the center of the dry ingredients. Pour in 1½ cups (360 mL) of buttermilk. Using your fingers, mix everything together to make a soft but not sticky dough. Add some of the remaining ¼ cup (60 mL) of buttermilk, if necessary.

3. Tip the dough out onto a lightly floured surface and knead lightly a few times. It is important not to over-knead the dough as this will toughen it. A few turns is sufficient. Shape the dough into an 8-inch round.

4. Place on the prepared baking sheet. Using a sharp knife, cut a cross in the top, about ½ inch deep.

5. Bake for 25 to 30 minutes. Test that the loaf is done by turning it over and tapping it on the bottom with your knuckles. It should sound hollow.

6. Place on a wire rack to cool, then cut into slices to serve. Soda bread is best eaten on the same day, but leftovers can be stored in an airtight container for up to 2 days. It can also be wrapped tightly and frozen for up to 3 months.

Victoria Scones

These rich scones are baked in rounds, scored into wedges. The cherries on top make them especially pretty. They earn their name, as they're fit for a queen. *Makes 4*

PREP TIME: 10 minutes **BAKE TIME:** 10 minutes

1⅔ cups (225 grams) self-rising flour (see tip on page 22), plus more for dusting
Pinch salt

¼ cup (50 grams) cold butter, cut into bits
¼ cup (50 grams) fine granulated sugar (caster sugar)

1 large free-range egg
7 tablespoons (100 mL) whole milk
4 glacé cherries, cut into quarters

1. Preheat the oven to 400°F/200°C. Line a rimmed baking sheet with parchment paper and set aside.

2. Sift the flour and salt into a bowl. Drop the butter into the bowl and quickly rub it into the flour using your fingertips and a snapping motion. The mixture will resemble fine dry bread crumbs when done. Stir in the sugar.

3. In another bowl, beat the egg and milk together. Remove and set aside a tiny bit to brush on top of the scones.

4. Add the egg-milk mixture to the flour mixture and stir it in with a butter knife to make a soft dough. Tip out the dough onto a lightly floured surface and knead gently a few times.

5. Cut the dough into 4 equal pieces. Shape each piece into a round, roughly ½ inch thick. Place each round on the prepared baking sheet. Using a sharp knife, score the top of each round into 4 sections, without cutting all the way down through the rounds. Brush the reserved egg-milk mixture on top of each scone, and lightly push a piece of cherry into the center of each quarter.

6. Bake for 10 to 15 minutes, until well risen and golden brown. Transfer to a wire rack to cool. Enjoy at room temperature with some butter and jam. These are best eaten the same day, but you can store leftovers in an airtight container.

CHAPTER 4

Cakes and Loaves

Battenberg Cake, 64

Victoria Sponge Cake

Historically, it is said that this cake was originally prepared by one of Queen Victoria's chefs for her birthday. It caught on with the public and has been a popular cake ever since. It makes a great centerpiece for the tea table and is quite simply delicious. *Makes 1 (7-inch) cake*

PREP TIME: 10 minutes **BAKE TIME:** 25 minutes

¾ cup (1½ sticks/170 grams) butter, softened

¾ cup plus 2 tablespoons (170 grams) fine granulated sugar (caster sugar)

¼ teaspoon vanilla extract

3 large free-range eggs, lightly beaten

1¼ cups (170 grams) self-rising flour (see tip on page 22)

3 tablespoons raspberry jam

Icing (confectioners') sugar or additional fine granulated sugar (caster sugar), for dusting

1. Preheat the oven to 350°F/180°C. Generously butter two 7-inch layer cake tins, line the base with parchment paper, and set aside.

2. Using an electric hand mixer or a stand mixer, cream the butter, sugar, and vanilla until fluffy and light in color. Beat in the eggs a bit at a time, beating well with each addition. If the mixture starts to curdle and split, add a tablespoon of the flour mixture.

3. Using a metal spoon, fold in the flour. Use a cutting motion and try not to knock too much of the air out of the mixture. Divide the batter evenly between the prepared baking tins. Level off the surface of each cake and then make a slight dip in the centers using the back of a metal spoon.

4. Bake in the center of the oven for about 25 minutes. The cakes should be well risen and golden brown and should spring back when lightly touched near the center. A toothpick inserted in the center should come out clean.

5. Cool in the pan for 5 minutes. Run a knife around the edge of each cake and then carefully tip out the cake onto a wire rack, gently pulling off the paper. Cool completely.

6. Place one cooled cake layer onto a serving plate, bottom-side up. Spread with the jam, all the way to the edges. Top with the other layer, right-side up. Dust with icing sugar or caster sugar to finish. This will keep for up to 4 days tightly covered.

Variation Tip: You can add a layer of vanilla buttercream icing to the center of the cake along with the jam. To make a simple buttercream, using an electric hand mixer, beat together ¼ cup (50 grams) softened butter, 1 cup (130 grams) sifted icing (confectioners') sugar, and 1 tablespoon whole milk until thick and creamy. Spread over the bottom layer and then top with the jam. Finish as directed.

Coffee and Walnut Cake

This is one of my all-time favorite cakes. With its moist coffee-flavored sponge and coffee buttercream icing, it always pleases. As a bonus, it is an amazingly easy cake to make. *Makes 1 (8-by-4-inch) loaf cake*

PREP TIME: 15 minutes, plus 1 hour to cool **BAKE TIME:** 45 minutes

For the cake
½ cup (120 mL) milk
⅓ cup (75 grams) butter, cut into bits
1 tablespoon instant coffee granules
½ cup (95 grams) fine granulated sugar (caster sugar)
½ cup (60 grams) chopped toasted walnuts, plus toasted walnut halves, for decoration
1 large free-range egg, lightly beaten
1 cup (140 grams) self-rising flour (see tip on page 22), sifted

For the coffee buttercream icing
Scant ½ cup (100 grams) butter, softened slightly
1⅓ cups (160 grams) icing (confectioners') sugar, sifted
1 teaspoon instant coffee, dissolved in 1 teaspoon boiling water
1 to 3 teaspoons whole milk, as needed

To make the cake

1. Preheat the oven to 325°F/160°C. Generously butter an 8-by-4-inch loaf tin and line with baking parchment, leaving an overhang for lifting out the finished cake when done. Set aside.

2. Combine the milk, butter, and coffee granules in a saucepan. Cook over medium heat, stirring, for several minutes, until the coffee has dissolved completely.

3. Remove from the heat and stir in the sugar and chopped walnuts. Let cool until you can stick your finger in it, then beat in the egg with a wooden spoon until well combined. Stir in the flour just to combine.

4. Spoon the batter into the prepared loaf tin, smoothing over the top. Bake in the center of the oven for 40 minutes, or until risen and a toothpick inserted in the center comes out clean.

5. Leave to cool in the tin for 5 minutes, then turn out onto a wire rack to cool completely.

To make the coffee buttercream icing

6. Combine the butter, sugar, coffee, and 1 teaspoon of milk in a bowl and beat together until thick and creamy, adding only enough milk to give you a proper spreading consistency.

7. Spread the icing over the top of the cooled loaf and then decorate with toasted walnut halves. This cake will keep tightly covered for up to 4 days.

Battenberg Cake

This traditional teatime bake has been appearing in British cookery books for over two centuries. Another name for it is church window cake, as the finished cake is thought to resemble the appearance of the stained-glass windows of a church. It only looks complicated and is much easier to make than one would suppose. *Makes 1 (7-inch square) cake*

PREP TIME: 45 minutes, plus 45 minutes to cool **BAKE TIME:** 30 minutes

¾ cup (1½ sticks/170 grams) butter, softened

Scant 1 cup (175 grams) fine granulated sugar (caster sugar), plus more for dusting

3 large free-range eggs, lightly beaten

1¼ cups (175 grams) self-rising flour (see tip on page 22)

A few drops red food coloring

2 to 3 tablespoons vanilla buttercream icing

2 to 3 tablespoons warmed and sieved apricot jam

⅔ pound (275 grams) natural almond paste (marzipan)

1. Preheat the oven to 325°F/160°C. Generously butter a 7-inch square tin, line with parchment paper, and set aside.

2. Using an electric hand mixer or a stand mixer, beat the butter and sugar together until light and fluffy. Beat in the eggs, a little bit at a time. If the mixture curdles, add a spoonful of the flour. Stir in the flour until smooth.

3. Transfer half the batter to a separate bowl. Tint one bowl of batter pink using a few drops of red food coloring.

4. Spoon the batters into the prepared baking tin, placing the plain batter on one side and the pink batter on the other side. Smooth the top gently without mingling the batters into each other.

5. Bake on the center rack for 30 to 35 minutes. When done, the top should spring back when lightly touched near the center, and a toothpick inserted in the center should come out clean.

6. Cool in the pan for 5 minutes, then carefully tip out the dough onto a wire rack to finish cooling.

7. Once the cake is completely cool, using a serrated knife, trim all the edges away from the cake, and then cut the cake into 4 equal long sections, 2 plain and 2 pink.

8. Place one of each color cake section side by side and spread a little buttercream icing between them to help them adhere. Repeat with other 2 sections. Spread a little warm jam on top of one of the 2-section blocks and place the other 2-section block on the jam, alternating the colors for a checkerboard pattern.

9. Dust the countertop with some granulated sugar. Roll the marzipan out on the granulated sugar into a thin oblong layer, about 7 inches long and roughly wide enough to wrap all the way around the cake with about a ½-inch overlap. Brush with some of the warm apricot jam.

10. Place the checkerboard sponge on top of the marzipan, placing it into the middle, perpendicular to the short side of the marzipan rectangle. Bring the marzipan up over the cake to cover it completely and press it lightly into place, with a bit of an overlap in the center. Brush more jam on the overlap so it seals shut and holds in place.

11. Place the cake on a serving plate, seam-side down. Using the dull edge of a knife, lightly mark the top of the marzipan in the traditional crisscross pattern. Cut into slices to serve. Store any leftovers in an airtight container for up to 4 days.

Classic Lemon Drizzle Cake

I cannot think of anyone who does not immediately get excited at the sight of a lemon drizzle cake, buttery and moist with a tart lemon syrup glaze. Enjoy it cut into thick slices to serve along with hot cups of tea. *Makes 1 (8-by-4-inch) loaf*

PREP TIME: 10 minutes **BAKE TIME:** 40 minutes

For the cake
¾ cup
(1½ sticks/170 grams)
butter, softened
Scant 1 cup (175 grams)
fine granulated sugar
(caster sugar)

3 large free-range eggs,
lightly beaten
1¼ cups (175 grams)
self-rising flour (see tip
on page 22), sifted
Finely grated zest and
juice of 1 medium lemon

For the drizzle
¼ cup (50 grams) fine
granulated sugar
(caster sugar)
Finely grated zest and
juice of 1 medium lemon

To make the cake

1. Preheat the oven to 350°F/180°C. Butter an 8-by-4-inch loaf tin and then line it with parchment paper, overlapping the edges for ease of removal. Set aside.

2. Using an electric hand mixer or a stand mixer, beat the butter and sugar until light and fluffy. Beat in the eggs one at a time, mixing them in well after each addition. If the mixture curdles, add a spoonful of the flour.

3. Gently fold in the flour and then stir in the lemon zest and juice to combine. Spoon the batter into the prepared pan and smooth over the top.

4. Bake on the center rack for 40 to 45 minutes, until well risen and golden brown. The top should spring back when lightly touched and a toothpick inserted in the center should come out clean.

5. While the cake is baking, whisk the sugar, lemon zest, and juice together until the sugar has dissolved. Set aside.

6. While the cake is still warm, prick it all over the top using the tines of a fork or a toothpick. Slowly drizzle the lemon syrup liberally and evenly over the top, allowing it to soak in.

7. Turn out the cake, lifting by the parchment, onto a wire rack and remove the paper carefully. Leave to cool completely before cutting into slices to serve. Store leftovers tightly covered for up to 3 days.

Madeira Cake

Contrary to the title, this delicious cake contains no madeira, nor is it related to Madeira in Portugal. It is one of the more popular British cakes, being dense and delicious and lightly flavored with lemon. I find it to be similar in texture to a North American pound cake. Traditionally it is decorated in the center with long strips of candied lemon peel. It goes down well with a hot cup of tea. *Makes 1 (8-by-4-inch) loaf cake*

PREP TIME: 15 minutes **BAKE TIME:** 1 hour

Heaping ¾ cup (115 grams) all-purpose flour

Heaping ¾ cup (115 grams) self-rising flour (see tip on page 22)

Scant 1 cup (175 grams) fine granulated sugar (caster sugar)

Finely grated zest of 1 medium lemon

¾ cup (1½ sticks/170 grams) butter, softened

3 large free-range eggs, lightly beaten

1 to 2 tablespoons whole milk

Thin slivers candied lemon peel, for garnish

Icing (confectioners') sugar, for dusting (optional)

1. Preheat the oven to 350°F/180°C. Generously butter an 8-by-4-inch loaf tin. Line with parchment paper, and set aside.

2. Sift both flours together into a bowl and set aside.

3. Measure the sugar into another bowl and rub the lemon zest into it until very fragrant. Drop in the butter and, using an electric hand mixer or stand mixer, cream together until light and fluffy. Beat in the eggs, a little bit at a time, until well incorporated. If the mixture curdles, beat in a spoonful of the flour. Fold in the flours using a metal spoon until thoroughly incorporated. Stir in just enough milk for a soft, droppable batter.

4. Spoon the batter into the prepared pan, smoothing over the top. Bake on the center rack for 20 minutes.

5. Carefully remove from the oven and lay the lemon peel on top, then return the cake to the oven to bake for 40 additional minutes, until golden brown and a toothpick inserted in the center comes out clean. Cool in the tin for 10 minutes before transferring to a wire rack to cool completely.

6. If desired, dust the cake with icing sugar before cutting into thin slices to serve. Store any leftovers in an airtight container for up to 5 days.

Traditional Swiss Roll

This is a childhood favorite: a delicious fat-free sponge, rolled up with a jam filling and cut into thick slices to serve. Of course, you can get a bit more creative and fill it with lemon curd, whipped cream, fresh fruit, and so on. It is a quick and easy cake to make. You will need a 9-by-13-inch Swiss roll tin to bake this in. *Serves 6 to 8*

PREP TIME: 10 minutes **BAKE TIME:** 10 minutes

4 large free-range eggs
½ cup (95 grams) fine granulated sugar (caster sugar), plus more for dusting

¾ cup (105 grams) self-rising flour (see tip on page 22)

Heaping ¼ cup strawberry or raspberry jam

1. Preheat the oven to 425°F/220°C. Lightly butter a 9-by-13-inch Swiss roll tin, line the bottom with parchment paper, and set aside.

2. Combine the eggs and sugar in the bowl of a stand mixer, and using the whisk on high, whisk them together until light and frothy. Continue to mix on high until the mixture leaves a ribbon trail when you lift the whisk from the bowl. (Alternatively, you can use an electric hand mixer, although it may take you longer.)

3. Using a spatula, fold in the flour a little bit at a time, and take care not to knock the air out of the egg/sugar mixture. Don't overmix or the cake will be tough and not as light. Pour into the prepared baking tin and gently shake to level it out, making sure the batter gets into all the corners. This is important because of the short bake time and high temperature.

4. Bake in the center of the oven for 10 minutes, until the cake is golden brown and the edges have begun to shrink away from the sides of the pan.

5. Meanwhile, lay out a sheet of parchment paper larger than the baking tin on the countertop and liberally dust it with sugar.

6. Invert the baked cake onto the sugar-dusted parchment paper. Remove the tin and, working quickly, carefully peel off the parchment paper. Make a shallow cut/score along one short edge of the cake, about 1 inch from the edge. Do not cut all the way through; this is only for ease of rolling. Leave to cool for a few minutes.

7. Spread a layer of jam all over the surface of the warm cake and, starting at the short edge where you made the cut, start to roll up the cake firmly.

8. Place the roll on a cake dish or platter, seam-side down. Cool completely before cutting into slices with a serrated knife to serve. Store any leftovers in an airtight container for up to 3 days.

Sticky Toffee Cake

Not to be confused with the pudding, this delightful cake embodies all of the elements of the perennial British favorite sticky toffee pudding. It has the same rich, moist date and brown sugar cake topped off with a lush brown sugar and cream frosting. *Makes 1 (7-by-11-inch) cake*

PREP TIME: 15 minutes, plus 1 hour to cool **BAKE TIME:** 45 minutes total

For the cake

8 ounces (225 grams)
   pitted Medjool dates
1¼ cups (300 mL) water
1 teaspoon baking soda
Heaping ¾ cup
   (170 grams) soft light
   brown sugar, packed
½ cup (1 stick/110 grams)
   butter, softened

1 teaspoon vanilla extract
2 large free-range eggs,
   lightly beaten
1⅓ cups (190 grams)
   self-rising flour (see tip
   on page 22)

For the icing

½ cup (100 grams)
   soft light brown
   sugar, packed
6 tablespoons (90 mL)
   heavy cream
2 tablespoons butter,
   softened
3½ tablespoons icing
   (confectioners')
   sugar, sifted

To make the cake

1. Preheat the oven to 350°F/180°C. Butter a 7-by-11-inch baking tin, line the base with parchment paper, and set aside.

2. Using a pair of kitchen scissors, snip each date into 3 or 4 pieces. Put the dates in a saucepan along with the water. Bring to a boil and boil for about 10 minutes, until most of the water has been absorbed and the dates have softened. Remove from the heat and stir in the baking soda. Set aside to cool.

3. Using a wooden spoon, cream together the brown sugar, butter, and vanilla extract until light and fluffy. Gradually beat in the eggs and then fold in the cooled date mixture. Stir in the flour to combine.

4. Spoon the batter into the prepared baking tin, smoothing the top over. Bake on the center rack for 30 to 35 minutes until risen and just set. Remove from the oven and cool in the tin for 15 minutes before tipping out onto a wire rack to cool completely.

To make the icing

5. Combine the sugar, cream, and butter in a saucepan. Heat over medium-low heat, stirring, until the sugar has dissolved. Bring to a boil, then leave to cook without stirring for exactly 4 minutes, until golden brown. Remove from the heat and allow to cool completely.

6. When cold, beat in the icing sugar until smooth. Using the back of a wet metal spoon, smooth it over top of the cold date cake. Leave to set before cutting into bars to serve. Store any leftovers in an airtight container for up to 5 days.

Traditional Christmas Cake

All over Great Britain, people go to great lengths to bake a beautiful fruitcake every year for Christmas. It is usually baked in early November, five to six weeks before Christmas, then wrapped in a brandy-soaked cloth and fed with more brandy biweekly up until the day it is savored. These are often covered with a layer of marzipan as well as a fondant icing and decorated with ribbons and small figures for the day, and served cut into thin slices late in the afternoon on Christmas Day. Many people enjoy theirs with some crumbled cheese on the side. *Makes 1 (9-inch round) cake*

PREP TIME: 15 minutes, plus overnight to soak **BAKE TIME:** 4½ hours

3 cups (450 grams) dried
  currants

1 generous cup
  (175 grams) raisins

1 generous cup
  (175 grams) sultanas

¼ cup (50 grams) glacé
  cherries, rinsed, dried,
  and halved

¼ cup (50 grams) finely
  chopped candied citrus
  peel (see tip)

⅓ cup (80 mL) good
  brandy, plus more for
  soaking the cake

1⅔ cups (225 grams)
  all-purpose flour

½ teaspoon mixed spice
  (see page 8)

¼ teaspoon freshly
  grated nutmeg

Pinch salt

1 cup (2 sticks/225 grams)
  butter

1 cup plus 2 tablespoons
  (225 grams) soft light
  brown sugar, packed

4 large free-range eggs,
  lightly beaten

2 tablespoons dark
  molasses

¼ cup (50 grams)
  coarsely chopped
  blanched almonds

Finely grated zest of
  1 medium lemon

Finely grated zest of
  1 medium orange

1. The evening before you are going to bake the cake, combine the currants, raisins, and sultanas in a large glass bowl, along with the cherries and candied citrus peel. Mix well and then stir in the brandy. Cover the bowl with a plate and leave to sit overnight, giving it an occasional stir.

2. In the morning, preheat the oven to 275°F/140°C. Generously butter a deep 9-inch round baking tin and then line it with 2 layers of parchment paper, buttering each layer. Set aside.

3. Sift the flour into a bowl along with the mixed spice, nutmeg, and salt. Set aside.

4. In a separate bowl, cream the butter and brown sugar together until light and fluffy, using an electric hand mixer. Beat in the eggs, a little bit at a time. If the mixture curdles, add a spoonful of the flour mixture. Fold in the flour mixture to combine well.

5. Fold in the dark molasses along with the steeped fruits and any brandy left in the bowl, the chopped almonds, and the grated citrus zests. Mix well and then spread the mixture into the prepared pan, pressing it down lightly. Place the prepared baking tin on a baking sheet.

6. Take a double thickness of newspaper and tie it around the outside of the cake tin, making sure it extends about an inch above the tin. Top with a large square of parchment paper with a 1-inch hole cut out of the center.

7. Place the tray with the cake tin on the lowest rack of the oven. Bake for 4½ to 4¾ hours, until the cake springs back when lightly touched and a toothpick inserted in the center comes out clean.

8. Place the cake, in the tin, on a wire rack to cool for 30 minutes, then remove the newspaper and discard. Carefully tip the cake out onto the wire rack and remove the baking parchment. Let cool completely.

9. Soak a double thickness of cheesecloth in some brandy and wrap the cake in this. Place into a tin, tightly cover, and leave in a dark spot until ready to decorate. Spoon a few tablespoons of brandy over the top of it twice a week until then.

Ingredient Tip: I like to order my candied citrus peels whole and then chop them myself. You can purchase them online. See page 76 for a recipe to make your own.

Technique Tip: Don't stint on the recommended paper linings and wrappings for the cake. Because of the long, slow cooking, these are necessary to help keep the cake moist.

DIY Candied Citrus Peels

If you are really keen on candied citrus peels, you can make your own. You will need the peels of citrus fruits, such as grapefruit, oranges, lemons, etc. Remove the peels and a fair amount (not too thick) of the pith (the bitter white part). Blanch the peels several times in boiling water. To do this, cut the peels into strips and put them in a saucepan. Cover with cold water, bring to a boil for 5 minutes, and drain. Repeat this process three times. If your peels still taste quite bitter, repeat again. Grapefruit peels sometimes need to be blanched a few more times.

Once they are blanched, make a simple syrup by using equal parts water and granulated sugar, enough to completely submerge your peels. Bring the water and sugar to a boil, allow the sugar to dissolve completely, and then add the peels. Reduce to a simmer and simmer the peels until soft and slightly translucent, 45 minutes to 1 hour.

Set up a drying rack over some parchment paper. Carefully remove the peels from the syrup and lay them out in a single layer on the drying rack. Leave them to dry overnight. (Keep any syrup left in the pan. It makes a great sweetener for teas or other beverages.) Optionally, once the peel has dried, you can roll it in granulated sugar to coat, but it is lovely just as it is.

Store the candied peel in an airtight container in a cool, dark place for several months.

Bara Brith

Bara brith is a Welsh quick bread/cake. It contains no fat at all, yet it's incredibly moist and delicious. Loaded with fruit, this treat is fabulous cut into thin slices and served with soft butter for spreading. You will need to plan ahead, as the fruit needs to soak overnight in cold tea. *Makes 1 (8-by-4-inch) loaf*

PREP TIME: 15 minutes, plus overnight to soak **BAKE TIME:** 2 hours

2½ cups (350 grams) mixed dried fruits (raisins, sultanas, currants)

1¼ cups (300 mL) strongly brewed tea, cold

1¾ cups (250 grams) all-purpose flour

2 teaspoons baking powder

2 teaspoons mixed spice (see page 8)

Pinch salt

⅔ cup (130 grams) fine granulated sugar (caster sugar)

1 large free-range egg, lightly beaten

1. Put the dried fruit in a bowl. Pour the cold tea over top and stir to combine. Cover the bowl with a plate and leave to sit overnight. Do not drain.

2. The next morning, preheat the oven to 350°F/180°C. Butter an 8-by-4-inch loaf tin and line the bottom and up both long sides with parchment paper, leaving an overhang for ease of lifting out. Set aside.

3. Sift the flour, baking powder, mixed spice, and salt together into a bowl. Stir in the sugar to combine.

4. Add the soaked fruit, along with any juices in the bowl, and the beaten egg. Mix well.

5. Spoon the batter into the prepared loaf tin, smoothing the top level. Bake in the center of the oven for 2 hours, until well risen and golden brown. A toothpick inserted in the center should come out clean. Cool in the tin for 10 minutes before lifting the loaf out to a wire rack to cool completely. Store in an airtight container for up to 2 weeks.

Scottish Dundee Cake

Dundee cake is a traditional Scottish fruitcake. Unlike the Traditional Christmas Cake (page 74), this has a light batter and no candied cherries in it, containing only raisins and currants. It is not quite as labor-intensive as the traditional fruitcake, but it's every bit as delicious. The top is decorated with whole blanched almonds. *Makes 1 (7-inch round) cake*

PREP TIME: 15 minutes **BAKE TIME:** 2 hours 15 minutes

1¼ cups (175 grams) self-rising flour (see tip on page 22), sifted

½ teaspoon mixed spice (see page 8)

Pinch salt

Scant 1 cup (175 grams) fine granulated sugar (caster sugar)

Finely grated zest of 1 large orange

¾ cup plus 1 tablespoon (175 grams) butter

3 large free-range eggs, lightly beaten

1 cup (150 grams) dried currants

1 cup (150 grams) raisins

6 tablespoons (80 grams) chopped mixed candied citrus peel

1 tablespoon Scottish whisky

16 to 20 whole blanched almonds

1. Preheat the oven to 325°F/160°C. Butter a deep 7-inch round cake tin, line with parchment paper, and set aside.

2. Sift together the flour, mixed spice, and salt. Set aside.

3. Rub the sugar and orange zest together until fragrant. Add the butter and beat together until light and fluffy. Beat in the eggs, a little bit at a time, until thoroughly combined. If the mixture curdles, stir in a teaspoon of the flour mixture. Stir in the flour mixture thoroughly. Stir in the currants, raisins, and candied peel along with the whisky, combining well.

4. Spoon into the prepared baking tin, smoothing over the top. Bake for 1½ hours. Remove from the oven and place the blanched almonds decoratively on top in two concentric circles. Return the cake to the oven and bake for an additional 45 minutes. The cake is done when golden brown and a toothpick inserted in the center comes out clean. Transfer to a wire rack and allow to cool completely before removing from the cake tin. Store in an airtight container for up to a month.

CHAPTER 5

Sweet and Savory Pies and Tarts

Cornish Pasties, 84

Sausage Rolls

These classic puff pastry rolls filled with a savory sausage filling are popular all over the UK. They are great for parties, picnics, lunches, and game nights. Cut into smaller pieces, they also make great appetizers. *Makes 12*

PREP TIME: 10 minutes **BAKE TIME:** 15 minutes

1¼ pounds (500 grams) good-quality sausage meat

1 large onion, minced

¾ cup (90 grams) fine dry bread crumbs

1 large free-range egg, beaten and divided

Salt

Freshly ground black pepper

1 sheet ready-made all-butter puff pastry, thawed if frozen

All-purpose flour, for dusting

1. Preheat the oven to 425°F/220°C. Line a large baking sheet with parchment paper and set aside.

2. Crumble the sausage meat into a bowl. Add the minced onion, bread crumbs, and half of the beaten egg, along with some salt and pepper. Mix everything together well, using your hands to combine. Divide the mixture into 3 equal portions.

3. Unroll the puff pastry and lay it out on a lightly floured countertop. Using a lightly floured rolling pin, roll the pastry out to a 12-by-16-inch rectangle. Cut the rectangle crosswise into 3 long strips.

4. Shape each third of the sausage meat mixture into a log the length of each strip of pastry, by rolling it between the palms of your hands. Place one meat log down the center of each pastry strip.

5. Brush one long edge of each strip with some of the remaining beaten egg. Roll the pastry up over the meat to enclose, overlapping the edges with the egg-brushed edge facing down on the bottom edge. Gently press closed.

and flatten them slightly between the palms of your hands until you have a little pastry roughly 2 inches in diameter. Place them 2 inches apart on the prepared baking sheet. Gather up and re-roll scraps of pastry as needed.

5. Brush the tops of each pastry with milk and sprinkle with a bit of demerara sugar. Using a sharp knife, cut 2 small slits in the top of each pastry.

6. Bake for 10 to 15 minutes, until golden brown. Scoop off onto a wire rack to cool completely before serving. Store any leftovers in an airtight container for up to 3 days.

Ingredient Tip: You can purchase candied citrus peels whole and then chop them yourself. See page 76 for a recipe to make your own.

Flaky Pastry

This is a quick and easy alternative to puff pastry and makes a great casing for pies, turnovers, and tarts. You can make it ahead and freeze for convenience. *Makes 8 ounces (225 grams)*

PREP TIME: 15 minutes, plus 30 minutes to chill

1⅔ cups (225 grams) all-purpose flour, plus more for dusting

⅛ teaspoon fine sea salt

2 tablespoons fine granulated sugar (caster sugar) (if using for a sweet bake)

¾ cup (1½ sticks/ 170 grams) butter, softened

¼ to ½ cup (60 to 120 mL) cold water

1. Sift the flour and salt into a bowl. Stir in the sugar, if using.

2. Divide the butter into 4 equal portions. Add one portion of butter to the flour mixture and incorporate it using a butter knife, along with just enough cold water for a soft dough that is not sticky.

3. Tip the dough out onto a lightly floured surface. Using a floured rolling pin, roll the dough into a rectangle roughly ¼ inch thick.

4. Using a pastry brush, brush off any excess flour from the surface of the dough. Cut another portion of the butter into bits and evenly space over two-thirds of the surface of the pastry. Fold the pastry in thirds, bringing the end third without the butter to the center first and covering with the opposite end.

5. Press the edges together with your fingers and then give the pastry a half turn. Roll out again to a rectangle ¼ inch thick.

6. Repeat steps 4 and 5 two more times until you have used up all the butter. Wrap in plastic wrap and chill in the refrigerator for 30 minutes, then proceed as directed in the recipe you are using it in. Alternatively, you can wrap the pastry tightly and freeze for up to 3 months. Thaw in the refrigerator overnight before using.

Homemade Mincemeat

This is the tastiest mincemeat tart/pie filling. It is nice and fruity and beautifully spiced. Once you realize how very easy it is to make your own, you will never buy a jar of it again! *Makes 1 pound (enough for about 3 dozen mince pies)*

PREP TIME: 15 minutes, plus 12 hours to rest

1 cup (150 grams) dried currants

¾ cup packed (125 grams) raisins

⅓ cup (25 grams) blanched almonds, finely chopped

1 sweet apple, peeled, cored, and grated using the large holes of a box grater

½ cup (50 grams) shredded beef or vegetable suet (see tip)

1 knob preserved stem ginger, finely chopped (see tip)

2 tablespoons calvados (French apple brandy)

1 tablespoon dark brown sugar, packed

¼ teaspoon ground cinnamon

¼ teaspoon ground nutmeg

⅛ teaspoon ground cloves

Finely grated zest and juice of 1 medium lemon

1. Combine the currants, raisins, almonds, apple, suet, ginger, calvados, sugar, cinnamon, nutmeg, cloves, zest, and juice in a large bowl. You can use your hands to make sure everything is evenly mixed.

2. Cover the bowl with a clean towel and set aside on the counter for at least 12 hours in order to meld the flavors together. Transfer to a container with a tight-fitting lid and store in the refrigerator until ready to use.

3. Bring to room temperature prior to use.

Ingredient Tip: Suet can be purchased from any good butcher and in some grocery shops. It can also be purchased online. Alternatively, you can use an equal quantity of grated frozen vegetable shortening. Preserved stem ginger can be purchased online; try Opies Chinese Stem Ginger.

Mince Pies

These mini pies are very much a British Christmas tradition. Small, crisp, and buttery pastry cases filled with a delicious filling of spiced fruits and nuts, dusted or not with sifted icing sugar, always go down as a real treat during the holidays. You can use a ready-made mincemeat filling if you wish, but the pies are exponentially better if you make your own filling from scratch. It just wouldn't be Christmas without a few dozen or more of these to munch on! *Makes 24*

PREP TIME: 25 minutes, plus 30 minutes to chill **BAKE TIME:** 25 minutes

2½ cups (350 grams) all-purpose flour, plus more for dusting

Pinch salt

⅓ cup (75 grams) cold lard, cut into bits

⅓ cup (75 grams) cold butter, cut into bits

Ice water, as needed

1¼ pounds (560 grams) mincemeat, home-made (page 99) or store-bought

Milk, for brushing

Icing (confectioners') sugar, for dusting

1. Sift the flour and salt into a large bowl. Drop in the lard and butter and rub them into the flour, using a snapping motion with your fingertips, until the mixture resembles fine dry bread crumbs. Work quickly so the fat doesn't melt into the flour.

2. Using a fork, add ice water, 1 tablespoon at a time, until the mixture forms a dough that leaves the sides of the bowl. Shape into a disk and wrap tightly in plastic wrap. Place into the refrigerator to chill for 30 minutes.

3. Preheat the oven to 400°F/200°C. Lightly butter 2 muffin tins.

4. Divide the pastry in half. Using a lightly floured rolling pin, roll half of the pastry out on a lightly floured surface to ¼ inch thickness. Cut into 24 rounds using a 3-inch fluted pastry cutter. Fit a round into each hole of the muffin tins. (They don't need to come all the way up the sides.) Fill each with 1 heaping tablespoon of mincemeat.

Yeasted Breads

Chelsea Buns, 108

English Muffins

These round, flattish yeasted breads are baked on a griddle pan or in a skillet. Once baked, they are meant to be split open with a fork and toasted. This method of tearing them open creates lots of nooks and crannies that, once toasted, crisp up nicely, perfect for your butter to melt into. *Makes 8 to 10*

PREP TIME: 20 minutes, plus 1 hour to rise **BAKE TIME:** 15 minutes

Scant 5 cups (675 grams) strong white bread flour, plus more for dusting

2 teaspoons fine granulated sugar (caster sugar)

2¼ teaspoons fast-acting yeast

1½ teaspoons fine sea salt

Scant 2 cups (450 mL) lukewarm whole milk

1 teaspoon fine cornmeal, for dusting

Canola oil, for greasing

1. Lightly dust a large baking sheet with flour and set aside.

2. Combine the flour, sugar, yeast, and salt in the bowl of a stand mixer. Whisk together to combine by hand. Begin to pour in the milk, slowly, in a steady stream, with the mixer on low to medium. Stop the mixer and switch to a dough hook. (See tip for electric hand mixer instructions.)

3. Knead the dough using the dough hook for about 10 minutes, until the dough is smooth and elastic.

4. Turn the dough out onto a lightly floured surface and, using a lightly floured rolling pin, roll the dough out to ½ inch thickness.

5. Cut into rounds using a 3-inch cookie cutter, taking care not to twist the dough. Place the rounds on the floured baking sheet, leaving space between them to rise. Dust the tops with the cornmeal. (You can re-roll the scraps to cut more, but they won't be as perfect to look at as your first cuts, so do try to get as many as you can from the first lot.)

6. Cover loosely with lightly oiled plastic wrap and set aside in a warm place to rise until they have doubled in size, about 1 hour.

7. Lightly grease a griddle pan or a heavy-bottomed skillet with oil. Heat over medium heat until you can feel the warmth from the pan when you hold your hand about an inch over the top.

8. Place the rounds in the pan two or three at a time, then immediately turn the heat down to low. Cook on each side until golden brown and well risen, about 7 minutes per side. Scoop the muffins onto a wire rack to cool before splitting and toasting.

9. These will keep tightly wrapped or in an airtight container for up to 4 days. You can also freeze them, tightly wrapped, for up to 2 months.

Technique Tip: You can make these with an electric hand mixer if you wish. Just mix up to the kneading part and then finish them by tipping the dough out onto a lightly floured surface and kneading it by hand until the dough is smooth and elastic. Proceed as directed.

Chelsea Buns

These dense, fruited buns are as popular in the UK as cinnamon rolls are in North America. The buns were originally made and sold in the eighteenth century at the Chelsea Bun House in the Pimlico area of London. They are delicious served warm and buttered along with a nice hot cup of tea or coffee. *Makes 9*

PREP TIME: 30 minutes, plus 2 hours to rise **BAKE TIME:** 30 minutes

1⅔ cups (225 grams) strong bread flour, divided, plus more for dusting

2¼ teaspoons regular dried yeast

1 teaspoon fine granulated sugar (caster sugar)

½ cup (120 mL) warm milk

Pinch salt

1 heaping tablespoon lard, softened

1 medium free-range egg, lightly beaten

¼ cup (50 grams) butter, melted, plus more butter for greasing and serving (optional)

¼ cup (50 grams) soft light brown sugar, packed

⅓ cup (50 grams) raisins

⅓ cup (50 grams) dried currants

⅓ cup (50 grams) sultanas

¼ cup (25 grams) mixed candied peel

¼ cup (60 mL) honey

1. Combine ⅓ cup (50 grams) of flour, the yeast, sugar, and milk in a bowl. Whisk together until smooth, then cover lightly with a tea towel and set aside in a warm place for 20 minutes. It will become quite frothy.

2. Meanwhile, combine the remaining 1⅓ cups (175 grams) of flour and the salt in a separate bowl, and drop in the lard. Using your fingertips, rub the lard into the flour until well combined.

3. Stir the yeast mixture into the flour mixture along with the beaten egg to make a soft dough. Tip out the dough onto a lightly floured surface and knead for about 5 minutes, until you have a nice smooth dough. Shape into a ball.

4. Lightly oil a clean bowl and add the ball of dough, turning the dough to oil the top. Cover with a piece of plastic wrap and set aside in a warm place to rise until doubled in size, about 1½ hours.

5. Generously butter an 8-inch round cake tin.

6. Tip the dough out onto a lightly floured surface and knead gently to knock the air out. Using a lightly floured rolling pin, roll the dough out to a 9-by-12-inch rectangle. Brush the melted butter evenly over the surface of the dough. Sprinkle the brown sugar and dried fruits and peel evenly over the top, leaving about ⅓ inch free all the way around the rectangle.

7. Working from one long edge, roll the dough up tightly as if you were making a jelly roll. Brush the other long edge of the dough with water and seal carefully, pinching it shut. Cut the roll crosswise into 9 equal pieces. Place the rolls, cut-side up, in the prepared cake tin, placing one roll in the center and the remaining 8 around the outside. Cover the tin with oiled plastic wrap and set aside in a warm place for another 30 minutes to rest and rise again.

8. Preheat the oven to 375°F/190°C.

9. Bake for 30 to 35 minutes, until risen and golden brown. Remove from the oven and carefully tip the buns out onto a wire rack, right-side up.

10. Brush the honey over the tops of the buns while still warm. Pull apart and serve warm, with or without butter for spreading.

Iced Buns

Soft and yeasty with a delicious icing glaze and glacé cherry topping, these delicious buns were made famous in the 2003 British comedy film *Calendar Girls*. Children everywhere, both old and young, love them. *Makes 8*

PREP TIME: 20 minutes, plus 1 hour 45 minutes to rise **BAKE TIME:** 10 minutes

1½ tablespoons butter
⅓ cup (80 mL) water
Scant ⅓ cup (70 mL) whole milk
2 tablespoons fine granulated sugar (caster sugar)

1¾ cups (250 grams) strong bread flour, plus more for dusting
2¼ teaspoons fast-acting yeast
1 teaspoon fine sea salt

1 medium free-range egg
½ cup (65 grams) icing (confectioners') sugar, sifted
1 tablespoon water
4 glacé cherries, halved

1. Combine the butter, water, milk, and sugar in a saucepan. Warm the mixture over low heat until lukewarm. It should not be hot to the touch. If it is too hot, you will kill the yeast. If you think it is too hot, let it cool to lukewarm.

2. Combine the flour and yeast in the bowl of a stand mixer fitted with a dough hook. Add the salt around the edges of the bowl. Pour in the milk mixture and the egg. Mix together on low for 4 to 5 minutes to combine all the ingredients. Increase the speed to medium and mix for an additional 6 minutes, until smooth and satiny.

3. Scrape out the dough onto a lightly floured surface and knead for a few minutes. Transfer to a lightly oiled bowl. Cover with lightly oiled plastic wrap and set aside in a warm place to rise for 1 hour. The dough should double in size. (Alternatively, you can do this with an electric hand mixer, but it will take you a bit longer to get a smooth satin-textured dough.)

4. Lightly grease a rimmed baking sheet.

5. Divide the dough into 8 equal pieces. (You can weigh the full dough on a scale, then divide by 8. Each portion should weigh the same amount.) Shape each piece into a round bun, then place them on the prepared baking sheet, seam-side down, leaving plenty of space in between each. Cover lightly with oiled plastic wrap and set aside in a warm place to rise for an additional 45 minutes. Again, they should double in size.

6. Preheat the oven to 425°F/220°C.

7. Bake for 7 to 8 minutes, until light golden brown and fluffy. They should be golden brown on the undersides also, and sound hollow when tapped on the underside. Transfer to a wire rack to cool completely.

8. Once completely cooled, whisk the icing sugar together with just enough water to give you a nice thick and sticky glaze icing. Dip the tops of the cooled buns into this icing, pop them back onto the baking tray, icing-side up, and place half a glacé cherry in the middle of each. Leave to set before serving. These are best eaten the same day.

Technique Tip: For optimum flavor, don't glaze and decorate until you are ready to serve!

Hot Cross Buns

These spiced and fruity buns are an Easter tradition all over the UK, though they are available in the shops all year round now. Nothing beats the delicious flavor of a freshly baked hot cross bun, split, toasted, and spread with butter. These buns normally have a pastry cross baked into the top, but it is also quite acceptable to cut a cross on top if you prefer. They are glazed after baking with a water-sugar glaze. You can also pipe a cross on top with a thick glacé icing after they cool (see tip). *Makes 1 dozen*

PREP TIME: 30 minutes, plus 2 hours to rise **BAKE TIME:** 15 minutes

For the buns

3¼ cups (450 grams) strong white bread flour, plus more for dusting

¼ cup (50 grams) fine granulated sugar (caster sugar)

2¼ teaspoons fast-acting yeast

1 teaspoon salt

1 teaspoon mixed spice (see page 8)

1 teaspoon ground cinnamon

½ teaspoon freshly grated nutmeg

3½ tablespoons butter, melted and cooled

⅔ cup (160 mL) luke-warm milk

¼ cup (60 mL) luke-warm water

1 large free-range egg, lightly beaten

½ cup (75 grams) dried currants

⅓ cup (50 grams) chopped candied peel

For the pastry crosses (optional)

⅓ cup (50 grams) plain all-purpose flour

2 tablespoons butter

Water as needed

For the glaze

2 tablespoons water

2 tablespoons granu-lated sugar

1. Combine the flour, sugar, yeast, salt, mixed spice, cinnamon, and nutmeg in a large bowl. Mix them completely. In a measuring cup with a spout, whisk together the melted and cooled butter, milk, water, and egg. Make a well in the center of the dry ingredients and pour in the wet, then add the currants and candied peel on top.

2. Mix with a wooden spoon to form a soft dough. Tip the dough out onto a lightly floured surface. Knead by hand for about 10 minutes until you have a smooth and elastic dough. Shape the dough into a smooth ball. Add the ball of dough to an oiled

bowl, turning to coat it with oil. Cover with oiled plastic wrap and set aside in a warm place to rise until doubled in size, about 1½ hours.

3. Butter 2 rimmed baking sheets.

4. Tip the risen dough out onto a lightly floured surface and knead it gently for 2 to 3 minutes. Divide the dough into 12 equal pieces. (You can weigh the dough on a scale and then divide it by 12. This is the weight each piece of dough should be.) Shape each piece into a round, poking any currants or peel that pop out back into the dough.

5. Place the buns spaced well apart on the prepared baking sheets. Flatten them slightly with the palm of your hand and cut a cross into the top of each one with a sharp knife. Cover lightly with greased plastic wrap and set aside to rise in a warm place until doubled in size, about 30 minutes.

6. Preheat the oven to 425°F/220°C.

7. While the buns are rising, you can make the pastry crosses, if you like. Put the flour in a small bowl and rub in the butter. Add only enough water to make a stiff dough, then roll out onto a lightly floured surface using a floured rolling pin. Cut into thin strips, no more than ⅓ inch wide. Moisten one side of the pastry strips and lay in a cross pattern over the top of each bun.

8. Bake the buns for 15 minutes, until golden brown. They should sound hollow when tapped on the bottoms when done. While the buns are baking, prepare the sugar glaze by gently heating the water and sugar together until the sugar dissolves. Brush this mixture over the hot buns as soon as they come out of the oven.

Variation Tip: To make a glacé icing to pipe crosses on top, whisk together ½ cup (65 grams) icing (confectioners') sugar and just enough cold water to make a thick glaze. Pop this into a small resealable plastic bag. Cut a small part from one corner of the baggie and use this to pipe crosses onto the tops of the completely cooled buns.

Old-Fashioned Hovis Loaf

This is a much-beloved whole-wheat bread in the UK. Typically, it is baked using strong white bread flour with the addition of wheat germ. A bit of dark treacle is added for sweetness, which also serves to give it a lovely brown color. There is an iconic advertisement for the store brand that shows a young boy walking his push bike up a steep cobbled street, a loaf of fresh Hovis bread in his basket. This vision never fails to tug on the heartstrings and make one long for an older, simpler time. *Makes 1 loaf*

PREP TIME: 30 minutes, plus 2 hours to rise BAKE TIME: 30 minutes

Scant 1¼ cups (280 mL) lukewarm water

1 tablespoon dark treacle or blackstrap molasses

1½ teaspoons regular dried yeast

3⅔ cups (500 grams) strong bread flour, plus more for dusting

7 tablespoons (110 grams) wheat germ

1½ teaspoons salt

1 tablespoon canola oil

1. Combine the lukewarm water and treacle in a large measuring cup and stir to dissolve. Add the yeast and stir. Leave to proof for 10 minutes. The mixture should look nice and bubbly and have a definite yeasty fragrance.

2. Whisk the flour, wheat germ, and salt together in a bowl. Add the yeast mixture along with the oil and stir everything together into a soft dough. It should be a bit tacky.

3. Tip the dough out onto a lightly floured surface. Knead well for about 10 minutes, until you have a smooth, satiny elastic dough, adding flour as needed to keep the dough from sticking. Shape into a ball and place in a lightly oiled bowl, turning to coat the top with oil. Cover with oiled plastic wrap and place in a warm place to rise until doubled in size, about 1 hour.

4. Generously butter an 8-by-4-inch loaf tin and set aside.

5. Tip the risen dough out onto a lightly floured surface and knead gently for 2 to 3 minutes to knock out any air. Shape the dough into a loaf and smooth the top and ends. Place in the prepared loaf tin. Cover loosely with lightly oiled plastic wrap and place in a warm place for an additional hour to rise. At the end of that time, it should almost fill the pan.

6. Preheat the oven to 375°F/190°C.

7. Bake for 30 to 35 minutes, until well risen and nicely browned. When done, the loaf should sound hollow on the bottom when lightly tapped. Tip the loaf out onto a wire rack and cool completely.

Crumpets

Crumpets are small, round yeasted breads cooked on a griddle pan. Soft and spongy and filled with lovely holes, these are perfect for holding all that butter and jam spread on top. These are the perfect addition to a tea party! You will need 4-inch metal cooking rings to cook these. *Makes 8*

PREP TIME: 15 minutes, plus 1 hour to rise **BAKE TIME:** 10 minutes

1⅓ cups plus 1 tablespoon (330 mL) whole milk	1⅔ cups (225 grams) all-purpose flour	2¼ teaspoons fast-acting yeast
1 teaspoon fine granulated sugar (caster sugar)	1 teaspoon fine sea salt	Canola oil, for greasing

1. Put the milk and sugar in a saucepan and heat gently over medium-low heat to dissolve the sugar. The milk should not be hot; it should only be lukewarm. If it gets too hot, allow it to cool to lukewarm. Remove the pan from the heat and pour the milk into a large measuring cup with a pouring spout.

2. Sift the flour into a bowl and whisk in the salt and yeast. Make a well in the center. Pour in the lukewarm milk and whisk both together until you have a smooth, lump-free batter. Cover with a clean tea towel and set aside in a warm place to rise for 1 hour.

3. When you are ready to cook the crumpets, preheat the oven to 250°F/125°C. Heat a tiny bit of oil in a large heavy-bottomed nonstick skillet over low heat. Generously coat four 4-inch cooking rings with oil. Place them in the skillet. Spoon a heaping tablespoon of crumpet batter into each ring.

4. Cook for 3 to 4 minutes, until the surface of the crumpets are covered with tiny air bubbles. Once the bubbles begin to pop, remove the rings and carefully turn the crumpets over. The crumpets should be golden brown on the underside. Cook for 1 minute longer.

5. Keep the crumpets warm in the oven while you cook the remainder of the crumpets, re-oiling the rings and the pan.

Measurement Conversions

	US STANDARD	US STANDARD (OUNCES)	METRIC (APPROXIMATE)
VOLUME EQUIVALENTS (LIQUID)	2 tablespoons	1 fl. oz.	30 mL
	¼ cup	2 fl. oz.	60 mL
	½ cup	4 fl. oz.	120 mL
	1 cup	8 fl. oz.	240 mL
	1½ cups	12 fl. oz.	355 mL
	2 cups or 1 pint	16 fl. oz.	475 mL
	4 cups or 1 quart	32 fl. oz.	1 L
	1 gallon	128 fl. oz.	4 L
VOLUME EQUIVALENTS (DRY)	⅛ teaspoon	———	0.5 mL
	¼ teaspoon	———	1 mL
	½ teaspoon	———	2 mL
	¾ teaspoon	———	4 mL
	1 teaspoon	———	5 mL
	1 tablespoon	———	15 mL
	¼ cup	———	59 mL
	⅓ cup	———	79 mL
	½ cup	———	118 mL
	⅔ cup	———	156 mL
	¾ cup	———	177 mL
	1 cup	———	235 mL
	2 cups or 1 pint	———	475 mL
	3 cups	———	700 mL
	4 cups or 1 quart	———	1 L
	½ gallon	———	2 L
	1 gallon	———	4 L
WEIGHT EQUIVALENTS	½ ounce	———	15 g
	1 ounce	———	30 g
	2 ounces	———	60 g
	4 ounces	———	115 g
	8 ounces	———	225 g
	12 ounces	———	340 g
	16 ounces or 1 pound	———	455 g

	FAHRENHEIT (F)	CELSIUS (C) (APPROXIMATE)
OVEN TEMPERATURES	250°F	120°C
	300°F	150°C
	325°F	180°C
	375°F	190°C
	400°F	200°C
	425°F	220°C
	450°F	230°C

Resources

BOOKS

Mary Berry's Ultimate Cake Book, Mary Berry, 1994, BBC Books

This was one of the first books I purchased when I moved to the UK in 2000 and has been an invaluable resource for great classic recipes for cakes, biscuits, traybakes, scones, and more. I highly recommend.

Delia Smith's Complete Cookery Course, Delia Smith, 1992, BBC Books

I received this book for Christmas from my husband in 2003. It is a wonderful resource for how to cook British, from soup to nuts and everything in between. It has excellent conversion tables as well.

New British Classics, Gary Rhodes, 1999, BBC Books

This was the first cookbook I purchased when I moved to the UK in 2000. It, too, has been invaluable in my journey toward becoming an accomplished British cook and baker. It features good, solid recipes of the old favorites with a modern twist.

Be-Ro Home Baked Recipes, Be-Ro Flour

This is a great basic baking book, covering scones, biscuits, cakes, pastry, pies, and all things in between. If you can get your hands on one of these, you have a treasure. Mine was a gift from a friend.

SHOPPING

Amazon has everything you need as far as baking-related materials and ingredients are concerned and is an invaluable resource for baking pans and British ingredients.

Amazon.com

British Food Shop is a great source of British ingredients. It carries everything from jams to spreads to essential baking ingredients, including suet, dark treacle, a variety of sugars and flours, and preserved ginger in syrup.

BritishFoodShop.com

British Corner Shop is also a great resource for British ingredients, carrying a wide variety of British goods and ingredients.

BritishCornerShop.co.uk

Index

Acknowledgments

To Callisto Media and Anne Lowrey, thank you so very much for affording me the opportunity to share my love of British baking with the world.

To my mother, and her mother, and her mother before her, generations of good cooks who fed their families well and who inspired me to want to do the same.

To my children, who were my guinea pigs throughout the years and upon whom I cut my culinary teeth.

To my father, sister, and brother who have always been my biggest fans, but especially to my father and mother, who gave me wings and encouraged me to use them. Family—it's not a small thing. It's everything.

About the Author

 **Marie Rayner** is a retired professional chef, food blogger, and cookbook author. She began her culinary career working as a pastry chef at a hotel back in the 1970s, then took time off to raise a family. In 2000 she moved to the UK, where she worked as a personal chef for several years before retiring from the trade several years ago. In 2009 she started the award-winning food blog The English Kitchen (TheEnglishKitchen.co), where she shares her lifetime of cooking experience with tried-and-true recipes, along with many beloved and traditional British recipes. She does all the testing, so you don't have to. Marie is the author of several cookbooks, including *Recipes from the Big Blue Binder* and *The English Kitchen: An Anglophile's Love Note to English Cuisine*. She created an award-winning recipe for the British Turkey Federation in 2012, which went on to win a prestigious Turkey Award at the national level. She and her blog have been highlighted in *The Times* of London and the Canadian *HELLO!* magazine. Her motto is "Food doesn't have to be complicated to be delicious."

CPSIA information can be obtained
at www.ICGtesting.com
Printed in the USA
JSHW011201100122
21900JS00004B/39